JACKSONVILLE & COMPANY

The Junior League of Jacksonville, Florida, Inc.

The purpose of the Junior League of Jacksonville, Inc. is to promote voluntarism, to develop the potential of its members for voluntary participation in community affairs and to demonstrate the effectiveness of trained volunteers.

Copies of JACKSONVILLE & COMPANY may be obtained from the Junior League of Jacksonville, Inc.
c/o JACKSONVILLE & COMPANY
2165 Park Street
Jacksonville, Florida 32204
or by mailing an order blank from the back of the book to the above address.

Copyright ©1982
ISBN: 0-9609338-0-8
The Junior League of Jacksonville, Florida, Inc.
First Edition   October 1982   20,000

All profits realized from the sale of
JACKSONVILLE & COMPANY are returned to the community through profits of the Junior League of Jacksonville, Inc.

Printed by
S.C. Toof & Co.
Memphis, Tennessee

Committee

Chairman	Drema Houchins Farmer
Co-Chairman	Harriet Talley Beardsley
Design	Monett Powers Kent
Co-Chairman	Langhorne Kirill Stoneburner
	Elizabeth Donegan Daniel
	Meredith Mori Mason
Entertainment Section	Cornelia Covington Smithwick
Editing	Winifred Wootton Booher
Herb Cooking	Sara Carver Frazier
Marketing and Promotion	Susan Shanklin Threlkel
	Patricia Igoe Hannan
	Ann Davis Baker
	Susan Herbertson Adams
Recipe Solicitation	Susannah Davis Sands
Sustainer Committee	Annette White King
	Barbara Horne Arnold
	Ann James Doswell
	Carol Hart Kohlhaas
	Linda Crank Moseley
	Margrett Yallalee Rennard
	Patricia Portman Sanow
	Sally Holcomb Surface
	Winifred Sessoms Wootton
Testing	Karen Guernsey Johnston
Co-Chairman	Cindy Brocato Lobrano
Advisors	Carol Blume Baumer
	Tillie Kidd Fowler
	Alice Jones Stanly
Wine Consultant	Benjamin G. Bell, Master Knight of the Vine Professional, Professional Sommelier Guild
Artist	Gail Spratt

The Junior League of Jacksonville, Inc. extends sincere appreciation to all who submitted recipes. We regret that we were unable to include all of them because of similarities and lack of space.

Contents

Introduction 7
Appetizers 9
Salads & Molds 37
Fish & Seafood 63
Poultry 85
Meats 111
Vegetables 133
Grains & Breads 157
Cheese, Eggs, Rice & Pasta 179
Sauces, Dressings, Pickles & Jellies 203
Soups, Sandwiches & Beverages 221
Desserts 249
Cakes & Pies 271
Cookies & Candies 297
Cooking with Herbs 315
Entertaining "Jacksonville Style" 333
Index 355

Jacksonville & Company celebrates cooking and entertaining, Jacksonville style, with fresh recipes, tempting menus and creative ideas for festive settings on a scale either grand or small. The inviting watermelon basket on the cover speaks of superb food beautifully presented. The gala museum benefit, the small dinner beside the ocean, the oyster roast, the game feast, the galley supper, the tennis luncheon — all portray a city blessed with magnificent beaches, the wide expanse of the St. Johns River and a temperate climate. Jacksonville style is gathering out of doors the year-round; it is cosmopolitan cuisine enhanced by the warmth of southern hospitality; it is setting the stage with flair and imagination....Enjoy!

Appetizers

Shrimp With Creole Mustard

1	cup olive oil
1/2	cup white wine vinegar
8	scallions, finely chopped
2	tablespoons snipped parsley
2	tablespoons finely chopped celery
1	tablespoon Zatarain's creole mustard
1	teaspoon salt
1/2	teaspoon paprika
1/2	teaspoon pepper
2	pounds large shrimp

Servings: 8
Preparation time: 1 hour
Marinating time: 6 hours or overnight

- In a bowl, blend first 9 ingredients.
- Steam shrimp in lightly salted water. Shell and devein.
- Pour sauce over shrimp and marinate for 6 hours or overnight.
- Serve shrimp on a bed of lettuce.
- You may also marinate artichokes or mushrooms with shrimp.

Chilled Shrimp With Saffron Dressing

1	pound large fresh shrimp
1	cup dry white wine
1	tablespoon olive oil
1	cup V-8 juice
2	tablespoons fresh lemon juice
1	tablespoon fresh parsley
1/8	teaspoon dried thyme
1/2	bay leaf
1	medium onion, chopped
1	clove garlic, minced
1/4	teaspoon pepper
1	teaspoon powdered saffron
1/2	teaspoon salt
	Lettuce leaves
	Lemon slices

Servings: 4
Preparation time: 10 minutes
Cooking time: 10 minutes
Chilling time: 2 hours

- Peel and devein shrimp.
- Combine first 13 ingredients in a large saucepan. Simmer over low heat for 5 minutes.
- Remove shrimp from sauce with a slotted spoon and refrigerate.
- Strain sauce and allow to chill for 2 hours.
- To serve, place shrimp on lettuce. Spoon reserved sauce over shrimp and garnish with lemon slices.

APPETIZERS

Shrimp Remoulade

4	tablespoons horseradish mustard	
1/8	cup tarragon vinegar	
2	tablespoons catsup	
1	tablespoon paprika	
1/2	tablespoon cayenne pepper	
1	tablespoon salt	
1	clove garlic, minced	
1/3	cup salad oil	
1/2	cup finely chopped green onions with tops	
1/2	cup finely chopped celery	
1/2	cup finely snipped parsley	
2	pounds shrimp, peeled, deveined and cooked	

Servings: 6
Preparation time: 45 minutes
Chilling time: 3 to 4 hours

- Mix mustard, vinegar, catsup, paprika, pepper, salt and garlic.
- Add oil, beating with a wire whisk.
- Add onions, celery and parsley.
- Pour dressing over shrimp and chill for several hours.
- Serve on a bed of chopped lettuce.

Shrimp With Mayonnaise Dressing

1	pound medium shrimp
1	cup mayonnaise
2	tablespoons mustard
1/2	teaspoon lemon juice
1/4	teaspoon salt
1	clove garlic, minced
1/4	teaspoon black pepper
1/8	teaspoon Tabasco sauce

Servings: 4 to 6
Preparation time: 30 minutes
Cooking time: 5 minutes
Chilling time: overnight

- Boil shrimp for 5 minutes in salted water. Cool. Peel and devein shrimp.
- Combine next 6 ingredients and stir thoroughly.
- Add Tabasco, then shrimp. Toss lightly.
- Chill overnight.

Marinated Shrimp

1	tablespoon salt
1	bunch celery tops
2	bay leaves
2	quarts water
2	pounds fresh shrimp
2	medium onions, sliced thin and separated into rings
2	tablespoons capers
1	cup vegetable oil
1/2	cup white vinegar
2	teaspoons celery seed
1	tablespoon salt
	Tabasco sauce to taste

Servings: 8 to 12
Preparation time: 30 minutes
Chilling time: 8 hours or overnight

- Boil salt, celery tops and bay leaves in water for 10 minutes.
- Add shrimp and return to a boil.
- Remove from heat and let stand for 10 minutes.
- Drain shrimp, rinse in cold water, peel and devein.
- Layer shrimp with onions and capers in a bowl.
- Mix oil, vinegar, celery seed, salt and Tabasco.
- Pour sauce over shrimp. Cover and chill for 8 hours or overnight.
- Serve with fresh French bread and a salad.

Shrimp Pâté

1	pound shrimp
1/4	cup finely chopped onion
3	tablespoons lemon juice
4	tablespoons butter
1	8-ounce package cream cheese
4	tablespoons mayonnaise
1	teaspoon garlic salt
1	teaspoon snipped fresh parsley

Servings: 10 to 12
Preparation time: 45 minutes
Chilling time: 6 hours

- Boil shrimp. Peel, clean and mince shrimp.
- Mix remaining ingredients in a food processor on high.
- Fold in shrimp by hand.
- Pack into a crock or appropriate serving container. Refrigerate for at least 6 hours.
- Serve with plain crackers.

Spicy Shrimp Spread

1	8-ounce package cream cheese, softened	Servings: 12
1/4	cup mayonnaise	Preparation time: 15 minutes
5	green onions, finely chopped	Chilling time: 6 hours
1/2	teaspoon horseradish	
1/2	tablespoon dry mustard	
	Garlic salt to taste	
1/2	pound cooked shrimp, chopped	

- Mix all ingredients together, adding shrimp last.
- Chill for 6 hours.
- Serve with crackers.

Shrimp Balls

1	pound shrimp, cooked, shelled, deveined and chilled
1	teaspoon Worcestershire sauce
3	tablespoons cream cheese
1	tablespoon chili sauce
2	teaspoons horseradish
1/4	cup finely chopped celery
1	hard-boiled egg, chopped
1	tablespoon grated onion
1	tablespoon finely chopped parsley
3/4	teaspoon salt
1/8	teaspoon pepper
1	cup finely snipped parsley

Servings: 2-1/2 dozen shrimp balls
Preparation time: 1 hour
Chilling time: 4 hour

- Finely chop shrimp in a blender or food processor.
- Add next 10 ingredients.
- Mix well.
- Form mixture into small balls.
- Roll in chopped parsley.
- Chill in refrigerator for 4 hours.

Shrimp Butter

4	pounds shrimp, cooked, peeled and deveined
1	medium white onion, finely chopped
1	cup butter, melted
1/3	cup lemon juice
	Salt and pepper to taste
	Dry mustard to taste
2	ounces brandy

Servings: 30
Preparation time: 10 minutes
Chilling time: 12 hours

- Mince shrimp or chop in a food processor until crumbly.
- Add remaining ingredients and mix until a paste is formed.
- Pack mixture in a greased mold.
- Chill for 12 hours.
- Unmold and serve with melba toast.

Hot Crabmeat Dip

1	8-ounce package cream cheese
3	tablespoons mayonnaise
1	teaspoon Dijon mustard
1/2	cup sour cream
2	tablespoons dry white wine
8	ounces fresh flaked crabmeat
	Garlic salt to taste
	White pepper to taste

Servings: 12
Preparation time: 10 minutes
Cooking time: 10 minutes

- Combine cream cheese, mayonnaise, mustard and sour cream in the top of a double boiler over simmering water.
- Stir until smooth and well blended.
- Gradually add wine.
- Add crabmeat and blend.
- Season with garlic salt and white pepper.
- Pour into a chafing dish. Serve with crackers or miniature pastry shells.

Hot Shrimp or Crab Dip

2	8-ounce packages cream cheese
1	hot chili pepper
1	sweet banana pepper
1	tablespoon hot chili pepper juice (from jar)
1	tablespoon banana pepper juice (from jar)
1	tablespoon garlic juice
1	medium tomato
1	medium onion
1	pound crabmeat or shrimp or 1/2 pound of each, cooked
	Doritos (plain)

Servings: 6 to 8
Preparation time: 15 minutes

- In a saucepan, slowly melt cream cheese over low heat.
- In a blender or food processor, blend peppers, juices, tomato and onion.
- Add pepper mixture to cream cheese and simmer for 10 minutes.
- Add crabmeat and/or shrimp.
- Serve in a chafing dish with Doritos.
- Make sure flame under chafing dish is low. Stir dip occasionally.

Crab Rangoon

1/2	pound fresh crabmeat, drained, picked and chopped
1	8-ounce package cream cheese, softened
1/2	teaspoon A-1 Sauce
1/4	teaspoon garlic powder
30 to 36	wonton wrappers
1	egg yolk, beaten
	Vegetable oil
	Hot Mustard Sauce (see Index)

Servings: 30 to 36 wontons
Preparation time: 30 minutes
Cooking time: 15 minutes

- Blend crabmeat, cream cheese, A-1 Sauce and garlic powder until mixture is the consistency of paste.
- Place 1 heaping teaspoon of this mixture on each wonton.
- Gather four corners of wonton together, pull up and twist, using egg yolk to moisten and bind.
- Deep fry in a wok or electric skillet.
- Serve with Hot Mustard Sauce.

Gourmet Crab Dip

1	8-ounce package cream cheese
2	tablespoons milk
1	pound fresh white crabmeat
2	tablespoons chopped onions or scallions
1/2	teaspoon salt
1/2	tablespoon horseradish
	Lemon juice to taste
	Pepper to taste
1	2-1/4-ounce package slivered almonds, toasted
1/4	cup chopped fresh parsley
	Parsley for garnish

Servings: 10
Preparation time: 10 minutes
Baking time: 20 minutes

* Preheat oven to 375° F.
* Combine first 10 ingredients in order given.
* Place in a small soufflé baking dish.
* Bake for 20 minutes.
* Serve with crackers or melba toast.
* Garnish with parsley.
* May be frozen or prepared 1 day ahead and refrigerated until baked.

Hot Crab Dip

1	pound lump crabmeat
2	8-ounce packages cream cheese, softened
1/2	pint sour cream
4	tablespoons mayonnaise
	Juice of 1/2 lemon
1	tablespoon Worcestershire sauce
1	teaspoon dry mustard
1/4	teaspoon garlic salt
1/2	cup sharp Cheddar cheese, grated
2	tablespoons milk
1	cup dry sherry
	Tabasco sauce to taste (optional)

Servings: 25
Preparation time: 25 minutes
Baking time: 50 minutes

* Preheat oven to 350° F.
* Combine crab, cream cheese, sour cream, mayonnaise, lemon juice, Worcestershire sauce, dry mustard, garlic salt, 3/4 of the cheese and milk.
* Stir in sherry.
* Pour into a buttered casserole.
* Top with remaining cheese.
* Bake for 50 minutes.
* Serve with melba toast, crackers or pastry cups.
* May do ahead but do not add sherry until time to bake.

Crab Swiss Rounds

1	pound lump white crabmeat
1/2	cup chopped green onions
1/2	cup chopped celery
1	cup Hellmann's mayonnaise
8	ounces Swiss cheese, grated
1/2	teaspoon salt
1/2	teaspoon pepper
	Party rye bread rounds

Servings: 30 rounds
Preparation time: 20 minutes
Broiling time: 3 to 5 minutes

- Clean and drain crabmeat.
- Add onions and celery.
- Add mayonnaise, cheese, salt and pepper.
- Turn on broiler.
- Mound 1 teaspoon of mixture on each rye bread round.
- Place on a greased baking sheet.
- Broil for 3 to 5 minutes or until brown around edges and bubbly on top.

Clams Monterey

1	pound Monterey Jack cheese, grated
3	6-1/2-ounce cans clams, drained and chopped
2	tablespoons finely chopped parsley
2	tablespoons chopped fresh chives
2	cloves garlic, finely minced
	Freshly ground black pepper to taste
	Red pepper to taste
8	slices pumpernickel bread

Servings: 8
Preparation time: 10 minutes
Baking time: 5 minutes

- Preheat broiler.
- Combine first 7 ingredients. Mix until well blended.
- Spread a generous amount of mixture on each slice of bread.
- Place bread on a cookie sheet.
- Broil until golden brown and bubbly, about 5 minutes.
- Cut into squares and serve immediately.

Oysters Rockefeller

1	dozen oysters on the half shell
1	tablespoon minced green onion
1	small clove garlic, minced
1	tablespoon chopped parsley
2	tablespoons butter, melted
	Salt and pepper to taste
2	tablespoons finely chopped fresh spinach
2	tablespoons Pernod or white wine
1/3	cup fine bread crumbs

Servings: 2
Preparation time: 30 minutes
Baking time: 8 minutes

- Preheat oven to 450° F.
- Carefully remove oysters from shells and drain.
- Wash shells and put one oyster in each. Place in a baking pan.
- Mix green onion, garlic, parsley and 1 tablespoon butter. Put a bit of mixture on each oyster.
- Sprinkle oysters with salt and pepper.
- Combine spinach and Pernod. Top each oyster with some of mixture.
- Sprinkle with bread crumbs and dot with remaining 1 tablespoon butter.
- Bake for 8 minutes.
- Serve immediately.

Avocado Appetizer

1	large or 2 small ripe avocados
1	teaspoon lemon juice
1/2	teaspoon Lawry's seasoned salt
1	8-ounce carton sour cream
1/2	teaspoon garlic powder
1	4-ounce can taco sauce
1/4	cup chopped scallions
5	ounces Monterey Jack cheese, grated

Servings: 8 to 10
Preparation time: 15 minutes
Chilling time: 2 hours or more

- Peel and remove seed from avocado.
- Slice avocado very thinly and arrange slices in a 9 or 10-inch glass pie plate.
- Sprinkle with lemon juice and salt.
- Spread sour cream over slices and sprinkle with garlic powder.
- Pour taco sauce over entire mixture and cover with plastic wrap.
- Refrigerate for 2 hours or more.
- Just before serving, sprinkle with scallions and grated cheese.
- Serve with large corn chips or tostadas.

Bacon Wraps

1	1-pound package bacon
1	1-pound package pitted dates
	Toothpicks
	Brown sugar

Servings: 36 wraps
Preparation time: 15 minutes
Baking time: 5 minutes

- Preheat oven to 400° F.
- Cut bacon slices in half. Cook in a skillet until soft but still pliable.
- Wrap a piece of bacon around each date. Fasten with a toothpick.
- Dip in brown sugar.
- Bake for 5 minutes or until crispy and brown.
- May be frozen after dipped in brown sugar.

Bacon and Onion Roll-Ups

1	8-ounce package cream cheese, softened
8	green onions, chopped
14	slices thin white bread, crusts removed
14	slices bacon, cut in thirds
	Plain wooden toothpicks

Servings: 42 roll-ups
Preparation time: 30 minutes
Cooking time: 15 minutes

- Preheat oven to 400° F.
- Combine cream cheese and onions.
- Spread cream cheese mixture on bread, roll up and slice into 3 pieces.
- Wrap bacon around bread and secure with a plain wooden toothpick. Colored toothpicks will run.
- Bake for 10 minutes.

Chicken Teriyaki

4	chicken breast halves, skinned and boned
1/2	cup soy sauce
1/4	cup orange juice concentrate
1/2	cup water
1	teaspoon grated lemon rind
2	teaspoons sugar
1/4	teaspoon ground ginger
1	clove garlic, minced
1	small onion, minced

Servings: 4
Preparation time: 10 minutes
Marinating time: 1 hour
Baking time: 50 minutes

- Cut chicken into bite-sized pieces.
- Put chicken in an ovenproof casserole.
- Combine remaining ingredients and pour over chicken.
- Marinate for 1 hour or longer.
- Preheat oven to 325° F.
- Bake for 50 minutes, uncovered, turning occasionally.
- Serve with toothpicks.

Boursin Stuffed Mushrooms

12	medium to large fresh mushrooms
	Melted butter
1	5-ounce package Boursin or Rondele cheese
	Paprika
	Parsley for garnish

Servings: 4 to 6
Preparation time: 10 minutes
Baking time: 15 minutes

- Preheat oven to 350° F.
- Remove stems from mushrooms and wipe caps with a damp cloth.
- Brush outside of caps with melted butter.
- Fill caps with cheese.
- Arrange stuffed mushrooms on a cookie sheet, sprinkle with paprika and bake for approximately 15 minutes.
- Stuffed caps may be refrigerated overnight before baking.
- Garnish with parsley.

Stuffed Mushroom Caps

12	fresh mushrooms, at least 1-1/2 inches in diameter
4	tablespoons butter
2	small shallots, finely chopped
4	tablespoons finely chopped parsley
	Juice of 1/2 lemon
1/4	cup fine dry bread crumbs
1	tablespoon white wine
	Salt and pepper to taste
3	tablespoons butter

Servings: 12 mushrooms
Preparation time: 30 minutes
Baking time: 5 minutes

- Wipe mushrooms. Remove and chop stems.
- Melt 2 tablespoons butter in a medium skillet. Sauté mushroom caps gently on both sides for a total of 3 minutes.
- Remove to a small baking pan, cup side up. Set aside.
- Melt 2 tablespoons butter in skillet. Sauté chopped stems, shallots and parsley until tender and juice has evaporated. Remove from heat.
- Add lemon juice, bread crumbs, wine, salt and pepper.
- Add more bread crumbs or wine as needed to make correct consistency for stuffing.
- Stuff each cap and dot with butter.
- May be refrigerated at this point.
- When ready to serve, bake at 375° F. for 5 minutes.

French Fried Mushrooms

1	-12-ounce can of beer
1	cup all-purpose flour
	Salt to taste
1	pound fresh mushrooms
	All-purpose flour
	Vegetable oil or shortening for frying

Servings: 6 to 8
Preparation time: 15 minutes, prepare 3 hours ahead
Cooking time: 5 minutes

- Combine beer, flour and salt.
- Leave undisturbed for 3 hours.
- Wash, dry and trim mushrooms.
- Shake mushrooms in a bag of flour and dip into batter.
- Deep fry until golden brown, approximately 5 minutes.

Sausage Filled Mushrooms

40	large fresh mushrooms, stemmed
2	tablespoons butter, melted
1	pound bulk sausage
1/2	cup bread crumbs
1	egg
1/2	cup pizza or spaghetti sauce
2	large slices mozzarella cheese

Servings: 40 mushrooms
Preparation time: 25 minutes
Cooking time: 15 minutes

- Preheat oven to 425° F.
- Wash and dry mushrooms.
- Dip mushrooms in butter.
- Brown sausage and drain off all grease.
- Combine sausage, bread crumbs, egg and spaghetti sauce.
- Stuff mushrooms with sausage mixture.
- Top with a 1-inch square of sliced mozzarella.
- Bake for 15 minutes.

Blue Cheese Stuffed Mushrooms

12 to 14	large fresh mushrooms
1/4	cup chopped green onions
3	tablespoons butter
1/4	cup crumbled blue cheese
1/3	cup fine dry bread crumbs
	Salt and pepper to taste

Servings: 4 to 6
Preparation time: 20 minutes
Baking time: 12 minutes

- Preheat oven to 350° F.
- Remove stems from mushrooms.
- Chop stems and cook with onions in butter until tender but not brown.
- Add blue cheese, 2 tablespoons bread crumbs, salt and pepper.
- Fill mushroom caps with mixture.
- Sprinkle remaining bread crumbs on top.
- Place caps on a baking sheet and bake for 12 minutes.

Mushroom and Sausage Hors d'Oeuvre

1	pound hot bulk sausage
3	cups chopped fresh mushrooms
1	small onion, chopped
1	clove garlic, minced
1	teaspoon lemon juice
1	teaspoon Worcestershire sauce
1	8-ounce can crescent rolls
1	8-ounce package cream cheese, softened
1	cup freshly grated Parmesan cheese

Servings: 12
Preparation time: 20 minutes
Baking time: 20 minutes

- Brown sausage in a large skillet. Drain off all grease.
- Add mushrooms, onion and garlic. Sauté until tender.
- Add lemon juice and Worcestershire.
- Preheat oven to 350° F.
- Press crescent roll dough into bottom and up sides of a jelly roll pan.
- Spread cream cheese on dough.
- Top with sausage mixture.
- Sprinkle with Parmesan cheese.
- Bake for 20 minutes or until golden.
- Cool for 10 minutes. Then cut into squares.

Hot Sausage In Sour Cream

2	pounds highly seasoned bulk sausage
1	8-ounce jar Major Grey's chutney
1	cup sherry
1	cup sour cream

Servings: 14
Preparation time: 10 minutes
Cooking time: 20 to 25 minutes

- Roll sausage into bite-size balls. Cook in a skillet.
- Pour off grease and remove sausage to a chafing dish.
- Put chutney in skillet. Add sherry and sour cream.
- Cook gently and pour over sausage.

Crémaillère

1/4	pound unsalted butter
1	cup all-purpose flour
2	cups milk
2	cups freshly grated Parmesan cheese
4	egg yolks, beaten
1	teaspoon salt
1/3	teaspoon cayenne pepper
1/4	teaspoon ground nutmeg
1	loaf unsliced bread, very fresh and very soft
	Oil for frying

Servings: 48 rolls
Preparation time: 45 minutes
Cooking time: 5 minutes

- Melt butter in a saucepan.
- Add flour, a small amount at a time. Cook slowly for 10 minutes, stirring constantly. Do not brown.
- Heat milk to boiling point. Add hot milk to butter mixture, mixing vigorously with a whisk.
- Simmer for 10 minutes, stirring constantly.
- Add cheese, stirring until melted.
- Blend in egg yolks, salt, cayenne and nutmeg. Simmer for 2 minutes until mixture becomes a very thick paste. Cool. This paste may be prepared one day ahead and refrigerated.
- Cut crust from bread and slice into 48 very thin slices.
- Spread cheese mixture over each slice. Roll into a cigarette shape.
- When ready to serve, fry rolls, 12 at a time, in very hot oil (400° F.), until brown. They brown almost immediately.
- Serve at once.

Chutney Dip

2	8-ounce packages cream cheese, softened
1/2	cup Major Grey's Best chutney, chopped
1/2	cup almonds, toasted
2	teaspoons curry powder
1/2	teaspoon dry mustard

Servings: 15 to 20
Preparation time: 10 minutes

- Mix all ingredients and refrigerate.
- Keeps indefinitely.
- Serve with crackers.

Kaiser Dippers

3	tablespoons butter
1	medium onion, chopped
1	cup chopped ham
1	cup chopped corned beef
1	clove garlic, minced
2	cups sauerkraut, drained and chopped
1/2	cup beef broth
6	tablespoons all-purpose flour
1	egg, lightly beaten
1/2	teaspoon salt
1	tablespoon Worcestershire sauce
1	tablespoon snipped parsley
2	eggs, beaten
2	cups bread crumbs
	Oil for deep frying
	Mustard
	Sour cream
	Toothpicks

Servings: 4 dozen appetizers
Preparation time: 15 minutes
Cooking time: 15 minutes
Chilling time: 3 hours

- Heat butter in a 10-inch skillet and sauté onion.
- Add ham, corned beef and garlic. Cook for 10 minutes.
- Stir in next 7 ingredients.
- Cook until thick, about 3 minutes.
- Cool. Cover and chill for several hours.
- Shape cold mixture into 1-inch balls.
- Dip balls in egg. Then roll in crumbs.
- Fry, a few at a time, in deep oil at 375° F. until lightly browned, about 2 to 3 minutes.
- Drain on paper towels.
- Serve warm with toothpicks or small forks for dipping in mustard or sour cream.

Vidalia Onion Spread

6	medium Vidalia onions or other sweet onions
1/2	cup cider vinegar
1	cup sugar
2	cups water
1/2	cup mayonnaise
1	teaspoon celery salt

Servings: 12
Preparation time: 10 minutes
Chilling time: 3 to 4 hours

- Slice onions paper thin.
- Mix with vinegar, sugar and water.
- Let stand in refrigerator for 3 to 4 hours.
- Drain well.
- Mix onions with mayonnaise and celery salt.
- Pour into a serving dish and surround with melba toast or crackers.
- This makes excellent filling for finger sandwiches.

Chile Rellenos Squares

3	cups grated Monterey Jack cheese
1	3-ounce can green chilies, drained and chopped
4	large eggs, beaten

Servings: 64 squares
Preparation time: 10 minutes
Baking time: 1 hour

- Preheat oven to 350° F.
- Sprinkle cheese and chilies evenly into the bottom of a greased 8-inch square pan.
- Pour eggs on top of cheese mixture.
- Bake for 1 hour.
- Allow to cool for 5 minutes. Cut into 1-inch squares.
- Serve warm or cold.

Caviar Egg Ring

8	hard-boiled eggs
1	small onion, minced
1/4	teaspoon dry mustard
2	tablespoons lemon juice
1/4	teaspoon monosodium glutamate
1/2	cup mayonnaise
1/2	cup margarine, melted but not hot
1	cup caviar
4	tablespoons snipped fresh parsley

Servings: 16
Preparation time: 15 minutes
Chilling time: 5 hours

- Chop eggs into 1/4-inch pieces.
- Mix onion, mustard, lemon juice and monosodium glutamate.
- Add mayonnaise and margarine.
- Gently fold in eggs.
- Pour into an oiled 1-quart ring mold. Chill for at least 5 hours.
- To serve, unmold carefully and fill center with caviar.
- Sprinkle with chopped parsley.

Caviar Supreme

1 envelope unflavored gelatin
1/4 cup water

Egg Layer
4 hard-boiled eggs, chopped
1/2 cup mayonnaise
1/4 cup chopped fresh parsley
Salt to taste
White pepper to taste
Hot sauce to taste

Avocado Layer
1 medium avocado, puréed
1 medium avocado, diced
1 shallot, minced
2 tablespoons lemon juice
2 tablespoons mayonnaise
Salt and pepper to taste
Hot sauce to taste

Sour Cream and Onion Layer
1 cup sour cream
1/4 cup minced onion

3 to 4 ounces black caviar
Lemon juice to taste
2 ounces pimento strips

Servings: 25
Preparation time: 45 minutes
Chilling time: overnight

- Line bottom and sides of a 1-quart soufflé dish with foil. Extend both ends of foil at least 4 inches beyond rim.
- Oil lightly.
- Soften gelatin in water in a cup.
- Dissolve gelatin by setting cup in a pan of hot water. Gelatin will be divided among the three layers.
- Combine all ingredients with 1 tablespoon gelatin mixture.
- Spread into bottom of prepared dish with a spatula.

- Combine all ingredients with 1 tablespoon gelatin mixture.
- Gently spread over egg layer.

- Mix sour cream and onion with remaining 2 tablespoons gelatin mixture.
- Spread over avocado layer.
- Cover dish tightly with plastic wrap and refrigerate overnight.
- Just before serving, place caviar in a fine sieve. Rinse gently under cold running water.
- Sprinkle lemon juice over caviar and drain.
- Lift mold out of dish onto serving platter, using foil extensions as handles.
- Spread caviar over top and create your own design on top using pimento strips.

Cottage Cheese Mold

4	tablespoons milk
1	16-ounce carton small curd cottage cheese
1/2	teaspoon Worcestershire sauce
3 to 4	celery leaves, finely chopped
1/4	medium sweet onion, finely chopped
3	tablespoons mayonnaise
1/2	teaspoon salt
1/4	teaspoon white pepper
	Juice of 1/2 large lemon
3	tablespoons milk
1-1/2	envelopes Knox unflavored gelatin
	Vegetable spray
	Chives or parsley for garnish
	Lettuce leaves
	Mayonnaise

Servings: 8
Preparation time: 15 minutes
Refrigeration time: 4 hours

- Combine first 9 ingredients in order listed by placing in a blender jar with blender running at low speed.
- Warm 3 tablespoons milk and add gelatin. Stir until thoroughly dissolved.
- Add mixture to blender and blend for 6 seconds.
- Spray a 1-quart ring mold with vegetable spray. Pour blended ingredients in mold and refrigerate until firm, approximately 4 hours.
- Unmold on a platter and fill center with marinated vegetables such as carrots, broccoli and string beans. Surround edge with cherry tomatoes.
- Garnish with chives or chopped parsley and serve on a bed of greens with extra mayonnaise.

Frosted Artichokes With Caviar

1	8-ounce package cream cheese, softened
2	tablespoons sour cream
2	teaspoons mayonnaise
1	teaspoon lemon juice
2	teaspoons grated onion
1	teaspoon garlic salt
1	8-1/2-ounce can artichokes, drained
1	2-ounce jar caviar

Servings: 2 cups
Preparation time: 15 minutes

- Combine first 6 ingredients.
- Chop artichokes and pack into a mound on a serving plate.
- Spread cream cheese mixture over artichokes.
- Sprinkle caviar over top.
- Serve with mild crackers.

Pâté Burgette

Pâté

2	pounds chicken livers
6	tablespoons butter
1/3	cup chopped onion
1	tablespoon dried chervil
1	tablespoon dried tarragon
4	tablespoons cognac
1/2	cup light cream
5	eggs
	Salt and pepper to taste
8	slices bacon
2	bay leaves

Servings: 24
Preparation time: 1-1/2 hours
Baking time: 1-1/2 hours
Must be made 1 day before serving.

- Preheat oven to 400° F.
- Clean and trim livers. Dry on paper towels. Then cut in half.
- Melt butter in a large skillet. Sauté onion and herbs.
- Remove skillet from heat. Add livers, cognac, cream, eggs, salt and pepper.
- Purée mixture in a blender or food processor, or mash in a bowl. Do not over process.
- Line a loaf pan with bacon. Put bay leaves on the bottom. Spoon in liver mixture.
- Place in a pan of hot water that is 1 inch deep.
- Bake for 1-1/2 hours.
- Cool completely on a rack.
- Cover and refrigerate overnight.
- The day of serving, unmold pâté and turn out onto a tray. Remove bacon and bay leaves. Smooth surfaces.
- Cover and chill until ready to glaze.

continued...

Pâté Burgette continued...

Glaze

1	envelope unflavored gelatin
1/4	cup cold water
1	cup white wine
1/2	teaspoon dried tarragon
1	teaspoon chopped fresh parsley

- Sprinkle gelatin over cold water in a saucepan. Let stand for 5 minutes.
- Add wine, tarragon and parsley.
- Stir over low heat until gelatin dissolves. Strain.
- Set pan in ice water. Allow to thicken for about 15 minutes, stirring occasionally.
- Paint entire pâté with glaze. Chill to set, about 1/2 hour.

Decoration

1	hard-boiled egg
1/2	teaspoon butter, softened
1	pimento, cut into 1/4-inch strips
1	ripe olive
1/2	green bell pepper
2	capers
1	bunch watercress

- Halve egg crosswise. Remove yolk and mash with butter. Set aside.
- Place pimento strips end to end around top edge of pâté. Put a slice of olive in each corner.
- Cut oval slices from egg white to be flower petals.
- Cut green pepper to make 2 stems and 2 leaves.
- Make 2 daisies of egg white petals and use yolk for centers. Dot both centers with a caper. Arrange leaves and stems.
- Surround loaf with a wreath of watercress.
- Serve with melba toast or French bread.

"The" Pâté

1	pound chicken livers
3/4	cup fresh mushrooms, sliced
1	cup butter
1/4	cup chopped green onions
1/3	cup cognac
1	teaspoon salt
1/8	teaspoon black pepper
1/8	teaspoon cayenne pepper
1/4	teaspoon ground allspice
1/8	teaspoon dried thyme
1	3-ounce package cream cheese, softened
	Mayonnaise
	Caviar

Servings: 8 to 10
Preparation time: 1 hour
Chilling time: 1 hour

- Wash, dry and chop chicken livers.
- Sauté mushrooms in butter for 5 minutes. Remove with a slotted spoon and set aside.
- Sauté green onions in same pan for 5 minutes.
- Add livers, stir and sauté for 5 minutes or until barely pink.
- Put liver mixture into a food processor or blender and mix well.
- Add mushrooms, cognac and seasonings.
- If mixture is too thick, thin with melted butter, 1 tablespoon at a time.
- Mold into a mound and cool in refrigerator.
- Ice mound with cream cheese that has been softened with mayonnaise.
- Spread caviar over all.
- May be done ahead.

Frosted Pâté

1	pound braunschweiger or liverwurst
1	clove garlic, crushed and minced
1/4	cup finely chopped fresh parsley
1/2	teaspoon dried basil, crushed
1/4	cup minced onion
1	8-ounce package cream cheese, softened
1	tablespoon mayonnaise
1/8	teaspoon Tabasco sauce
	Fresh parsley for garnish

Servings: 16
Preparation time: 20 minutes
Chilling time: 2 hours

- Mash braunschweiger in a bowl.
- Blend in next 4 ingredients.
- Shape into a mound on a serving plate.
- Chill until firm.
- Combine cream cheese, mayonnaise and Tabasco. Spread over pâté.
- Garnish with parsley.
- Serve with crackers.

Hot Appetizer Pie

1	8-ounce package cream cheese, softened
2	tablespoons milk
2	tablespoons minced onion
2	tablespoons minced green bell pepper
1/2	teaspoon pepper
1	2-1/2-ounce jar dried beef, chopped
1/2	cup sour cream
	Tabasco sauce to taste
1/4	cup chopped walnuts

Servings: 8 to 10
Preparation time: 15 minutes
Baking time: 15 minutes

- Preheat oven to 350° F.
- Blend first 5 ingredients.
- Stir in beef, sour cream and Tabasco.
- Spoon into a buttered shallow 1-quart baking dish.
- Sprinkle with nuts.
- Bake, uncovered, for 15 minutes.
- Serve hot with Triscuits.

Fried Zucchini

2	pounds zucchini
1/4	cup all-purpose flour
1	teaspoon salt
1/2	teaspoon pepper
2	eggs, beaten
2	tablespoons lemon juice
1-1/2	cups Pepperidge Farm herb bread crumbs
1/2 to 1	cup bacon grease

Servings: 6 to 8
Preparation time: 10 minutes
Cooking time: 15 minutes

- Wash zucchini. Do not peel.
- Cut into 1/4-inch slices.
- Combine flour, salt and pepper on waxed paper.
- Combine eggs and lemon juice in a bowl.
- Crush bread crumbs with a rolling pin or in a food processor until fine.
- Roll zucchini in flour mixture, then egg mixture, then crumbs.
- Fry in hot bacon grease until brown on both sides.
- Drain well on paper towels and serve immediately.

Asparagus-Cheese Canapes

1	loaf thin sliced white bread
1	8-ounce package cream cheese
1	6-ounce package Roquefort cheese
1	tablespoon Hellmann's mayonnaise
1	egg, beaten
1	15-ounce can Green Giant extra long asparagus spears
1/2	cup butter, melted

Servings: 60 to 75 canapes
Preparation time: 45 minutes
Freezing time: 1 hour
Baking time: 10 minutes

- Cut crust from bread. Roll each slice flat with a rolling pin (steaming crustless slices of bread in a colander over boiling water until damp will facilitate rolling bread).
- Mix cheeses and mayonnaise until smooth.
- Add egg and mix into a paste. Do not use a food processor as mixture will be too soft.
- Spead mixture to edges of each slice of bread.
- Place 1 asparagus spear on edge of bread and roll like a jelly roll.
- Smooth final edge and ends of roll.
- Brush all sides of rolls with melted butter. Place on a cookie sheet and quick freeze.
- When frozen, remove from freezer and cut each roll into thirds.
- Store in Zip-loc plastic bag in freezer.
- When ready to serve, remove amount needed and toast in a preheated 350° F. oven for 10 minutes or until golden brown.

Tennis Team Spinach Spread

1	10-ounce package frozen chopped spinach
1	8-ounce carton large curd cottage cheese
8	green onions, chopped
1	2-ounce jar pimentos, chopped
1/4	cup chopped celery
	Seasoned salt and pepper to taste

Servings: 2 cups
Preparation time: 30 minutes
Chilling time: 24 hours

- Cook spinach according to package directions. Drain well.
- Combine spinach with remaining ingredients.
- Refrigerate for 24 hours to blend flavors.
- Serve with crackers and raw vegetables.

Dallas Cowboy Dip

3	15-1/4-ounce cans black-eyed peas, drained
5 to 8	jalapeño peppers, remove seeds and chop
1	teaspoon jalapeño pepper juice
1/2	medium onion, chopped
1	4-ounce can green chilies, drained and chopped
1	clove garlic, crushed and minced
1/2	pound butter
1/2	pound sharp Cheddar cheese, grated

Servings: 5 cups
Preparation time: 20 minutes

- Combine first 6 ingredients.
- In the top of a double boiler, melt butter and cheese.
- Combine the two mixtures.
- Serve warm with corn chips.

Feta Phyllo Squares

1	10-ounce package frozen chopped spinach
1/2	pound phyllo leaves (found in frozen food section of market)
1	cup butter, melted
4	eggs
1	8-ounce package cream cheese, softened
1	pound Feta cheese

Servings: 48 squares
Preparation time: 30 minutes
Baking time: 30 minutes

- Cook spinach according to package directions. Drain well.
- Preheat oven to 375° F.
- Separate phyllo into 16 leaves. Cut to fit inside a 12 x 17-inch jelly roll pan.
- Lay 8 leaves in bottom of pan, brushing each with melted butter (use approximately 1/3 cup).
- Beat eggs until fluffy.
- Add cream cheese and Feta cheese, blending well.
- Add spinach and beat well.
- Pour mixture onto phyllo base.
- Top with remaining phyllo leaves, brushing each with melted butter.
- Drizzle remaining melted butter over top.
- Bake for 30 minutes.
- Cool for 15 minutes before cutting into squares.

Homemade Boursin Cheese

2	large cloves garlic, minced
1/2	cup minced fresh chives
1/4	cup minced fresh parsley
1	8-ounce package cream cheese, softened
8	ounces farmers cheese
	Salt and pepper to taste

Servings: 6
Preparation time: 15 minutes
Chilling time: 5 hours

- Combine all ingredients and mix thoroughly.
- Cover and chill for at least 5 hours.
- May be made ahead.
- May be frozen.

Salads & Molds

Cold Snapper Mold

1-1/2	pounds fresh red or pink snapper fillets
1	cup court bouillon or light chicken broth
2	tablespoons capers
	Juice of 1 lime
1/4	cup white wine
4	green onions, minced
1	envelope unflavored gelatin
1/3	cup water
2	cups mayonnaise, preferably homemade
	Salt and pepper to taste
	Bibb lettuce
	Ripe olives for garnish
	Cherry tomatoes for garnish

Servings: 8
Preparation time: 20 minutes
Cooking time: 5 minutes
Chilling time: 4 hours or overnight

- Poach snapper in bouillon for 3 to 5 minutes.
- Cool in broth.
- Remove any bones from fillets and flake to measure 2 cups of fish.
- Combine fish with capers, lime juice, wine and onions.
- Dissolve gelatin in water. Then add to fish.
- Stir in 1 cup mayonnaise.
- Add salt and pepper.
- Pat mixture into an oiled 4-cup mold.
- Cover and chill for several hours or overnight.
- When ready to serve, unmold onto bed of lettuce and frost with 1 cup mayonnaise.
- Garnish with olives and tomatoes.
- Serve as a luncheon dish, light supper or appetizer.

Chutney and Curry Chicken Salad

1/2	cup chutney	
3/4	cup mayonnaise	
1	teaspoon curry powder	
2	teaspoons grated lime peel	
1/4	cup fresh lime juice	
1/2	teaspoon salt	
4	cups cooked and diced white chicken meat	
1	cup pineapple chunks, drained	
1/2	cup chopped green onions	
1/2	cup slivered almonds, toasted	
	Butter or Bibb lettuce leaves	

Servings: 6
Preparation time: 15 minutes

- Combine first 6 ingredients. Mix well.
- Pour over chicken, pineapple, onions and almonds. Lightly mix together.
- Refrigerate.
- Serve on lettuce leaves.

Cobb Salad

1/3	cup salad oil
2/3	cup red wine vinegar
1	clove garlic, minced
1	teaspoon salt
1/2	teaspoon pepper
1	teaspoon sugar
1	teaspoon dry mustard
1	teaspoon paprika
1	teaspoon Worcestershire sauce
1/2	head iceberg lettuce, chopped
1/2	bunch watercress, chopped
1	bunch chicory, chopped
1	head romaine lettuce, torn
2-1/2	tablespoons minced fresh chives
3	tomatoes, chopped
2-1/2	cups cooked and diced white chicken
6	slices bacon, cooked and crumbled
2	hard-boiled eggs, diced
3	ounces blue cheese, crumbled
1	avocado, diced

Servings: 6
Preparation time: 20 minutes

- Early in the day, combine first 9 ingredients in a jar. Cover and shake well. Then refrigerate.
- When ready to serve, place remaining ingredients in a large salad bowl. Mix well, but gently.
- Pour salad dressing as needed over salad and toss.
- Serve immediately.

Chicken Salad Supreme

4	cups cubed cooked chicken
1-1/2	cups chopped celery
3	green onions, sliced
1	6-ounce can sliced water chestnuts, drained
2	medium pieces candied ginger, finely chopped
1	teaspoon salt
1	cup real mayonnaise
1/2	cup heavy cream, whipped
1/2	cup sliced seedless grapes

Servings: 6 to 8
Preparation time: 20 minutes
Chilling time: 1 hour

- Mix chicken, celery, onions, water chestnuts, ginger and salt.
- Fold mayonnaise into whipped cream and combine with chicken mixture.
- Chill for at least 1 hour.
- Garnish with grapes.
- A nice touch is to spoon chicken salad into center of a broccoli or spinach mold.

Chicken Stack-Up Salad

3	cups cubed cooked chicken
1/2	teaspoon curry powder
1/2	teaspoon salt
1/2	teaspoon paprika
1/4	teaspoon pepper
2	cups shredded iceberg lettuce
2	cups shredded romaine lettuce
1/4	cup chopped fresh parsley
1	medium onion, sliced
1	large cucumber, sliced
1	cup short pasta, cooked and drained
1	large green bell pepper, sliced thinly into rings
1-1/2	cups mayonnaise
2	tablespoons lemon juice
2	tablespoons milk
1	teaspoon salt
1/4	teaspoon pepper
1/4	cup chopped fresh parsley
2	tomatoes cut into wedges

Servings: 6
Preparation time: 30 minutes
Refrigeration time: overnight

- In a small bowl, combine first 5 ingredients. Toss to coat well.
- In a clear salad bowl, layer lettuce, chicken mixture, parsley, onion, cucumber, pasta and green pepper.
- Combine mayonnaise, lemon juice, milk, salt and pepper. Spread over salad.
- Cover and chill overnight.
- When ready to serve, sprinkle with parsley and garnish with tomato wedges.

SALADS & MOLDS

Tropical Chicken Salad

2	cups chicken, white meat, cooked and cubed
1	cup pineapple chunks, fresh or canned
1	orange, peeled and coarsely chopped
3	tablespoons salad oil
2	tablespoons lemon juice
1/2	cup white seedless grapes, halved
1/2	cup mayonnaise
1/4	cup slivered almonds, toasted
1/2	cup shredded coconut, toasted
	Lettuce leaves

Servings: 4
Preparation time: 30 minutes
Marinating time: 2 hours

- Combine and mix chicken, pineapple and orange.
- Combine oil and lemon juice.
- Marinate chicken mixture in oil and lemon juice.
- Drain chicken mixture.
- Add grapes and mayonnaise.
- Toss to combine.
- Garnish with almonds and coconut.
- Serve on lettuce leaves.

Rice and Shrimp Salad

1	cup sour cream
2	cups mayonnaise
2	tablespoons tarragon vinegar
3	tablespoons chopped parsley
3	tablespoons chopped chives
2	tablespoons chopped scallions
2	cups raw rice
3	tablespoons tarragon vinegar
3	tablespoons olive oil
1-1/2	pounds shrimp, cooked

Servings: 8
Preparation time: 30 minutes
Cooking time: 20 minutes

- Combine sour cream, mayonnaise, 2 tablespoons vinegar, parsley, chives and scallions in a jar.
- Cook rice according to package directions. When done and still hot, pour 3 tablespoons vinegar and olive oil over rice and mix.
- Add enough sour cream sauce to moisten rice. Then add shrimp.
- Serve at once.
- Leftover sour cream sauce may be stored in refrigerator for 2 weeks.
- May substitute chicken or ham for shrimp.

Cold Seafood and Pasta Salad

Mayonnaise

1	egg
1/2 to 1	cup vegetable oil
	Juice of 1 lemon
2	anchovy fillets (optional)
1/4	teaspoon dried orégano or dried tarragon
2	tablespoons capers

Salad

2	cups pasta, combination of small shapes
	Mayonnaise
1	head leaf lettuce
1/2	pound prawns or shrimp, cooked, shelled and deveined
	Lettuce for garnish
2 to 3	tablespoons capers for garnish
1	lemon, sliced for garnish
	Fresh snipped parsley for garnish

Servings: 6
Preparation time: 30 minutes
Chilling time: 30 minutes

- In a blender or food processor, blend egg briefly. Then add oil slowly until mixture begins to thicken.
- Add lemon juice, anchovy fillets and orégano. Blend until smooth.
- Stir in capers.
- Cook pasta in a large pot of boiling water until tender.
- Drain well and place in a bowl, tossing with mayonnaise.
- Line a serving bowl with lettuce. Stir prawns into pasta.
- Arrange pasta mixture on lettuce.
- Garnish with lettuce, capers, lemon slices and parsley.
- Store, covered, in the refrigerator and remove 30 minutes before serving.

Louis Pappas' Famous Greek Salad

Salad

10	large lettuce leaves
1	head iceberg lettuce, shredded
4	cups potato salad (recipe below)
2	cucumbers, peeled and sliced
2	tomatoes, quartered
1	avocado, peeled and sliced
8	green onions
2	green bell peppers, cut into thin circles
20	black olives
1/2	pound Feta cheese, crumbled
20	hot cherry or banana peppers
1	2-ounce can anchovies
1/2	bunch watercress
1	pound shrimp, cooked and shelled

Servings: 12
Preparation time: 1 hour
Cooking time: 40 minutes

- Place lettuce leaves around edge of a large oval platter.
- Cover with shredded lettuce.
- Mound potato salad in center of platter.
- Stack cucumber slices around potato salad.
- Lay tomato quarters around cucumbers.
- Put avocado slices between tomato quarters.
- Arrange green onions, green peppers and black olives on platter.
- Sprinkle Feta cheese on top.
- Garnish with hot peppers and anchovies.
- Arrange watercress and shrimp around edge of platter.
- Pour desired amount of dressing over all.

Dressing

1	cup olive oil
1	cup red wine vinegar
1/8	teaspoon dried thyme
1/8	teaspoon dried orégano
1/8	cup chopped parsley

- Combine all ingredients in a jar and shake well.

Potato Salad

2	pounds peeled white potatoes
1	cup real mayonnaise
3	tablespoons vinegar
1	large white onion, diced
2	teaspoons salt

- Boil potatoes in water until tender.
- Allow to cool and cut into cubes.
- Combine mayonnaise and vinegar.
- Combine onion, salt, mayonnaise mixture and potatoes. Mix together gently.

Cucumber Salmon Mousse

SALADS & MOLDS

Mousse

2	envelopes unflavored gelatin
1/4	cup cold water
2	13-1/2-ounce cans Consommé Madrilene
1	16-ounce can red salmon
3/4	cup finely chopped celery
1/4	cup minced green onion
3/4	cup finely chopped cucumber
2	cups sour cream
1/2	cup mayonnaise
1	tablespoon horseradish
1/2	teaspoon salt
1	3-ounce jar red caviar for garnish or sauce
	Parsley for garnish
	Lemon wedges for garnish

Red Caviar Sauce

1	cup mayonnaise
1/4	cup light cream
1	tablespoon lemon juice
1	tablespoon minced parsley
	Red caviar

Servings: 12
Preparation time: 30 minutes
Chilling time: 3 to 4 hours

- Soften gelatin in cold water for 5 minutes.
- Heat 1 cup consommé to simmering. Add to gelatin and stir until gelatin is dissolved.
- Stir in remaining consommé.
- Stir in salmon liquid from can and cool until liquid begins to thicken.
- Pick skin and bones from salmon.
- Flake salmon and combine with celery, onion and cucumber.
- Fold salmon and vegetables into gelatin mixture.
- Combine sour cream, mayonnaise, horseradish and salt.
- Fold mixtures together.
- Spoon into a greased 2-quart mold.
- Chill until firm.
- When ready to serve, run a knife around edge of mold.
- Place a hot wet towel over bottom of mold and invert onto serving plate.

- Combine all ingredients and chill.
- Serve with mousse.

Thousand Island Mold with Fresh Seafood

2	envelopes unflavored gelatin
1/2	cup cold water
1-1/2	cups mayonnaise
1	cup chili sauce
1/4	teaspoon Tabasco sauce
1/2	teaspoon sugar
1/4	teaspoon salt
6	hard-boiled eggs, sliced
1	cucumber, chopped
1	cup chopped celery
1/3	cup chopped scallions
1	pound fresh crabmeat or fresh shrimp, shelled and cooked
2	tablespoons fresh lemon juice
	Bibb lettuce as needed
	Watercress sprigs as needed
	Parsley for garnish

Servings: 8
Preparation time: 20 minutes
Chilling time: 6 hours

- Soften gelatin in cold water. Dissolve by stirring in the top of a double boiler over hot water for 3 minutes.
- Combine gelatin, mayonnaise, chili sauce, Tabasco sauce, sugar and salt. Blend well.
- Chill in refrigerator until slightly thickened.
- Gently fold in eggs, cucumber, celery and scallions.
- Pour mixture into an oiled 8-cup ring mold. Refrigerate for at least 6 hours.
- Combine seafood with lemon juice.
- Prepare a platter with a bed of Bibb lettuce leaves and watercress sprigs.
- Unmold salad ring onto lettuce. Fill center with seafood.
- Garnish with parsley and serve immediately.

Watercress Salad with Turkey and Bacon

Dressing

1-1/2	cups olive oil
2/3	cup red wine vinegar
1	egg yolk
1	tablespoon Dijon mustard
1/8	teaspoon dried orégano
1/8	teaspoon dried thyme
1/8	teaspoon dried basil
1/8	teaspoon paprika
	Ground nutmeg to taste
1/2	teaspoon salt
1/8	teaspoon pepper
1	teaspoon Worcestershire sauce
6	drops Tabasco sauce
2	cloves garlic, peeled

Servings: 8
Preparation time: 15 minutes

- Mix olive oil and vinegar in a large bowl.
- Using a wire whisk, mix in remaining ingredients. Stir until smooth and velvety.
- Pour in a covered jar and keep refrigerated.
- This dressing will yield approximately 2-1/2 cups.

Salad

5	bunches watercress
10	bacon slices, fried and crumbled
1-1/2	cups diced smoked turkey
1	avocado, peeled and cut into cubes

- Assemble all ingredients in a large salad bowl.
- Toss lightly with dressing.
- Serve on chilled plates.

Seafood and Pasta Salad Pescara

1	pound of short pasta (macaroni, shells, swirls)
3	cups fresh seafood, cooked and diced
3/4	cup fresh diced tomato
1/4	cup finely snipped fresh dill weed
1/2	cup diced shallots
3	tablespoons capers
1/4	cup diced red pimentos
1/4	cup diced ripe olives
1/2	cup lemon juice
1/4	cup Dijon mustard
1	tablespoon vinegar
2	tablespoons vegetable oil
1/2	cup ripe olives, pitted and halved
1/2	cup grated zucchini

Servings: 8
Preparation time: 1 hour
Cooking time: 10 minutes

- Cook pasta until tender and drain.
- Put pasta in a large serving bowl. Toss with seafood, 1/2 cup tomatoes, dill, shallots, capers, pimentos, olives and lemon juice.
- Mix mustard and vinegar until smooth. Then add oil.
- Pour dressing over salad and toss well.
- Decorate top of salad with remaining 1/4 cup tomatoes, olive halves and grated zucchini.
- Serve at room temperature or slightly chilled.
- Serve with Parmesan bread and fresh cantaloupe slices.
- May be done ahead.

Tuna Mousse with Cucumber Sauce

Mousse

3/4	cup cold water
3	envelopes unflavored gelatin
3	7-ounce cans of waterpacked tuna, drained and flaked
1-1/2	cups finely chopped celery
8	pimento-stuffed olives, finely chopped
2	cups mayonnaise
1-1/2	teaspoons salt
3	tablespoons lemon juice
3	teaspoons capers

Sauce

1	unpeeled cucumber, finely chopped
1	tablespoon grated onion
1/4	cup mayonnaise
2	teaspoons vinegar
1	tablespoon chopped parsley
1/2	cup sour cream
	Salt and pepper to taste

Servings: 10
Preparation time: 30 minutes
Chilling time: 4 to 5 hours

- In the top of a double boiler, soften gelatin in cold water.
- Place over simmering water and stir until dissolved. Cool.
- Add remaining ingredients to gelatin and mix well.
- Chill in an oiled 2-quart mold until set.

- Combine all ingredients.
- Chill.
- Serve with mousse.

Roast Beef Salad with French Mustard Dressing

Salad

2	pounds cooked roast beef
2	medium Bermuda onions
1	pound green beans
2	pounds Idaho potatoes, boiled and thinly sliced
2	cups cherry tomatoes
1/4	cup minced shallots
3	tablespoons beef broth
	Minced chives for garnish
	Minced parsley for garnish

Dressing

1/2	cup red wine vinegar
2	tablespoons Dijon mustard
1	teaspoon salt
	Pepper to taste
1	cup olive oil

Servings: 6 to 8
Preparation time: 40 minutes

- Cut roast beef into 1/4 X 2-inch strips.
- Slice onions and separate into rings.
- Cook green beans in boiling water until just tender. Drain and run under cold water.
- Trim ends off beans and cut into 1-inch pieces.
- Combine all ingredients and mix well.
- Toss beans with half of the dressing and put in refrigerator.
- Combine potatoes, shallots and beef broth. Mix well.
- Add remaining dressing to potatoes, mixing gently.
- To assemble, layer onion slices around the outside of a large platter.
- Make a ring of green beans, then potatoes, then tomatoes. Mound roast beef in the center and top with a rosette of onion rings.
- Sprinkle with chives and parsley.
- Dressing may be prepared ahead of time and kept in refrigerator. Bring to room temperature before serving.

Gourmet Beef Salad Vinaigrette

1-1/2	pounds sirloin beef roast, cooked
3/4	pound fresh mushrooms, halved
1	cup artichoke hearts, halved
3	tomatoes, peeled and chopped
2	tablespoons fresh lemon juice
1/4	cup red wine vinegar
1/2	teaspoon salt
1/2	teaspoon lemon pepper
1/2	cup sliced scallions
3/4	cup salad oil
1/4	teaspoon dry mustard
1/8	teaspoon dried rosemary
1/8	teaspoon dried thyme
1/8	teaspoon dried marjoram
1/8	teaspoon white pepper
2	heads Bibb lettuce
	Watercress sprigs for garnish
	Tomato wedges

Servings: 6 to 8
Preparation time: 30 minutes
Chilling time: 4 hours

- Carve meat into 1/8-inch thick slices. Cut into strips 1 inch wide and 3 inches long.
- Place in a large bowl.
- Add mushrooms, artichoke hearts and tomatoes.
- In a separate bowl, combine next 11 ingredients. Mix thoroughly.
- Pour marinade over beef mixture.
- Cover and chill for 4 hours.
- Stir occasionally.
- Line a platter with Bibb lettuce. Arrange meat mixture attractively in center.
- Use as much marinade as you like over it.
- Surround salad with tomato wedges.
- Garnish with watercress sprigs.
- May substitute flank steak for sirloin.
- Beef and vegetables may be marinated separately. Then arrange attractively on platter.

Tabouli

1	cup bulgur wheat
	Boiling water
2	large green onions, finely chopped
1	large tomato
1	cucumber
1	bunch of parsley, about 2 cups
1	small clove garlic, crushed and minced
1/4	cup lemon juice
1/8	cup olive oil
2	teaspoons salt
	Pepper to taste

Servings: 8
Preparation time: 30 minutes
Chilling time: 2 to 3 hours

- Put wheat in a bowl and cover with boiling water. Let wheat stand while you prepare all vegetables. Then drain off excess water.
- Chop all vegetables very finely.
- Combine vegetables, wheat, lemon juice, oil, salt and pepper.
- Refrigerate for 2 to 3 hours to let flavors ripen before serving.
- Great as a salad, but equally good when used as a filling for pita bread pockets.

Artichoke-Rice Salad

1	package chicken-flavored (or paella-flavored) rice mix
4	green onions, thinly sliced
1/2	green bell pepper, chopped
12	pimento-stuffed olives, sliced
2	6-ounce jars marinated artichoke hearts
3/4	teaspoon curry powder
1/2	cup mayonnaise

Servings: 6 to 8
Preparation time: 30 minutes
Cooking time: 15 to 20 minutes

- Cook rice according to package directions, omitting butter.
- Place rice in a large bowl. Cool.
- Add onions, green peppers and olives.
- Drain artichoke hearts, reserving marinade. Cut hearts in half.
- Combine artichoke marinade, curry powder and mayonnaise.
- Add artichoke hearts to rice mixture.
- Toss with dressing and chill.
- This may be used as a side dish. If shrimp, chicken or ham is added, it may serve as a main course.

Georgia Coleslaw

1/2	pound bacon
1/4	small head red cabbage, shredded
1/4	small head green cabbage, shredded
1	large carrot, shredded
1/2	cup diced green bell pepper
1/2	cup chopped onion
1	shallot, minced
1	cup mayonnaise
1/2	cup sour cream
1/4	cup cold beef broth or stock
2	teaspoons white wine vinegar
1/2	teaspoon chili powder
1/2	teaspoon salt
1/4	teaspoon dry mustard
1/8	teaspoon white pepper
2	tablespoons light cream
	Sprigs of watercress for garnish

Servings: 8 to 10
Preparation time: 30 minutes
Chilling time: 1 hour

- Cook bacon in large frying pan until crisp. Drain on paper towels, reserving 3 tablespoons of bacon drippings.
- In a large mixing bowl, combine red and green cabbage, carrot, pepper, onion and shallot.
- In a separate bowl, whisk together mayonnaise, reserved drippings, sour cream, broth and vinegar. Add chili powder, salt, mustard and white pepper. Whisk in enough cream to thin to a desired consistency.
- Add dressing to slaw and toss well.
- Crumble bacon, reserving half for garnish. Add remainder to slaw and toss to mix.
- Cover and refrigerate for at least 1 hour.
- Serve garnished with watercress and reserved bacon.

Mushroom Salad

1/2	pound fresh mushrooms, sliced
1/2	cup sliced celery
1/2	cup chopped green bell pepper
1/4	cup salad oil
1/4	cup red wine vinegar
3	tablespoons chopped onion
2	tablespoons chopped dill weed
1	teaspoon chervil
1/4	teaspoon salt
1/4	teaspoon sugar

Servings: 4
Preparation time: 20 minutes

- Combine mushrooms, celery and green pepper in a salad bowl.
- Combine remaining ingredients. Pour over mushroom mixture and toss lightly.
- Let salad sit and soak in dressing before serving.

Parslied Salad with Homemade Croutons

Salad

8	tablespoons light olive oil	
6	tablespoons red wine vinegar	
1	teaspoon dried orégano	
1	teaspoon ground black pepper	
1	teaspoon salt	
6	green onions, chopped	
2	medium tomatoes, chopped	
4	tablespoons chopped fresh parsley	
1	large head iceberg lettuce, torn into bite-size pieces	

Servings: 4 to 6
Preparation time: 45 minutes
Standing time: 1 hour

- Combine olive oil, wine vinegar and spices. Mix until well blended.
- Add onions, tomatoes and parsley. Let stand for 1 hour.
- Just before serving, mix lettuce with dressing. Toss.
- Serve with croutons.

Croutons

3	large rounds Arabic bread	
1/2	cup light olive oil	
1/2	cup butter	
2	tablespoons dried parsley, flaked	
1	teaspoon dried orégano	
1	teaspoon dried chives	

- Cut bread into bite-size pieces.
- Melt olive oil and butter in a large sauté pan. Add spices and stir to blend.
- Add bread, mixing well to cover all pieces with oily mixture.
- Sauté for 8 minutes or until light brown and crisp.

Ensalada de Fruta

Salad

	Romaine or Boston lettuce	
5	ripe bananas, sliced	
3	ripe avocados, sliced	
1/2	purple onion, thinly sliced	

Dressing

8	tablespoons olive oil	
4	tablespoons wine vinegar	
	Salt and pepper to taste	

Servings: 8
Preparation time: 10 minutes

- In an attractive serving bowl, place lettuce around sides and on bottom.
- Place bananas, avocados and onion in layers on lettuce.
- Put oil, vinegar, salt and pepper in a glass jar. Shake vigorously.
- Drizzle over salad. Toss salad carefully.

Wild Rice Salad with Oriental Vegetables

Vinaigrette

3	tablespoons wine vinegar
1/2	teaspoon salt
	Pepper
2/3	cup olive oil
2	tablespoons Dijon mustard
3	tablespoons lemon juice
3/4	teaspoon crushed rosemary

Salad

2	cups raw wild rice
1/3	cup olive oil
4	cups chicken broth
2/3	cup sliced water chestnuts
1/2	cup sliced red bell pepper
1/4	cup minced shallots
	Salt and pepper to taste
3/4	pound snow peas
1/2	pound fresh mushrooms, thinly sliced
	Parsley for garnish

Servings: 8
Preparation time: 25 minutes
Cooking time: 50 minutes
Chilling time: 1 hour

- Combine all ingredients in a covered container. Shake vigorously.

- Rinse and drain wild rice.
- Heat olive oil in a saucepan. Add wild rice and chicken broth. Cover.
- Bring rice to a boil, reduce heat to low, and continue cooking for 45 minutes or until rice is tender.
- Transfer rice to a bowl and mix with 1/2 cup vinaigrette dressing.
- Add water chestnuts, red peppers, shallots, salt and pepper.
- Chill for 1 hour.
- Steam snow peas until slightly crisp. Cut into 1-inch diagonal pieces.
- Add sliced mushrooms and toss with 1/2 cup vinaigrette dressing.
- Transfer rice to a large serving bowl. Make a "well" in center of rice. Mound snow peas and mushrooms in it.
- Garnish with parsley.

SALADS & MOLDS

Vegetable Pasta Salad

1	8-ounce box macaroni twists
1/2	bunch broccoli, broken into flowerets
1/2	medium head cauliflower, broken into flowerets
1	dozen cherry tomatoes, halved
1/2	cup freshly grated Parmesan cheese
1	medium onion, sliced paper thin
	Best Salad Dressing (see Index)

Servings: 6
Preparation time: 30 minutes
Chilling time: 1 hour

♦ Cook twists according to package directions.
♦ Cook broccoli in boiling water until just tender. Rinse under cold water. Drain until dry. Separate flowerets into small pieces.
♦ Cook cauliflower until fork tender. Rinse under cold water. Drain until dry.
♦ Mix vegetables, macaroni, cheese and onion. Chill for at least 1 hour.
♦ Toss with Best Salad Dressing just before serving.

Frozen Tomato Salad

1	envelope unflavored gelatin
1/4	cup cold water
2	cups tomato juice, divided
1	8-1/4-ounce can crushed pineapple
1/2	cup mayonnaise
1/2	cup cottage cheese, sieved
1/8	teaspoon dry mustard
1/4	teaspoon dry ginger
1/2	teaspoon red pepper
1	teaspoon grated onion
1-1/2	teaspoons salt
	Tabasco sauce to taste

Servings: 8
Preparation time: 20 minutes
Freezing time: 6 hours

♦ Soak gelatin in cold water. Then dissolve in 2/3 cup hot tomato juice.
♦ Add remaining ingredients.
♦ Pour mixture into a container, cover and freeze.
♦ Stir 3 times, 30 minutes apart, to prevent flaking.
♦ Serve with an ice cream scoop.

Wilted Lettuce Salad

8	slices bacon
1/3	cup vinegar
1	teaspoon water
1/4	teaspoon sugar
2 to 3	heads Bibb lettuce, torn
4	green onions, sliced

Servings: 4
Preparation time: 15 minutes
Cooking time: 5 minutes

- Fry bacon until crisp, reserving grease. Drain on paper towel and then crumble.
- Mix vinegar, water and sugar. Set aside.
- In a large salad bowl, combine lettuce, onions and bacon.
- Just before serving, heat bacon grease. When hot, carefully pour in vinegar mixture.
- Stir once and pour hot dressing over lettuce and toss.
- Serve immediately.
- May substitute spinach for Bibb lettuce.
- Delicious with homemade soup or stew.

Spinach Salad Mold

2	10-ounce packages frozen chopped spinach
3	hard-boiled eggs, chopped
3/4	cup mayonnaise
1	10-ounce can consommé, hot
2	envelopes unflavored gelatin
1-3/4	teaspoons salt
3	teaspoons Worcestershire sauce
2	tablespoons lemon juice
1/8	teaspoon Tabasco sauce
6 to 8	lettuce leaves
	Cherry tomatoes for garnish

Servings: 6
Preparation time: 20 to 30 minutes
Chilling time: 3 to 4 hours

- Cook spinach according to package directions. Drain well.
- Combine spinach, eggs and mayonnaise.
- Dissolve gelatin in consommé. Then fold into spinach mixture.
- Stir in all seasonings.
- Turn into an oiled 2-quart mold.
- Chill for 3 to 4 hours.
- Unmold on bed of lettuce and garnish with cherry tomatoes.

Layered Spinach Salad

1	pound fresh spinach, deveined and cleaned
12	slices cooked bacon, crumbled
4	hard-boiled eggs, chopped
1/2	head romaine lettuce
1	10-ounce package Birdseye tiny peas, defrosted
1	red onion, chopped
1/2	pound fresh mushrooms, sliced
	Salt and pepper to taste
1	teaspoon sugar
2	cups mayonnaise
1	cup sour cream
1	cup grated Swiss cheese

Servings: 8 to 10
Preparation time: 45 minutes
Chilling time: 5 hours or overnight

- Use a 9 X 13-inch dish or salad bowl.
- Put spinach on the bottom.
- Next layer bacon, then hard-boiled eggs.
- Break romaine lettuce into bite-size pieces and put on top of eggs.
- Sprinkle on peas, then onion.
- Place mushrooms on top of onion.
- Sprinkle salt, pepper and sugar on top of mushrooms.
- Blend together mayonnaise and sour cream.
- Add Swiss cheese and mix well.
- Pour evenly on top of salad and spread to cover completely.
- Refrigerate for at least 5 hours or overnight.

Bermuda Salad

Salad
1	large head romaine lettuce, torn
1	head iceberg lettuce, torn
1	cup croutons
1	tablespoon freshly ground black pepper

Dressing
1	teaspoon dry mustard
3	cloves garlic, cut and crushed
1	teaspoon salt
	Worcestershire sauce to taste
	Dried orégano to taste
4	tablespoons wine vinegar
4 to 5	tablespoons salad oil
2	tablespoons chopped parsley
8	anchovies, cut
	Juice of 2 lemons
1/2	cup freshly grated Parmesan cheese

Servings: 8
Preparation time: 15 minutes

- Tear lettuce and place in a salad bowl.
- Sprinkle with croutons and pepper.
- Add dressing and toss to coat evenly.

- Mix mustard, garlic and salt.
- Add Worcestershire and orégano.
- Mix well with vinegar and oil.
- Add parsley and anchovies, then lemon juice and cheese. Mix well.

Tangy Squash Salad

5	medium yellow (summer) squash, thinly sliced
1/2	cup thinly sliced green onions
1/2	cup thinly sliced green bell pepper
1/2	cup thinly sliced celery
2	tablespoons wine vinegar
3/4	cup sugar
1	teaspoon salt
1/2	teaspoon pepper
2/3	cup salad oil
1-1/3	cups cider vinegar
1	clove garlic, crushed

Servings: 8
Preparation time: 25 minutes
Chilling time: 12 hours

- Combine squash, onions, green pepper and celery in a 3-quart mixing bowl. Toss lightly.
- In a separate bowl, combine remaining ingredients. Stir well and spoon over vegetables.
- Chill for approximately 12 hours, stirring occasionally.
- Drain and serve.
- This is attractive served on spinach or lettuce leaves.
- May be kept in refrigerator for 4 to 5 days.

Salade de Maison

Dressing

2	anchovy fillets, crushed
1	small clove garlic, minced
1/8	teaspoon dry mustard
1/2	cup light olive oil
2	tablespoons wine vinegar
	Juice of 1/2 lemon
1/2	teaspoon Worcestershire sauce
	Crushed dried tarragon leaves to taste
	Salt and freshly ground black pepper to taste

Servings: 8
Preparation time: 20 minutes
• Combine all ingredients in a jar. Shake well.
• May be made ahead.

Salad

1	pound fresh spinach
1	head Boston lettuce
3	Belgian endive
1	pint cherry tomatoes, halved
1	cup pine nuts

• Tear greens into bite-size pieces.
• Add tomatoes and pine nuts.
• Toss with dressing just before serving.

Orange Avocado Toss

5	cups lettuce, torn into bite-size pieces
1-1/3	cups thinly sliced cucumber
1	avocado, seeded, peeled and sliced
2	tablespoons sliced green onion
1	11-ounce can mandarin orange sections, drained
1/2	teaspoon grated orange peel
1/4	cup fresh orange juice
1/2	cup salad oil
2	tablespoons sugar
2	tablespoons red wine vinegar
1	tablespoon lemon juice
1/4	teaspoon salt

Servings: 8
Preparation time: 10 minutes
• In a large salad bowl, combine lettuce, cucumber, avocado, onions and oranges.
• Combine remaining ingredients in a jar. Cover and shake well.
• Just before serving, pour dressing over salad and toss lightly.

Watercress and Orange Salad

Salad
3	bunches watercress
2	red onions, sliced
2	11-ounce cans mandarin oranges, drained
2 to 3	avocados, sliced

Dressing
6	tablespoons wine vinegar
3	teaspoons Dijon mustard
1/4	teaspoon cayenne pepper
3	tablespoons poppy seeds
2	teaspoons lime juice
1	teaspoon onion juice
1/3	cup vegetable oil or more to taste
3	tablespoons honey

Servings: 10
Preparation time: 10 minutes
- Wash watercress and pat dry.
- Add remaining ingredients and toss with dressing.

- Combine all ingredients in a jar and shake well.

Salade Niçoise

Salad
3	medium tomatoes, cut into eighths
6	radishes, sliced
1	head Boston lettuce
1	bunch watercress
1	7-ounce can solid white tuna, drained and flaked
2	hard-boiled eggs, quartered
8	ripe olives
1	small Bermuda onion, thinly sliced
3	tablespoons chopped parsley

Servings: 4
Preparation time: 20 minutes
- Arrange all ingredients attractively on a platter or in a salad bowl.

Dressing
1/2	cup vegetable oil
2	tablespoons olive oil
1	tablespoon Dijon mustard
2	tablespoons cider vinegar
1	teaspoon honey

- Put all ingredients in a blender. Blend for 30 seconds.
- Pour dressing over salad.

Mandarin Orange Salad

Dressing

1	teaspoon dry mustard
1	teaspoon salt
	Pepper to taste
1/2	teaspoon Worcestershire sauce
1/2	cup salad oil
1/4	cup sugar
1/4	cup tarragon vinegar
2	teaspoons minced parsley
1	red onion, thinly sliced

Servings: 8
Preparation time: 15 minutes
Refrigeration time: 2 hours

- Combine all ingredients and refrigerate for at least 2 hours.

Salad

4	heads Bibb lettuce, torn
1	bunch watercress
2	11-ounce cans mandarin oranges
1/2	cup slivered almonds, toasted

- Just before serving, shake dressing and pour over lettuce and watercress.
- Toss oranges and slivered almonds with greens. Serve immediately.

Marinated Broccoli Ring

2/3	cup salad oil
1/3	cup tarragon vinegar
1	teaspoon salt
1/2	teaspoon prepared mustard
1/4	teaspoon pepper
1	tablespoon sugar
2	tablespoons grated Parmesan cheese
1-1/2	pounds fresh broccoli, cut into stalks
1/2	pound fresh mushrooms, sliced
2	tomatoes, sliced
	Escarole

Servings: 5 to 6
Preparation time: 40 minutes
Chilling time: 24 hours

- Mix first 7 ingredients in a jar. Shake well.
- Cook broccoli in a small amount of seasoned water for 9 minutes. Drain.
- Place broccoli in a large shallow dish.
- Drizzle 1/2 cup dressing over top.
- Chill for 24 hours.
- Line a serving platter with escarole.
- Layer broccoli and sliced tomatoes.
- Pile mushrooms in center.
- Drizzle remaining dressing over tomatoes and mushrooms.

Fish & Seafood

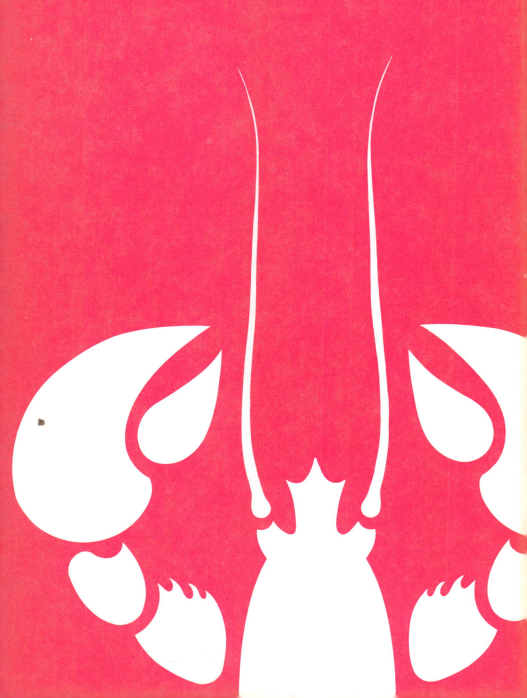

Quenelles Superior

2	pounds fish fillets, snapper or flounder
1	pound raw shrimp, shelled
1-1/2	pounds fish fillets, snapper or flounder
3/4	cup milk
1/4	teaspoon salt
2	tablespoons butter, melted
1/2	cup plus 2 tablespoons all-purpose flour
2	eggs, beaten
2	tablespoons butter
1	egg white, slightly beaten
1/8	teaspoon salt
1/8	teaspoon white pepper

Sauce

3/4	cup water
3/4	cup dry white wine
1	lemon, sliced
1	medium onion, sliced
3/4	pound shrimp in shells
2	tablespoons butter
2	tablespoons warm brandy
1	cup heavy cream
2	tablespoons cornstarch mixed with 1 tablespoon water

Servings: 8
Preparation time: 1 hour
Baking time: 40 minutes

- Line a 12-cup ring mold with 2 pounds fish fillets. Set aside.
- In a food processor or blender, mix shrimp and 1-1/2 pounds fish until well blended.
- Preheat oven to 350° F.
- In a small saucepan, heat milk, salt and butter until bubbling.
- Add flour all at once. Stir vigorously until ball of dough is formed.
- Remove from heat, cool slightly and beat in eggs.
- Add minced seafood, butter, egg white, salt and pepper.
- Pour into fish-lined ring mold.
- Bake ring mold for 40 minutes in a large pan filled with 2 inches of water.
- Unmold on a platter and pour half the sauce on top.
- Serve remainder of sauce to accompany individual servings.

- In a saucepan, bring water, wine, lemon and onion to a boil. Simmer for 5 minutes.
- Add shrimp and simmer for 5 minutes.
- Remove shrimp. Discard onion and lemon. Reserve broth.
- Remove shells from shrimp.
- Put shells in a separate saucepan with butter. Mash them with a spoon as they simmer.
- Add brandy and ignite.
- Add reserved shrimp liquid and reduce to 1 cup liquid.
- Strain shells from liquid.
- Return liquid to pan. Add cream and cornstarch mixture. Stir until thickened.
- Add shrimp to sauce.
- Sauce may be made ahead and chilled.

FISH & SEAFOOD

Baked Stuffed Red Snapper

1   3-pound whole red snapper, dressed

Stuffing
1-1/2 cups bread cubes
1/4 cup milk
1 large white onion, chopped
1 tablespoon vegetable oil
    Salt and pepper to taste
1/2 pound crabmeat or shrimp

Sauce
1 tablespoon vegetable oil
2 large white onions, chopped
1/2 green bell pepper, chopped
1/2 cup chopped celery
40 ounces canned tomatoes
2 cups water
    Garlic powder to taste
    Salt and pepper to taste
3 bay leaves
    Sprig of thyme
1/2 teaspoon dried orégano

Servings: 6
Preparation time: 1 hour
Baking time: 2 hours

- Soak bread cubes in milk. Squeeze dry.
- Sauté onion in oil.
- Add bread and cook with onion for 15 minutes, stirring to prevent browning.
- Season with salt and pepper.
- Add crabmeat.
- Stuff mixture in cavity of fish and place in a large baking dish.
- Preheat oven to 350° F. and prepare sauce.

- Sauté onions, pepper and celery in oil until tender.
- Add remaining ingredients.
- Cook for 10 minutes.
- Pour sauce over stuffed fish.
- Bake for 1-1/2 to 2 hours, basting often.
- Dish may be prepared in the morning, refrigerated and reheated.

Herbed Flounder

1	teaspoon dried dill weed
1	teaspoon dried thyme
1	pound fresh fillet of flounder
2	tablespoons finely minced parsley
1	shallot, minced
2-1/2	tablespoons olive oil
	Salt and pepper to taste
	Lemon wedges for garnish
	Parsley for garnish

Servings: 2
Preparation time: 10 minutes
Cooking time: 25 to 30 minutes

- Sprinkle a baking dish with dill and thyme. Arrange fish in dish.
- Combine parsley, oil and shallot.
- Salt and pepper fish. Pour parsley mixture over fish. Cover dish tightly with foil and place on a rack over boiling water in a steamer, casserole or frying pan.
- Steam on top of stove until flesh is white and firm, approximately 30 minutes.
- Serve in baking dish with lemon wedges and small clusters of parsley.
- Excellent with fresh asparagus.

Company Fish Fillets

1-1/2	tablespoons salt
1/2	cup white wine
3	pounds any white fish fillets
1-1/2	cups fine dry bread crumbs
3/4	cup mayonnaise
3/4	cup sour cream
1/3	cup chopped onion
	Paprika

Servings: 8
Preparation time: 10 minutes
Cooking time: 10 minutes

- Preheat oven to 500° F.
- Butter a shallow baking dish.
- Combine salt and wine. Marinate fish fillets in this mixture for at least 2 hours.
- Pat fish dry and roll in bread crumbs.
- Place fish in baking dish.
- Combine mayonnaise, sour cream and onion. Pour over fillets.
- Sprinkle with more bread crumbs and paprika.
- Bake, uncovered, for 10 minutes.
- Serve hot.
- Will keep in oven on low or on a warming tray.

Crab Fondue

1	8-ounce package cream cheese
6	ounces Swiss cheese, grated
1/2	cup milk
1/4	teaspoon lemon pepper seasoning
1/4	cup sherry
	Salt to taste
	White pepper to taste
1	pound crabmeat
1	loaf French bread, cut into 1-inch cubes

Servings: 4
Preparation time: 15 minutes
Cooking time: 10 minutes

- In the top of a double boiler, combine first 7 ingredients.
- Cook and stir over simmering water until cheese melts and all ingredients are blended.
- Stir in crabmeat.
- Serve in a fondue pot with French bread.

Deviled Crab

1	pound crabmeat, fresh or frozen
2	eggs, separated
1-1/2	cups bread crumbs
	Juice of 1 lemon
1	teaspoon dry mustard
2	teaspoons salt
2	tablespoons Worcestershire sauce
1/2	teaspoon Tabasco sauce
1/2	cup mayonnaise
1/2	cup butter, melted
8 to 10	coquille shells or crab shells
	Vegetable cooking spray
1	teaspoon butter for each shell
	Paprika to taste
	Lemon slices for garnish
	Parsley for garnish

Servings: 4 to 6
Preparation time: 15 minutes
Baking time: 15 minutes

- Preheat oven to 400° F.
- Flake crabmeat with a fork.
- Add egg yolks, bread crumbs, lemon juice, mustard, salt, Worcestershire and Tabasco. Mix well.
- Add mayonnaise, then butter.
- Beat egg whites until stiff. Fold into crab mixture.
- Spray coquille shells or crab shells with vegetable cooking spray.
- Stuff shells with crab mixture.
- Top each portion with 1 teaspoon butter and sprinkle with paprika.
- Bake for 15 minutes.
- Garnish with lemon slices and parsley.
- This dish may be prepared in individual shells or in a 9 X 13-inch baking dish.

Crab or Shrimp Mornay

1/2	cup butter
1/2	cup all-purpose flour
1/4	cup chopped onion
1/2	cup chopped green onion
2	tablespoons chopped parsley
2	cups light cream
1	cup dry white wine
2-1/2	teaspoons salt
1/4	teaspoon cayenne pepper
2-1/2	ounces Swiss cheese, minced
	Fresh artichokes, boiled, leaves scraped and bottoms quartered
1	tablespoon lemon juice
2	pounds lump crabmeat
1/2	pound fresh mushrooms, sliced
3	tablespoons grated Romano cheese

Servings: 8 to 10
Preparation time: 30 minutes
Baking time: 40 minutes

- Preheat oven to 350° F.
- Melt butter in a 2-quart saucepan. Stir in flour and cook for 5 minutes over medium heat, stirring often.
- Add onions. Cook for 2 to 3 minutes without browning.
- Stir in parsley. Gradually add cream. Heat thoroughly.
- Add wine, salt and pepper.
- Blend well and bring to a simmer, stirring occasionally.
- Add Swiss cheese. Stir, cover and remove from burner. Allow to cool to lukewarm.
- Stir in scrapings from artichoke leaves and lemon juice.
- In a 3-quart casserole, make alternate layers of crabmeat, quartered artichoke bottoms and mushrooms. Use sauce between layers and on top.
- Sprinkle Romano cheese over top.
- Bake, uncovered, for 40 minutes.
- If top is not browned, turn oven to broil and brown for 3 to 5 minutes.
- This dish is better if made ahead of time to allow flavors to blend.
- May substitute 3 pounds shrimp, boiled and peeled for the crabmeat.

Maryland Crab

1	pound fresh lump crabmeat
1/2	teaspoon salt
1/8	teaspoon cayenne pepper
3	tablespoons butter
3	dashes Worcestershire sauce
1	tablespoon chopped parsley
4	crab shells
2	tablespoons butter
	Paprika for garnish

Servings: 4
Preparation time: 25 minutes
Baking time: 15 minutes

- Preheat oven to 375° F.
- Mix first 6 ingredients carefully with a fork to avoid breaking lumps of crabmeat.
- Put mixture in shells.
- Top with a pat of butter.
- Sprinkle with paprika.
- Bake for 15 minutes.

Crabmeat Crêpes

Crêpe Batter

1	cup cold water
1	cup cold milk
4	large eggs
1/2	teaspoon salt
2	cups all-purpose flour
4	tablespoons margarine, melted
1	teaspoon vegetable oil

Servings: 12
Preparation time: 1-1/2 hours
Refrigeration time: 2 hours
Cooking time: 25 minutes

- In an electric blender, mix water, milk, eggs, salt, flour and butter for 1 minute.
- Refrigerate for 2 hours.
- Oil a 6 to 7-inch frying pan.
- Heat over medium to low heat.
- Pour 1/4 cup batter in skillet and tilt to completely cover bottom.
- Cook crêpe about 1 minute, until edges turn light brown.
- Turn crêpe and cook another 30 seconds.
- Slide crêpe onto a platter.
- Place waxed paper between crêpes.
- Crêpes may be frozen.

Filling

3	tablespoons minced scallions
3	tablespoons butter
1-1/2	cups fresh crabmeat
	Salt and pepper to taste
1/4	cup dry vermouth

- Sauté scallions in butter.
- Add crabmeat and heat for 1 minute.
- Add salt, pepper and vermouth.
- Simmer until liquid evaporates. Set aside.

continued...

Crabmeat Crêpes continued...

Sauce

1/3	*cup dry vermouth*
2	*tablespoons cornstarch blended with 2 tablespoons milk*
1-1/2	*cups heavy cream*
1/4	*teaspoon salt*
1-8	*teaspoon white pepper*
1	*cup grated Swiss cheese*
2	*tablespoons butter*
	Paprika

- Preheat oven to 425° F.
- Pour vermouth in a skillet and boil until reduced to 1 tablespoon.
- Stir in cornstarch mixture.
- Add cream, salt and pepper. Stir occasionally until thickened.
- Stir in 1/2 cup cheese.
- Blend half the cheese sauce into crabmeat filling.
- Place a heaping tablespoon of filling on lower third of each crêpe.
- Roll crêpe into a cylinder.
- Arrange crêpes closely in a lightly buttered 9 X 13-inch baking dish.
- Spoon remaining sauce on top of crêpes and sprinkle with 1/2 cup Swiss cheese.
- Dot with butter.
- Sprinkle with paprika.
- Refrigerate until ready to bake.
- Bake for 20 minutes.

Crab Stuffed Artichoke Entrée

4	artichokes
2	tablespoons minced green onions
1	clove garlic, minced
2	small bay leaves, crumbled
4	tablespoons butter
1/4	cup all-purpose flour
1/8	teaspoon pepper
3/4	cup clam juice
1/4	cup dry white wine
1	pound crabmeat
1/4	cup grated Parmesan cheese
1	1-ounce triangle Gruyère cheese

Servings: 4
Preparation time: 30 minutes
Cooking time: 30 minutes
Baking time: 30 minutes

- Preheat oven to 375° F.
- Cut off top third of artichoke. Trim base and tips of leaves.
- Cook artichokes in boiling salted water for 25 minutes or until tender.
- Drain upside down and let cool.
- Remove choke by gently removing a few center leaves and scooping out the fuzzy center.
- Place artichokes in an 8 X 8 X 2-inch baking dish.
- In a medium skillet, sauté onions, garlic and bay leaves in butter until tender but not brown.
- Blend in flour and pepper.
- Add clam juice.
- Cook quickly, stirring constantly, until mixture thickens and bubbles.
- Stir in wine, crab and Parmesan cheese.
- Spoon into artichokes and place a fourth of the Gruyère cheese on top of each.
- Pour boiling water around artichokes in baking dish to 1/2-inch depth.
- Cover loosely with foil.
- Bake for 25 to 30 minutes.
- Serve with rice pilaf and drawn butter as a main course.

Michael Field's Broiled Shrimp with Tarragon

2	pounds large fresh shrimp
1/4	cup butter
1/4	cup olive oil
2	teaspoons lemon juice
1/4	cup finely chopped shallots
1	tablespoon finely chopped garlic
1	tablespoon finely chopped fresh tarragon or 1 teaspoon dried tarragon
	Freshly ground black pepper to taste
	Salt to taste
2	tablespoons finely chopped parsley
1	tablespoon finely chopped fresh tarragon

Servings: 6
Preparation time: 1 hour
Cooking time: 10 minutes

- Peel and devein shrimp. Wash and pat dry. Set aside.
- Melt butter in a large flat ovenproof dish that will hold shrimp in one layer.
- Stir in olive oil, lemon juice, shallots, garlic and tarragon.
- Add shrimp and turn until coated with seasoned olive oil.
- Preheat broiler.
- Season shrimp with salt and pepper.
- Place dish 3 inches from heat and broil for 5 minutes, basting shrimp with pan juices.
- Turn shrimp and sprinkle with salt.
- Broil for 5 more minutes and continue basting.
- Mix parsley and tarragon. Sprinkle over shrimp.
- Serve from baking dish.

Shrimp and Crabmeat Fondue in Bread Cups

Bread Cups
12	slices white bread
1/2	cup butter
	Garlic salt to taste

Fondue
1/2	cup butter
	Garlic salt to taste
1/2	pound fresh mushrooms, sliced
1/2	cup chopped green onions
3	rounded tablespoons all-purpose flour
1-1/2	cups Half and Half
3/4	cup white wine
1	pound fresh raw shrimp, shelled and deveined
1/2	pound crabmeat
1	cup grated sharp Cheddar cheese
	Seasoned salt to taste
	Pepper to taste
1/2	cup chopped parsley for garnish

Servings: 8
Preparation time: 40 minutes
Baking time: 40 minutes

- Preheat oven to 300° F.
- Trim crusts from bread.
- Melt butter and season with garlic salt.
- Press bread into muffin tins and spread with garlic butter.
- Bake for 35 to 40 minutes or until quite crisp.

- Melt butter in a large heavy skillet. Season with garlic salt.
- Sauté mushrooms and onions until tender.
- Sprinkle with flour and stir to blend.
- Add Half and Half and wine.
- Cook over moderate heat, stirring constantly until thickened.
- Add shrimp, crabmeat and cheese.
- Simmer until shrimp are done.
- Season with salt and pepper.
- Transfer mixture to a chafing dish or fondue pot to serve.
- Spoon fondue into bread cups and sprinkle with parsley.
- Serve immediately.

Baked Stuffed Shrimp

1-1/2	cups boxed bread crumbs
2	cloves garlic, pressed
1	medium onion, grated
1/2	green bell pepper, grated
1/4	cup butter, melted
1	tablespoon Worcestershire sauce
	Juice of 1 lemon
1/2	teaspoon paprika
1/2	teaspoon dried marjoram
1	egg, beaten
	Salt and pepper to taste
	Chicken broth to moisten
40	large raw shrimp, peeled, deveined and split down back
20	slices bacon, halved crosswise and partially cooked
	Toothpicks

Servings: 5
Preparation time: 40 minutes
Baking time: 10 to 15 minutes

- Combine first 12 ingredients.
- Stuff each shrimp with 1 teaspoon of mixture.
- Preheat oven to 400° F.
- Wrap each shrimp with 1/2 slice bacon.
- Secure with a toothpick.
- Place shrimp in a baking dish and bake for 10 to 15 minutes, until bacon is browned.

Grilled Shrimp Marinated in Cognac

12	large shrimp, shelled and deveined
1/4	cup cognac
1/2	teaspoon salt
1/4	teaspoon pepper
1/2	teaspoon dried basil
6	slices bacon, cut in half

Servings: 2
Preparation time: 15 minutes
Marinating time: 1 hour
Cooking time: 15 to 20 minutes

- Marinate shrimp in cognac, salt, pepper and basil for at least 1 hour, but no longer than 2 hours.
- Wrap shrimp with bacon and string on skewers.
- Grill on a charcoal grill for 15 to 20 minutes, rotating skewers to cook shrimp evenly.
- May be broiled in oven.

Shrimp and Crab Soufflé

1	loaf sliced white bread
1/2	cup butter, softened
1	pound fresh crabmeat
1	pound fresh shrimp, cooked
1	pound sharp Cheddar cheese, grated
6	eggs
1	tablespoon prepared mustard
1/2	teaspoon white pepper
6	cups Half and Half

Servings: 12
Preparation time: 15 minutes
Baking time: 30 to 40 minutes
- Preheat oven to 400° F.
- Butter a 4-quart casserole.
- Spread butter on bread.
- Quarter slices of bread.
- Place a layer of bread in casserole, add a layer of seafood, then a layer of cheese, repeating until all ingredients are used. Use bread and cheese as top layer.
- Beat eggs slightly. Add mustard and pepper.
- Combine egg mixture with Half and Half. Pour over casserole.
- Bake for 30 to 40 minutes or until knife inserted in middle comes out clean.

Shrimp Creole

1-1/2	pounds fresh shrimp
1/2	cup chopped onion
1/2	cup chopped green bell pepper
2	cloves garlic, finely chopped
1/2	cup bacon drippings
4	tablespoons all-purpose flour
1	tablespoon brown sugar
1	teaspoon chili powder
	Seasoned salt and pepper to taste
2	cups canned stewed tomatoes
1/2	cup white wine

Servings: 6
Preparation time: 30 minutes
Cooking time: 20 minutes
- Peel shrimp and wash. Cut large shrimp in half. Set aside.
- Cook onion, green pepper and garlic in bacon drippings until tender.
- Blend in flour, sugar and seasonings.
- Add tomatoes. Cook until thick.
- Add shrimp and wine. Simmer, uncovered, for 20 minutes.
- Serve on a bed of rice.

Shrimp Rothbury

4	tablepoons butter
1	pound large raw shrimp, shelled and deveined with tails left on
	Salt to taste
	White pepper to taste
1	tablespoon chopped fresh chives
1	tablespoon chopped fresh parsley
1	tablespoon chopped fresh dill
1	teaspoon chopped fresh basil or 1/4 teaspoon dried basil
1/4	cup cognac, warmed

Servings: 2
Preparation time: 20 to 30 minutes
Cooking time: 6 to 8 minutes

- Melt butter in a large, heavy skillet or sauté pan.
- Add shrimp to sizzling butter.
- Cook over high heat stirring constantly until they turn pink, about 6 to 8 minutes. TAKE CARE NOT TO OVERCOOK.
- While cooking shrimp, sprinkle with salt, white pepper, chives, parsley, dill and basil.
- Turn off heat when shrimp are cooked. Add warmed cognac to hot pan. Ignite and shake pan gently until all flames die.
- Serve at once with pan juice in a casserole or individual ramekins.
- Serve with a salad, French or Cuban bread and white wine.

New Orleans Style Shrimp

1	pound butter
5	pounds headless shrimp (do not peel)
2	cups butter or 2 cups olive oil
5	cloves garlic, minced
3	bay leaves
	Basil to taste
	Salt to taste
5	heaping tablespoons coarsely ground black pepper
	Juice of 5 lemons

Servings: 8 to 10
Preparation time: 15 minutes
Cooking time: 40 to 50 minutes

- Preheat oven to 375° F.
- Melt butter in a large open pan.
- Add remaining ingredients, stirring to coat shrimp with liquid.
- Bake, uncovered, in the oven for 40 to 50 minutes.
- When cooking is complete, remove from oven and allow to cool.
- Good when served with a tossed salad and French bread. Bread may be dipped in the butter sauce.

Shrimp and Crabmeat Madeira

1	pound fresh shrimp
1/2	pound fresh lump crabmeat
4	tablespoons butter
3	tablespoons chopped green onions
1/2	pound fresh mushrooms, sliced
1/2	cup Madeira wine
1	teaspoon dried tarragon
1	tablespoon fresh lemon juice
2	teaspoons tomato paste
2	egg yolks
3/4	cup heavy cream
1/2	teaspoon salt
1/4	teaspoon pepper
1/4	cup chopped fresh parsley

Servings: 4
Preparation time: 15 minutes
Cooking time: 15 minutes

- Shell and devein shrimp. Pick through crabmeat.
- Melt butter in a large heavy skillet.
- Sauté onions until just tender. Add mushrooms and sauté until liquid evaporates.
- Add shrimp and cook until pink. Add crabmeat.
- Add Madeira. Simmer until wine is reduced by two thirds.
- Stir in tarragon, lemon juice and tomato paste.
- Reduce heat to low.
- Combine egg yolks and cream. Very slowly add to seafood, mixing constantly.
- Add salt, pepper and parsley.
- Serve over thin noodles.

Shrimp Scampi Puerta Verde

3	pounds large shrimp, shelled
1	pound butter
1/4	cup lemon juice
12	shallots, finely chopped
3	cloves garlic, finely minced
1/4	cup Worcestershire sauce
1	tablespoon Tabasco sauce
2	teaspoons salt
1/4	cup white wine
1/8	cup chopped chives
1/4	teaspoon dry mustard

Servings: 6
Preparation time: 20 minutes
Cooking time: 10 minutes

- Wash shrimp and drain well.
- Melt butter in a large heavy skillet.
- Sauté shrimp in butter for 5 minutes or until just done.
- Remove shrimp to a hot platter.
- Add remaining ingredients to butter.
- Simmer sauce for 2 to 3 minutes to blend flavors.
- Pour sauce over shrimp.

Scampi Bread

1	pound butter, softened
1/2	cup finely chopped parsley
1/4	cup finely chopped green onions
1-1/2	tablespoons finely minced garlic
1	tablespoon white wine
1-1/2	teaspoons salt
1	teaspoon freshly ground black pepper
1/4	cup finely chopped almonds
1	loaf French bread, about 2 feet long
1-3/4	pounds raw shrimp
1/4	cup white wine

Servings: 8
Preparation time: 30 minutes
Baking time: 35 minutes

- Preheat oven to 400° F.
- Combine the first 8 ingredients to make seasoned butter.
- Slice top third off loaf of French bread. Set aside top.
- Hollow out bottom of loaf and grind removed bread into crumbs.
- Shell and devein shrimp. Chop into chunks.
- In the following order, layer in the hollowed loaf: half of seasoned butter, shrimp, 1 tablespoon white wine sprinkled over shrimp, remaining seasoned butter, reserved bread crumbs.
- Sprinkle loaf with 1/4 cup white wine.
- Place loaf on a cookie sheet and bake, uncovered, for 35 minutes. Cover with bread lid for last 10 minutes of baking.
- To serve, cut into slices.
- For variations, use 2 round loaves of bread or individual hard rolls.

Shrimp Vermouth

1-1/2	pounds fresh shrimp
4	tablespoons butter
3/4	cup Martini and Rossi red vermouth
1/3	cup A-1 Sauce
	Tabasco sauce to taste
1	clove garlic, minced
2	tablespoons chopped parsley

Servings: 4
Preparation time: 20 minutes
Cooking time: 10 minutes

- Peel and devein shrimp.
- Melt butter in a large heavy skillet.
- Add vermouth, A-1 Sauce, Tabasco, garlic and parsley. Simmer for 5 minutes.
- Add shrimp and cook until pink, about 5 minutes.

Scampi Jacksonville

1-1/2	pounds shrimp
1/2	cup butter
1/2	teaspoon salt
1/4	teaspoon fresh cracked black pepper
2	cloves garlic, minced
1/4	cup chopped parsley
	Juice of 1 lemon
1	cup dry white wine
1	tablespoon all-purpose flour
	Parsley for garnish

Servings: 4
Preparation time: 20 minutes
Cooking time: 10 minutes

- Shell and devein shrimp.
- Heat 1/4 cup butter in a large skillet.
- Sauté shrimp over medium heat for 5 minutes or until pink.
- Remove shrimp and set aside.
- Melt remaining 1/4 cup butter in skillet.
- Add salt, pepper, garlic and parsley. Cook for 1 minute.
- Add lemon juice and white wine. Cook until mixture is reduced by a fourth.
- Add flour and whisk until dissolved.
- Return shrimp to sauce and heat through.
- Garnish with parsley.

Oysters with Herb Butter

1/3	cup butter, melted
1	tablespoon snipped parsley
1	tablespoon finely chopped chives
1	tablespoon chervil (optional)
1	shallot, finely minced
1/2	teaspoon salt
1/8	teaspoon pepper
2 to 3	dozen oysters
2	tablespoons lemon juice
3/4	cup bread crumbs
3/4	cup grated Swiss cheese

Servings: 6
Preparation time: 10 minutes
Baking time: 10 minutes

- Preheat oven to 450° F.
- Mix butter with herbs, shallots, salt and pepper.
- Place 4 to 6 oysters in each of 6 individual baking shells, or put oysters in a shallow baking dish.
- Sprinkle oysters with lemon juice.
- Drizzle herb butter over oysters.
- Toss together bread crumbs and cheese. Spoon mixture over oysters.
- Bake for 10 minutes or until oysters are done and topping is brown.

Baked Oysters

4	tablespoons butter
2	cups soda cracker crumbs
1/2	cup chopped parsley
1	teaspoon salt
1/4	teaspoon paprika
1-1/2	pints select oysters
1/2	cup light cream
1/2	teaspoon Tabasco sauce

Servings: 4 to 6
Preparation time: 10 minutes
Baking time: 35 minutes

- Preheat oven to 350° F.
- Melt butter in a saucepan.
- Remove pan from heat. Stir in cracker crumbs, parsley, salt and paprika.
- Drain oysters and reserve juice.
- Sprinkle a third of the crumb mixture in a buttered 9-inch pie pan.
- Layer half the oysters on top, then a third of the crumbs, then the rest of the oysters.
- Top with a mixture of oyster liquor, cream and Tabasco.
- Sprinkle the remaining third of the crumbs on top.
- Bake for 35 minutes or until golden brown.

Oysters Rockefeller Casserole

1/4	cup butter
1	small onion, chopped
1/2	cup chopped celery
1	10-ounce package frozen chopped spinach, cooked and drained
1/4	cup fresh snipped parsley
1	pint fresh oysters, well drained
1-1/2	cups sour cream
1/2	cup Parmesan cheese
2	slices white bread, crumbled
	Paprika to taste
	Lawry's seasoned salt to taste

Servings: 4
Preparation time: 30 minutes
Baking time: 30 minutes

- Preheat oven to 350° F.
- Sauté onion and celery in butter until onion is transparent.
- Add spinach and parsley.
- Transfer mixture to a buttered 1-1/2-quart casserole.
- Place oysters on top of spinach mixture.
- Combine sour cream, Parmesan cheese and bread crumbs.
- Spread mixture on top of oysters.
- Sprinkle with paprika and seasoned salt.
- Bake for 30 minutes.
- Serve immediately.

Scallops Provençale

3	tablespoons olive oil
3	tablespoons butter
1	pound scallops
8	shallots, minced
8	green onions, minced
2	cloves garlic, minced
2	teaspoons dried basil
1	teaspoon dried tarragon
1/4	teaspoon dried thyme
1/2	cup dry white wine
4	cups tomatoes, drained and chopped
1/2	cup heavy cream
2	teaspoons sugar

Servings: 4
Preparation time: 10 minutes
Cooking time: 20 minutes

- Heat olive oil and butter in a skillet.
- Add scallops and sauté for several minutes. Remove scallops to a bowl using a slotted spoon.
- Add shallots and onions to skillet and sauté. Stir in garlic, herbs and wine. Cook for 1 minute.
- Stir in tomatoes. Cook over medium heat for 5 minutes, or until sauce is thick.
- Stir in cream and sugar.
- Return cooked scallops to skillet and gently mix to combine all ingredients.
- Serve over noodles.

Bay Scallops en Coquille

6	large scallop shells
1-1/2	pounds bay scallops
1	tablespoon chopped shallots
1/4	teaspoon salt
1/8	teaspoon white pepper
1/2 to 3/4	cup dry vermouth
1	cup heavy cream
1	tablespoon olive oil
4	tablespoons olive juice
1	tablespoon all-purpose flour
4	tablespoons butter, softened
	Snipped parsley for garnish
	Pimento-stuffed olive slices for garnish

Servings: 6
Preparation time: 15 minutes
Cooking time: 2 minutes

- Butter scallop shells.
- Wash scallops. Put in a saucepan with shallots, salt, pepper and vermouth.
- Bring liquid to a boil, cover and simmer over low heat for 2 minutes only.
- Remove scallops with a slotted spoon. Divide into scallop shells.
- Cook liquid remaining in saucepan over high heat until reduced to half.
- Add cream. Boil rapidly until cream is reduced and is consistency of syrup.
- Add olive oil and olive juice.
- Combine flour and butter to make a paste.
- Add to sauce.
- Reduce heat and stir until very smooth.
- Pour sauce over scallops.
- Sprinkle tops with parsley and put olive slices on each.
- Serve at once.

Artichoke and Seafood Casserole

1	14-ounce can artichoke hearts
1	pound medium shrimp, cooked, peeled and deveined
2	tablespoons butter
1/4	pound fresh mushrooms, sliced
4-1/2	tablespoons butter
4-1/2	tablespoons all-purpose flour
1-1/2	cups Half and Half
1	tablespoon Worcestershire sauce
1/4	cup dry sherry or vermouth
	Salt and pepper to taste
1/4	cup grated Parmesan cheese
	Paprika
	Chopped parsley

Servings: 6
Preparation time: 40 minutes
Baking time: 20 minutes

- Preheat oven to 375° F.
- Drain artichokes, quarter and arrange in a buttered 1-quart casserole.
- Place shrimp over artichokes.
- Sauté mushrooms in 2 tablespoons butter for 6 minutes. Spoon over shrimp in casserole.
- Make a cream sauce by melting 4-1/2 tablespoons butter over low heat.
- Add flour and blend over low heat for 3 to 5 minutes.
- Slowly stir in Half and Half. Blend until thick.
- Add Worcestershire, sherry, salt and pepper.
- Pour over contents of baking dish.
- Sprinkle Parmesan cheese on top. Dust with paprika.
- Bake for 20 minutes.
- Cover with parsley just before serving.

Poultry

Chicken Breasts and Artichokes in Champagne Sauce

Chicken

6	chicken breast halves, skinned and boned
	Lemon juice to taste
	Salt and pepper to taste
6	tablespoons butter

Champagne Sauce

1	10-1/2-ounce can chicken broth, chilled
4	tablespoons butter
4	tablespoons all-purpose flour
1	pint heavy cream
3/4	cup champagne
2	10-ounce packages frozen artichoke hearts, thawed

Servings: 6
Preparation time: 30 minutes
Baking time: 1 hour

- Preheat oven to 200° F.
- Rub chicken breasts on both sides with lemon juice, salt and pepper.
- Melt butter over low heat in a 9 X 13-inch casserole.
- Roll breasts in melted butter and arrange in casserole.
- Butter a sheet of waxed paper large enough to cover casserole and extend over edges.
- Cover casserole with waxed paper, buttered side down.
- Cover this with aluminum foil or lid.
- Place in oven for 6 minutes.
- Remove waxed paper.

- Open can of broth and remove hardened fat.
- Simmer broth but do not boil.
- In another saucepan, melt butter until it foams.
- Stir in flour.
- Stir until mixture begins to bubble.
- Add hot broth to this mixture and stir until thickened.
- Remove from heat.
- In a saucepan, heat cream until warm, but not hot.
- Add cream to broth mixture. Stir and blend.
- Add champagne.
- Cut artichoke hearts in half and arrange in casserole with chicken.
- Pour sauce over chicken.
- Bake for 1 hour.

Chicken Dijon

8	chicken breast halves	
6	tablespoons butter	
4	tablespoons all-purpose flour	
2	cups chicken broth	
1	cup Half and Half	
4	tablespoons Dijon mustard	

Servings: 8
Preparation time: 30 minutes
Cooking time: 30 minutes

- In a large skillet, sauté chicken in butter until well browned.
- Remove from pan.
- Add flour to pan and stir until smooth.
- Stir in broth and Half and Half, then mustard.
- Simmer chicken in sauce for 30 minutes.
- Serve over rice or noodles.

Chicken Archduc

Chicken

3	whole chicken breasts, skinned, boned and halved
1/4	cup calvados or cognac
	Cayenne pepper to taste

Filling

2	tablespoons butter
1/4	pound fresh mushrooms, thinly sliced
1	tablespoon lemon juice
3	ounces boiled ham, shredded
2	tablespoons dry sherry
1	tablespoon dried tarragon
1	small clove garlic, pressed
	Salt and pepper to taste
4	ounces Gruyère or Swiss cheese, grated
	Toothpicks
	Flour

Servings: 6
Preparation time: 1 hour
Cooking time: 30 minutes

- Pound chicken breasts lightly until they are 1/4-inch thick.
- Sprinkle with calvados and cayenne.
- Set aside.

- Heat butter and sauté mushrooms.
- Sprinkle with lemon juice.
- Add ham and sherry. Sauté for 1 minute.
- Add tarragon, garlic, salt and pepper.
- Remove from heat and cool.
- When cool add Gruyère cheese.
- Put a heaping tablespoon of filling in center of chicken breast.
- Roll up and secure with toothpicks.
- Dust lightly with flour.

continued...

Chicken Archduc continued...

Sauce

4	tablespoons butter
1	tablespoon vegetable oil
1/4	cup calvados or cognac
1	teaspoon tomato paste
1	teaspoon meat extract
2	tablespoons all-purpose flour
1	10-1/2-ounce can chicken broth
1	cup dry white wine
1/4	cup sherry
1	tablespoon red currant jelly
	Salt and pepper to taste
6	artichoke bottoms
6	slices Swiss cheese
3	tablespoons freshly grated Parmesan cheese

- Heat butter and oil in a heavy skillet.
- Over medium high heat, sauté chicken until browned.
- In a small pot, heat calvados, ignite and pour flaming over chicken.
- When flame dies, remove chicken to a plate.
- Remove pan from heat. Add tomato paste, meat extract and flour. Mix well.
- Add broth, wine, sherry, jelly, salt and pepper.
- Return to heat. Bring to boil, stirring constantly.
- Reduce heat and add chicken.
- Simmer for 15 minutes.
- Remove chicken and arrange on a serving dish.
- Put an artichoke bottom on top of each breast.
- Cover with a slice of Swiss cheese.
- Sprinkle with Parmesan cheese.
- Put under broiler until cheese melts.
- Spoon sauce over top.

Wild Rice and Chicken Tarragon

2	cups raw wild rice
4	tablespoons butter or margarine
1	small onion, finely chopped
1/2	pound fresh mushrooms
	Juice of 1/2 lemon
2	tablespoons all-purpose flour
1-1/4	cups chicken stock
1/2	cup dry white wine
1/2	teaspoon salt
1/4	teaspoon garlic salt
1/4	teaspoon crumbled dried tarragon
3	tablespoons freshly grated Parmesan cheese
4	whole chicken breasts, simmered until tender, then boned
1	tablespoon finely chopped parsley

Servings: 10
Preparation time: 45 minutes
Standing time: 1 hour
Baking time: 20 minutes

- Put rice in a large strainer. Wash thoroughly under cold running water.
- Let soak in water to cover for 1 hour. Drain.
- Cook in boiling salted water for 25 minutes, or until almost tender. Drain.
- Melt 2 tablespoons butter in a large frying pan. Add onions and sauté until golden.
- Wash mushrooms and remove stems. Leave caps whole.
- Add caps and stems to pan. Sprinkle with lemon juice.
- Cook gently, stirring occasionally, until mushrooms are tender.
- In another pan, melt remaining 2 tablespoons butter. Blend in flour, mixing to make a roux.
- Pour in stock and wine. Cook, stirring constantly, until thickened.
- Season with salt, garlic salt and tarragon. Stir in Parmesan cheese.
- Combine rice, mushrooms, chicken and three fourths of the sauce.
- Spoon into a buttered 2 or 3-quart casserole. Spoon remaining sauce over top.
- If not cooking immediately, refrigerate until 45 minutes before serving.
- Preheat oven to 350° F.
- Bake for 20 minutes. If refrigerated, bake for 30 to 35 minutes.
- Sprinkle with parsley just before serving.

Chicken Shish Kabobs

Marinade
2/3	cup soy sauce
1/4	cup vegetable oil
6	cloves garlic, minced
2	teaspoons monosodium glutamate
2	teaspoons ground ginger
2	teaspoons dry mustard
2	tablespoons molasses

Shish Kabobs
2	pounds chicken breasts, skinned, boned and cut into 1-inch cubes
1	pound large fresh mushrooms
4	onions, quartered
2	green bell peppers, cut into strips

Servings: 4
Preparation time: 20 minutes
Marinating time: 30 hours
Grilling time: 10 minutes

- Mix all ingredients in a glass bowl and leave at room temperature for 24 hours.
- Marinate chicken cubes for 4 to 6 hours, no longer.
- Set and light a charcoal grill or preheat oven to 350° F.
- Arrange chicken on skewers with mushrooms, onion quarters and pepper strips.
- Grill for 5 minutes on each side.
- May omit onions and substitute pineapple chunks.

Hungarian Chicken

4	chicken breast halves, skinned and boned
2	tablespoons butter
	Salt and pepper to taste
1/4	teaspoon cayenne pepper
1/4	teaspoon garlic salt
1-1/2	teaspoons paprika
3	tablespoons finely chopped shallots
2	tablespoons Dijon mustard
2/3	cup sour cream
1/3	cup heavy cream

Servings: 4
Preparation time: 15 minutes
Cooking time: 15 minutes

- Pound chicken to 1/8-inch thickness.
- In a frying pan, melt butter and sauté chicken.
- Sprinkle with seasonings and paprika until pinkish in color.
- Add shallots.
- Stir in mustard, then sour cream.
- Just before serving, stir in cream and mix well.
- Serve with wild rice or over egg noodles.

Breast of Chicken and Country Ham in Grape Sauce

Chicken and Ham

1/3	cup all-purpose flour
1/3	cup fine cracker crumbs
4	chicken breast halves, boned
	Salt and pepper to taste
2	tablespoons butter
2	tablespoons vegetable oil
4	thin slices country ham

Sauce

1	cup chicken stock
1/2	cup orange juice
3/4	cup seedless grapes
1/4	cup raisins
1/4	teaspoon light brown sugar
1/8	teaspoon ground nutmeg
1/8	teaspoon ground cinnamon
1	tablespoon cornstarch
1	tablespoon water

Servings: 4
Preparation time: 15 minutes
Cooking time: 40 minutes

- Combine flour and cracker crumbs.
- Season chicken breasts with salt and pepper.
- Roll in flour mixture.
- Heat butter and oil in a heavy skillet.
- Add chicken breasts and sauté until golden.
- Cover and simmer for 30 minutes or until just tender.
- Place each breast on a ham slice.

- Combine first 7 ingredients in a saucepan.
- Bring to a boil.
- Add cornstarch to water.
- Add cornstarch mixture to sauce to thicken.
- Pour over breasts before serving.

Chicken Teichgraeber

4	chicken breast halves, skinned and boned
2	eggs, slightly beaten
1/2 to 3/4	cup fine dry bread crumbs
1/2	cup butter
2	cups white wine
1/2	pound fresh mushrooms, sliced
	Snipped parsley for garnish

Servings: 4
Preparation time: 15 minutes
Cooking time: 30 minutes

- Pound chicken between sheets of waxed paper until very thin.
- Dip each piece of chicken in egg, then bread crumbs.
- Melt butter in a large heavy skillet until sizzling.
- Brown chicken pieces on both sides.
- Pour white wine over chicken.
- Cover and simmer for 20 minutes.
- Add mushrooms and simmer another 10 minutes.
- Sprinkle with parsley.
- Serve with rice or noodles.

Poulet à la Crème Joubine

2 to 3	pounds of chicken pieces
	Salt and pepper to taste
1/4	cup butter or margarine
1	pound onions, thinly sliced
2	tablespoons snipped fresh parsley
1	stalk celery, cut into 3 pieces
2	tablespoons white wine
1	tablespoon brandy
1/2	cup heavy cream

Servings: 4 to 5
Preparation time: 20 minutes
Cooking time: 40 minutes

- Generously sprinkle chicken with salt and pepper.
- Melt butter in a large deep heavy skillet.
- Brown chicken pieces in butter. Remove and set aside.
- Sauté onions for 2 to 3 minutes.
- Add parsley, celery, wine, brandy and chicken.
- Simmer until chicken is tender, about 30 to 40 minutes.
- Remove chicken pieces to a heated platter.
- Discard celery.
- Bring sauce mixture to a boil, breaking up onions into small pieces.
- Add cream and blend.
- Pour sauce over chicken.

Lemon Chicken

2-1/2	pound broiler-fryer or 6 chicken breast halves
1/2	cup lemon juice
1/4	cup olive oil
2 to 3	cloves garlic, minced
1	bay leaf
	Salt and coarsely ground black pepper to taste
	Parsley for garnish
	Lemon slices for garnish

Servings: 4 to 6
Preparation time: 20 minutes
Marinating time: 4 hours
Cooking time: 45 to 60 minutes

- Cut up and skin chicken.
- Rinse under cold water and pat dry with paper towels. Set aside.
- Combine lemon juice, olive oil, garlic, bay leaf, salt and pepper.
- Marinate chicken in mixture in the refrigerator for at least 4 hours, turning chicken occasionally to coat all sides.
- Remove chicken, reserving marinade.
- Preheat oven to 375° F.
- Bake chicken in a shallow greased baking dish for 45 minutes to 1 hour, basting with marinade.
- Serve cold or at room temperature.
- Garnish with parsley and lemon slices.

Fruited Honey Chicken

3	pounds chicken pieces
3/4	cup apple juice
1/2	cup orange juice
1/4	cup lemon juice
1	onion, finely chopped
	Salt and pepper to taste
1/2	cup vegetable oil
2	tablespoons honey
1/2	cup seedless raisins
1/2	cup chopped dried apricots
1/2	cup chopped pitted prunes
1	apple, unpeeled and chopped

Servings: 6
Preparation time: 10 minutes
Marinating time: 1 hour
Baking time: 45 minutes

- Marinate chicken in a mixture of fruit juices and onion for 1 hour.
- Remove chicken from marinade. Salt and pepper.
- Preheat oven to 350° F.
- Brown chicken pieces in oil.
- Add honey and fruits to marinade.
- Place chicken pieces in 9 X 13-inch baking dish and pour marinade over all.
- Cover and bake for 45 minutes, basting occasionally.

Lime Chicken with Melon

6	chicken breast halves, skinned and boned
1	clove garlic
2	tablespoons fresh lime juice
2	shallots or green onions, minced
1	teaspoon dried tarragon
1	teaspoon salt
1/4	teaspoon pepper
6	tablespoons butter or margarine
1/2	cup white wine or dry vermouth
1	medium honeydew melon, cut into 12 wedges
	Lime wedges for garnish

Servings: 6
Preparation time: 15 minutes
Baking time: 40 minutes
Chilling time: 3 hours

- Preheat oven to 400° F.
- Rub chicken with garlic clove.
- Place chicken in a 9 X 13-inch buttered baking dish.
- Sprinkle chicken with each of next 5 ingredients.
- Dot with butter and pour wine over all.
- Bake, uncovered, for 40 minutes. Baste every 10 minutes and turn chicken after 20 minutes.
- Allow to cool. Then refrigerate, covered, for 3 hours or overnight.
- Serve 2 slices of honeydew with each breast.
- Garnish with lime wedges.

Chicken Breasts with Almond Sauce

	Salt and pepper to taste
6 to 8	chicken breast halves, boned
4	tablepoons butter
1/4	cup slivered almonds
4	tablespoons all-purpose flour
1	cup chicken broth
1/2	cup water
1/4	cup white wine
1/2	pound fresh mushrooms, sliced
1	cup sour cream
2	scallions, chopped

Servings: 6 to 8
Preparation time: 20 minutes
Cooking time: 30 minutes

- Salt and pepper chicken.
- Melt butter in a large heavy skillet.
- Brown chicken in butter. Set aside.
- Brown almonds.
- Blend in flour, then liquids, stirring constantly.
- Bring to a boil.
- Add chicken and mushrooms.
- Cover and simmer for 30 minutes.
- A few minutes before serving, stir in sour cream.
- Garnish with scallions.
- Serve with rice.

Chicken and Spinach Crêpes

Prepare a basic crêpe batter yielding 12 crêpes. Filling and sauce recipes follow.

Filling

1	tablespoon butter
2	small onions, chopped
1/2	pound fresh mushrooms, sliced thin
1/2	10-ounce package frozen chopped spinach, cooked and drained
2	cups cooked and cubed chicken
4	tablespoons sour cream
2	tablespoons sherry
1/2	teaspoon salt

Servings: 6
Preparation time: 45 minutes
Baking time: 20 to 30 minutes

- Sauté onions and mushrooms in butter.
- Add remaining ingredients and heat through.
- Fill crêpes and place in a 9 X 13 X 2-inch dish.

Sauce

4	tablespoons butter
4	tablespoons all-purpose flour
1	cup milk
2	cups chicken broth
1/2	cup grated Parmesan cheese
1/2	cup grated Swiss cheese
1/4	cup sherry
	Salt to taste
	Cayenne pepper to taste

- Preheat oven to 350° F.
- Melt butter over medium heat. Add flour.
- Add milk slowly, stirring constantly, until mixture thickens.
- Add remaining ingredients, mixing well.
- Pour over crêpes and bake until bubbly.

Chicken Pie with Coachwheel Crust

Chicken Pie

4	pounds chicken
4	cups water
1	teaspoon salt
3	tablespoons butter
1-1/2	tablespoons all-purpose flour
1	cup Half and Half
2	tablespoons lemon juice
3	tablespoons chopped onion
	Salt and pepper to taste

Coachwheel Crust

1-1/2	cups all-purpose flour
1	tablespoon baking powder
1/2	teaspoon salt
3	tablespoons shortening
1/2	cup milk
3	whole pimentos, chopped
3/4	cup grated Cheddar cheese

Servings: 8
Preparation time: 45 minutes
Cooking time: 1 hour
Baking time: 30 minutes

- Simmer chicken in 4 cups salted water for 1 hour.
- Reserve 2 cups of broth.
- Cut meat from bones and set aside.
- Melt butter over low heat. Blend in flour.
- Add Half and Half and reserved chicken broth.
- Simmer and stir until thickened.
- Add lemon juice, onion, salt and pepper.
- Combine sauce with chicken.
- Pour into a greased 9 X 13-inch casserole.
- Top with coachwheel crust.

- Preheat oven to 400° F.
- Sift dry ingredients together.
- Cut in shortening.
- Sprinkle in enough of the 1/2 cup of milk to make dough hold together and form a ball.
- On a lightly floured surface, roll dough into a thin rectangular shape.
- Sprinkle with pimentos and cheese.
- Roll dough up from end to end like a jelly roll.
- Cut into 3/4-inch thick slices.
- Place slices on top of chicken in casserole.
- Bake for 30 minutes.

Spanish Chicken

8	chicken breast halves
	Salt and pepper to taste
	All-purpose flour
1	medium onion, chopped
2	cloves garlic, minced
30	pimento-stuffed green olives, sliced
1/4	cup all-purpose flour
1-1/2	tablespoons chili powder
3	tablespoons snipped parsley
2	teaspoons salt
1/2	teaspoon pepper
1	tablespoons Worcestershire sauce
3	cups water

Servings: 8
Preparation time: 15 minutes
Baking time: 1 hour, 10 minutes

- Preheat oven to 425° F.
- Salt and pepper chicken pieces.
- Dredge in flour.
- Arrange chicken pieces, skin side up, in a buttered 9 X 13-inch baking dish.
- Bake, uncovered, for 40 minutes.
- Sprinkle onion, garlic and olives over chicken.
- Combine remaining ingredients, adding water a little at a time to make a paste. Smooth all lumps from flour in paste. Then add remaining water.
- Pour mixture over chicken.
- Reduce oven temperature to 350° F.
- Cover chicken and bake another 30 minutes.
- Serve with rice.

Chicken in Gouda Sauce

6	tablespoons all-purpose flour
8	chicken breast halves, skinned and boned
6	tablespoons butter
2	chicken bouillon cubes
1	cup boiling water
1	cup chopped celery
1	cup chopped scallions
2	cups sliced fresh mushrooms
1	pint sour cream
7	ounces Gouda cheese, grated
	Salt and pepper to taste
4	tablespoons chopped parsley

Servings: 8
Preparation time: 30 minutes
Cooking time: 45 minutes

- Lightly flour chicken breasts and brown quickly in butter.
- Dissolve bouillon cubes in water.
- Pour bouillon over chicken. Simmer until just tender, about 30 minutes.
- Remove chicken to a warmed casserole.
- Simmer vegetables in broth until just tender.
- Add sour cream and cheese, stirring until blended and hot. Do not boil.
- Add salt and pepper.
- Pour sauce over chicken and sprinkle with parsley.
- Serve with rice or noodles.

Amelia Island Brunswick Stew

5-1/2	pound chuck roast
5	pound fresh ham or pork roast
	Salt and pepper to taste
8-1/2	pounds chicken pieces
12	cups water
2	stalks celery
2	small onions
2	carrots
2	bay leaves
5	24-ounce bags frozen baby lima beans
1-1/2	pounds new potatoes, peeled
5	10-ounce bags chopped onions
1/2	cup butter
1/2	of 1-1/8-ounce can celery seeds
1/2	of 2-ounce bottle of Tabasco sauce
3/4	cup salt
	Pepper to taste
1-1/2	cups sugar
2	ounces Worcestershire sauce
6	28-ounce cans tomatoes
5	10-ounce cans tomato paste
4	20-ounce packages frozen corn

Servings: 50
Preparation time: 1 hour
Cooking time: 16 hours

- The night before turn oven to 200° F.
- Season chuck roast and pork with salt and pepper. Roast slowly all night or for at least 8 hours in a covered roasting pan.
- Early in the morning, season chickens with salt and pepper. Place in two large pots, covering chicken with 6 cups of water.
- Place half of the celery, onions, carrots and bay leaves in each pot.
- Cover pots and simmer for 3 hours or until meat is tender and easily falls from bone.
- Cool roast, pork and chickens until they can be handled.
- Remove meat from liquid. Combine meat juices and chicken broth. Set aside.
- Remove chicken from bones. Cut all meat into 1 or 2-inch pieces.
- Divide liquid and meat evenly between two large pots and bring to a boil.
- Add half each of the lima beans, potatoes, onions, butter, celery seeds, Tabasco sauce, salt, pepper, sugar and Worcestershire sauce to each pot and again bring to a boil, stirring occasionally to prevent sticking.
- Add half of the tomatoes, tomato paste and corn to each pot.
- When stew comes to a boil again, reduce heat, cover and simmer 4 to 5 hours, stirring occasionally to prevent sticking.
- Serve with French bread and a grapefruit and avocado salad.

POULTRY

Arroz con Pollo

3	pounds chicken breasts and thighs or 1-1/2 fryer chickens
1/4	cup olive oil
1	medium onion, finely chopped
1	small green bell pepper, finely chopped
1	large tomato, peeled, seeded and chopped
2	cloves garlic, minced
1	bay leaf
1	tablespoon salt
1/4	teaspoon hot sauce
1/2	teaspoon marjoram
1	envelope Vigo yellow flavoring and coloring or the flavor packet from yellow rice package
1	cup chicken broth
1/2	cup dry white wine
2	cups raw rice
2-1/4	cups chicken broth
1	8-1/2-ounce can peas
1	pimento, cut in strips
8 to 10	green asparagus
1/2	cup dry white wine

Servings: 6
Preparation time: 1 hour
Baking time: 30 minutes

- Preheat oven to 325° F.
- Sauté chicken in oil until golden.
- Remove to a casserole.
- To drippings in skillet, add onion and green pepper.
- Sauté until transparent.
- Add tomato, garlic, bay leaf, salt, hot sauce and marjoram.
- Blend and cook 3 to 4 minutes.
- Return chicken to skillet.
- Mix Vigo seasoning in 1 cup chicken broth and 1/2 cup wine. Pour over chicken.
- Cover and simmer for 15 minutes.
- Add rice, 2-1/4 cups chicken broth and wine.
- Bring to a boil and transfer contents of skillet to a 3-quart casserole.
- Bake, covered, for 25 minutes.
- Remove from oven.
- Garnish with peas (stir some in and sprinkle others on top), pimentos and asparagus.
- Sprinkle with rest of wine.
- Allow to stand, covered, 15 to 30 minutes.
- May be kept 3 to 4 days in the refrigerator.

Chicken Persian

1/2	cup all-purpose flour
1/3	teaspoon ground cinnamon
1/3	teaspoon dried thyme
1	teaspoon salt
1/4	teaspoon white pepper
12	chicken thighs
1	tablespoon vegetable oil
1/2	cup clarified butter
1-1/2	cups chicken broth
1	green apple, chopped
1	large onion, chopped
2	tablespoons butter
3	ounces dried apricots, chopped
3	ounces Moist Pack prunes, chopped
3/4	cup white raisins, plumped in 2 tablespoons sherry
1-1/2	cups raw rice
2-1/2	cups chicken broth

Servings: 6
Preparation time: 40 minutes
Baking time: 50 minutes

- Blend flour, cinnamon, thyme, salt and white pepper.
- Dredge chicken in flour mixture.
- Sauté in oil and butter until golden. Remove from pan.
- Add 1-1/2 cups broth to pan.
- Simmer for 12 minutes. Set aside.
- Preheat oven to 350° F.
- Cook apple and onion in 2 tablespoons butter until almost tender.
- Add apricots, prunes and raisins. Cook briefly.
- Mix fruit mixture with rice. Add 2-1/2 cups broth.
- Pour into a buttered 9 X 13-inch casserole.
- Heat reserved broth and pour over rice.
- Arrange chicken on top.
- Bake for 50 minutes or until rice is tender, adding more broth if necessary.

Chicken Connemara

Chicken
6	chicken breast halves, skinned and boned
	Salt and pepper to taste
1/4	pound fresh mushrooms, sliced
1	large potato, peeled and minced
2	tablespoons butter
1/4	cup chopped fresh parsley
1	teaspoon salt
1/2	teaspoon pepper
6	slices smoked bacon

Whiskey Sauce
2	tablespoons butter
2	tablespoons all-purpose flour
1	cup heavy cream
	Salt and pepper to taste
2	tablespoons Irish whiskey
1/4	cup chopped parsley

Servings: 6
Preparation time: 30 minutes
Baking time: 40 minutes

- Preheat oven to 400° F.
- Salt and pepper each chicken breast.
- Slit a pocket in the side of each breast to prepare for stuffing.
- Sauté mushrooms and potato in butter until tender.
- Add parsley, salt and pepper. Cook another minute.
- Stuff each breast with a sixth of this mixture.
- Wrap each breast with a slice of bacon.
- Place breasts in a 9 X 13-inch baking dish. Bake for 40 minutes.

- In a small saucepan, melt butter.
- Stir in flour with a wire whisk.
- Add cream and simmer, stirring with whisk until thick and smooth.
- Add salt and pepper.
- Remove from heat. Stir in whiskey and parsley.
- Spoon sauce over each chicken breast before serving.

Coronation Chicken

Chicken
12	chicken breast halves, boned
1	cup white wine
1	cup water
1	tablespoon salt
3 to 4	peppercorns
1/2	cup chopped parsley
1	carrot, sliced
2	stalks celery, sliced
	Bouquet Garni to taste

Servings: 12
Preparation time: 30 minutes
Cooking time: 40 minutes

- Poach chicken for 40 minutes in a broth made of the remaining ingredients.
- Allow chicken to cool in broth.
- Remove from broth, pat dry, cover and chill.
- Reserve broth and cook down to 1 cup in volume.

continued...

Coronation Chicken continued...

Sauce

1	tablespoon vegetable oil
1/4	cup chopped onion
1	tablespoon curry powder
2	teaspoons tomato purée
1	cup reserved broth
1	bay leaf
1/2	teaspoon salt
1/4	teaspoon pepper
2	teaspoons sugar
2	cups mayonnaise
1	3-ounce jar puréed apricots (baby food)
4	tablespoons heavy cream
1/2	cup chopped parsley

• Heat oil in a heavy skillet. Sauté onion until transparent.
• Add next 7 ingredients.
• Bring to a boil and simmer, uncovered, for 5 to 10 minutes.
• Strain sauce and cool.
• Fold in mayonnaise, apricot purée and cream.
• Spoon sauce over chicken, coating well.
• Sprinkle parsley on top.

Durkee Chicken

8	chicken breast halves
	Salt and pepper to taste
1	10-ounce jar Durkee sauce
3/4	Durkee jar of water
1/2	cup butter, melted (may be reduced or omitted)
1/8	cup vinegar
1/8	cup fresh lemon juice
1/2	cup sugar
2	tablespoons Worcestershire sauce
1	lemon, cut into slices

Servings: 8
Preparation time: 10 minutes
Baking time: 1 hour, 10 minutes
• Preheat oven to 425° F.
• Salt and pepper chicken.
• Arrange chicken pieces, skin side up, in a greased 9 X 13-inch baking dish.
• Bake, uncovered, for 40 minutes. Drain all grease from chicken.
• Combine Durkee sauce, water, butter, vinegar, lemon juice, sugar and Worcestershire. Pour over chicken. Place lemon slices on top.
• Reduce oven temperature to 350° F.
• Cover chicken and bake another 30 minutes.
• Serve with rice or noodles.
• This sauce is great as a barbeque sauce for grilled chicken.

Chicken à la Habakov

	Juice of 1 lemon
1-1/2	pounds fresh mushrooms
6	tablespoons butter
2	tablespoons vegetable oil
	Salt and pepper to taste
5	tablespoons all-purpose flour
1	cup hot milk
1/2	cup grated Gruyère cheese
1	egg yolk
3	tablespoons finely chopped fresh tarragon
	Salt and pepper to taste
6	chicken breast halves, skinned, boned and flattened
2	tablespoons grated Parmesan cheese

Servings: 6
Preparation time: 1 to 1-1/2 hours
Baking time: 20 minutes

- Sprinkle lemon juice over mushrooms.
- Sauté mushrooms in 2 tablespoons butter and 1 tablespoon oil. Season with salt and pepper. Set aside.
- In a separate saucepan, melt 3 tablespoons butter and blend in 3 tablespoons flour.
- Add milk.
- Simmer until sauce is thick and smooth, stirring constantly.
- Remove from heat. Stir in cheese and egg yolk. Set aside.
- Combine remaining 2 tablespoons flour with tarragon, salt and pepper.
- Dip chicken breasts in flour mixture. Then roll lengthwise.
- Brown chicken in remaining 1 tablespoon oil and 1 tablespoon butter.
- Preheat oven to 400° F.
- Spoon mushrooms into a small, shallow baking dish that will just hold the chicken pieces. Place chicken on top. Pour sauce over all.
- Sprinkle with Parmesan cheese.
- Bake for 20 minutes or until brown.

Brandied Chicken with Currant Jelly Sauce

Chicken

16	whole chicken breasts, skinned and boned
1/2	cup butter
4	medium onions, thinly sliced
1	cup chicken broth
1	cup vermouth
4	cups heavy cream
	Salt, pepper and lemon juice to taste
4 to 5	tablespoons brandy
1	cup chopped parsley
2-1/2	pounds mushrooms, sautéed
1	pound bacon, cooked and crumbled

Sauce

3	12-ounce jars red currant jelly
3	tablespoons dry mustard

Servings: 32
Preparation time: 30 minutes
Baking time: 30 minutes

- Preheat oven to 350° F.
- Poach chicken in lightly salted water for 20 minutes.
- Cut into bite-size pieces. Set aside.
- Melt butter and sauté onions.
- Add chicken broth and vermouth. Reduce liquid by half.
- Add cream, salt, pepper and lemon juice. Simmer to thicken.
- Add brandy, parsley, chicken and mushrooms.
- Pour chicken mixture in 2 buttered 9 X 13-inch casseroles.
- Bake for 30 minutes. When done, sprinkle bacon on top.

- Combine jelly and mustard in a saucepan over low heat. Cook until jelly melts.
- Serve over chicken.

Coq au Vin Bourguignon

3	small frying chickens, split and backbone removed
	Salt and pepper to taste
1/2	pound salt pork, cut into 1/4-inch cubes
5	tablespoons butter
24	small white onions, peeled
1	clove garlic, minced
6	fresh medium mushrooms, sliced
1/2	teaspoon dried thyme
1	bay leaf
	Salt and pepper to taste
1	bottle Burgundy wine
3	tablespoons all-purpose flour
1	cup beef stock
	Parsley for garnish

Servings: 6
Preparation time: 20 minutes
Cooking time: 45 minutes

- Wash chicken and pat dry.
- Sprinkle liberally with salt and pepper. Set aside.
- Blanch pork in boiling water. Drain and pat dry.
- In a large heavy pot, heat 3 tablespoons butter and pork.
- Brown chicken in pot.
- Add onions, garlic, mushrooms, thyme, bay leaf, salt, pepper and wine.
- Bring to a boil.
- Cover and simmer for 15 minutes.
- Combine flour and remaining 2 tablespoons butter to form a paste. Stir into chicken.
- Add stock. Simmer 30 minutes more or until tender.
- Sprinkle with parsley before serving.
- Serve with boiled new potatoes and whole baby carrots.

Heavenly Turkey Hash

	Turkey carcass with meat
1	quart water
1	teaspoon salt
	Freshly ground black pepper
1	small onion, sliced
2	stalks celery, chopped
	Raw rice (about 1 cup)
1	onion, chopped
1	tablespoon lemon juice
1/2	teaspoon curry powder
2	8-ounce cans sliced water chestnuts
1/2	pound fresh mushrooms, sliced
	Mayonnaise (about 1/2 cup)
1/4	cup chopped parsley

Servings: 12 to 14
Preparation time: 40 minutes
Cooking time: 1 hour, 20 minutes

- Break turkey carcass into smaller pieces.
- Simmer carcass in water for 1 hour with salt, pepper, sliced onion and celery. Broth should be reduced to about half.
- Remove carcass from broth and cool.
- Remove meat from carcass, cutting into bite-size pieces.
- Measure broth. Then return meat and liquid to pot.
- Add half as much rice to pot as measured broth.
- Add chopped onion, lemon juice, curry powder, water chestnuts and mushrooms.
- Cover and simmer until liquid is absorbed and rice is tender.
- Correct seasonings.
- Stir in 1/4 cup mayonnaise for each cup measured broth.
- Stir in parsley.
- Serve immediately.
- This may be transferred to a 2-quart casserole, topped with cracker crumbs and baked at 350° F. for 15 minutes or until crumbs are brown.

Dove with Shallots and Wine

6	tablespoons butter
4	dove
	Salt and pepper to taste
2	tablespoons shallots, chopped
2	tablespoons fresh parsley, chopped
1-1/2	cups seedless grapes, halved
1	cup white wine
3	tablespoons brandy
4	toast points

Servings: 2
Preparation time: 35 minutes
Cooking time: 40 minutes

- Heat butter in a skillet.
- Brown dove over medium heat.
- Season with salt and pepper.
- Add shallots, parsley, 1/2 cup grape halves and 1/2 cup wine.
- Cover and simmer until dove are tender, turning occasionally.
- If necessary, add more wine. Dove should be covered half way with liquid at all times.
- When dove are tender, pour on brandy and ignite.
- Add remaining grapes and wine.
- Simmer, covered, for 10 minutes.
- Serve on toast points.
- Spoon grape and wine sauce over dove.
- Serve with wild rice.

Grilled Quail and Dove

30	birds (all quail, all dove or a combination)
1	pound bacon
	Toothpicks
1	pound butter, melted
3	tablespoons lemon juice
3	tablespoons white wine
	Cumberland Sauce (see Index)

Servings: 15
Preparation time: 15 minutes
Cooking time: 30 minutes

- Pick over all birds. Remove any feathers or cartilage.
- Rinse well and pat dry.
- Wrap each bird with 1/2 slice bacon across the breast. Secure with toothpick.
- Melt butter. Add lemon juice and white wine.
- Cook birds on a charcoal or gas grill over a low flame about 20 minutes. Baste constantly with butter sauce. Do not let birds dry out.
- Serve with Cumberland Sauce.

Bacon Wrapped Dove

4	dove
	Salt and pepper to taste
4	tablespoons butter
4	slices of bacon
	Toothpicks
	Aluminum foil

Servings: 2
Preparation time: 20 minutes
Baking time: 1 hour
- Preheat oven to 350° F.
- Salt and pepper cavity of dove.
- Put large pat of butter in cavity.
- Wrap dove in bacon, securing with toothpicks.
- Wrap in aluminum foil, sealing securely.
- Bake for 1 hour.
- Open foil for last 15 minutes of baking so birds and bacon may brown.

Wild Duck in Red Wine

1	duck
1	apple, quartered
1	orange, quartered
2	stalks celery
2	cups red wine
4	cubes beef bouillon
1/2	cup chopped green onions
1/4	pound fresh mushrooms, sliced
1/4	cup sliced water chestnuts

Servings: 2
Preparation time: 30 minutes
Cooking time: 1 to 2 hours
- Wash duck. Put apple, orange and celery in cavity.
- Place duck in a pot or roaster. Cover halfway with water.
- Add 1 cup red wine and bouillon cubes. Cook for 1 to 2 hours until duck is tender.
- Remove duck from pan.
- To the liquid in pan, add onions, mushrooms, water chestnuts and second cup of red wine. Cook over medium heat until liquid is reduced by half.
- Pour liquid over duck.

Duck à l'Orange

3	ducks
1	cup chopped celery
1	cup chopped onion
	Seasoned salt to taste
	Salt and pepper to taste
6	tablespoons butter
6	tablespoons all-purpose flour
1-1/2	cups duck broth
1-1/2	cups orange juice
1	tablespoon grated orange rind
	Sugar to taste
	Orange slices for garnish
	Parsley for garnish

Servings: 6
Preparation time: 30 minutes
Cooking time: 2 hours

- Place ducks in a large pot and cover with water.
- Season water with celery, onion, seasoned salt, salt and pepper.
- Simmer until done, about 1-1/2 hours.
- Cool ducks and remove meat from bones. Reserve broth.
- Melt butter in a large skillet. Blend in flour.
- Add duck broth and orange juice, stirring until thick and smooth.
- Add orange rind and sugar.
- Add duck meat to roux and simmer for 20 minutes.
- Serve over wild rice, garnished with orange slices and parsley.
- Accompany with chutney.

Mosquito Lagoon Duck Breasts

1/2	cup Worcestershire sauce
1/2	cup soy sauce
1/8	cup red wine vinegar
	Juice and rind of 4 lemons
	Salt and pepper to taste
	Monosodium glutamate
8	whole or 16 split duck breasts, skinned and boned
	Béarnaise sauce

Servings: 8
Preparation time: 10 minutes
Marinating time: 24 hours
Cooking time: 3 to 5 minutes

- Combine first 6 ingredients to make marinade.
- Marinate breasts for 24 hours, making sure breasts are covered in marinade.
- Cook, covered, on a very hot charcoal fire for 1-1/2 minutes on each side for very rare, or continue cooking until desired degree of doneness is reached.
- Serve with a Béarnaise sauce.
- Use as an entrée, or cut into bite-size pieces and serve with toothpicks as an appetizer.

Meats

Fillet of Beef with Port Butter

3	cups beef stock
1	cup tawny port
1	6-pound beef fillet, at room temperature, trimmed and tied
2	tablespoons minced shallots or minced onion
2	tablespoons tawny port
2	tablespoons red wine vinegar
8	tablespoons unsalted butter, melted
1/2	teaspoon salt
1/4	teaspoon coarsely ground black pepper

Servings: 12 to 14
Preparation time: 1-1/2 hours
Baking time: 1-1/4 hours

- Preheat oven to 450° F.
- Combine stock and 1 cup port in a saucepan. Boil until reduced to approximately 3/4 cup. Set aside.
- Place meat in oven and immediately reduce heat to 375° F. Roast meat to 125° F. on meat thermometer, about 1-1/4 hour.
- Set meat aside.
- Drain all but 1 tablespoon of fat from roasting pan.
- Add shallots, 2 tablespoons port and vinegar. Bring to boil, scraping sides and bottom of pan.
- Boil over moderate heat for 1 minute.
- Add original sauce and boil another 2 minutes.
- Remove from heat and mix in butter, 2 tablespoons at a time, with a wire whisk.
- Add salt and pepper.
- Slice fillet and spoon sauce over slices.
- Serve remaining sauce on the side.

Fillet of Beef with Green Peppercorns

4	pounds fillet of beef, trimmed and tied
2	tablespoons oil
1-1/2	teaspoons salt
1	teaspoon coarsely ground black pepper
3	tablespoons cognac, heated
1-1/2	cups brown stock
1	cup heavy cream
3	tablespoons whole green peppercorns
1	tablespoon lemon juice
	Salt and pepper to taste
3	tablespoons butter, softened
	Parsley and cherry tomatoes for garnish

Servings: 8
Preparation time: 25 minutes
Roasting time: 20 to 25 minutes

- Preheat oven to 450° F.
- In a large skillet, brown fillet in oil over moderately high heat. Salt and pepper meat.
- Transfer fillet to a roasting pan.
- Roast fillet for 20 to 25 minutes depending on thickness of meat.
- Let fillet stand for 10 minutes.
- Remove fat from skillet, add cognac and ignite. Shake pan and stir until flames die. (Do not use teflon skillet.)
- Add stock and cream. Over moderately high heat, reduce sauce to 2 cups.
- Add peppercorns, lemon juice, salt and pepper.
- Remove from heat and stir in butter.
- Slice fillet 1/2-inch thick and arrange on a platter.
- Spoon a little sauce over meat and serve the rest in a sauceboat.
- Garnish platter with parsley and tomatoes.

Steak "Au Poivre"

1/2	pound of steak per person
	Salt and pepper to taste
	Boursin pepper cheese or Boursin garlic and herb cheese
	Brandy to taste

Servings: depends on steak
Preparation time: 3 minutes
Cooking time: 5 to 10 minutes

- Cook steak according to your favorite method.
- When steak is done, sprinkle with salt and pepper.
- Preheat broiler.
- Spread Boursin cheese over steak.
- Sprinkle brandy over cheese.
- Broil for about 30 seconds to melt cheese.
- Serve at once.

Tournedos Madagascar

2	tablespoons butter
1	tablespoon vegetable oil
6	tournedos (remove any fat or bacon)
	Salt and pepper to taste
6	green onions, finely chopped
3/4	cup beef broth
1/2	cup dry red wine
1	teaspoon bovril
2	tablespoons green peppercorns
2	teaspoons cornstarch combined with 1/4 cup water

Servings: 6
Preparation time: 10 minutes
Cooking time: 15 minutes

- Heat butter and oil in a large heavy skillet.
- Season tournedos with salt and pepper. Brown for 3 minutes on each side. Remove from pan and set aside.
- Add onions and sauté for 3 minutes.
- Stir in broth, wine, bovril and peppercorns. Simmer over low heat for 5 minutes.
- Return tournedos to sauce and continue simmering to desired doneness.
- Thicken sauce with cornstarch and serve immediately.

Russian Chef's Stroganoff

1-1/2	pounds sirloin or tenderloin
	All-purpose flour
1	medium onion, chopped
1	clove garlic, minced
2	tablespoons olive oil
4	ounces fresh mushrooms, sliced
	Tabasco sauce to taste
1	teaspoon Worcestershire sauce
1	cup sour cream
2	ounces Madeira wine

Servings: 4
Preparation time: 30 minutes
Cooking time: 45 minutes

- Remove all fat from meat.
- Flour both sides and cut into 3/4-inch cubes.
- In a large heavy skillet, sauté onion and garlic in olive oil until tender but not browned.
- Add meat and brown lightly.
- Add mushrooms. Cook for 5 minutes.
- Add Tabasco and Worcestershire.
- Cover and simmer at least 30 minutes.
- Just before serving, add sour cream. Do not boil.
- Add Madeira. Do not substitute. Madeira is the secret.

World Champion Chili

3	pounds ground chuck	*Servings: 12 to 14*
1	pound ground pork	*Preparation time: 30 minutes*
2	large onions, chopped	*Cooking time: 1-1/2 hours*
6	cloves garlic, minced	
1	10-3/4-ounce can beef bouillon	
1	12-ounce can beer	
3	8-ounce cans tomato sauce	
1	16-ounce can tomatoes, finely chopped with juice	
1	teaspoon dried orégano	
1	tablespoon ground cumin	
3	tablespoons chili peppers, crushed	
1	teaspoon sugar	
1	teaspoon salt	
2	tablespoons masa flour (optional)	
	Chopped scallions	
	Grated Cheddar cheese	
	Crisp bacon	

- Brown meats, onions and garlic.
- Drain well.
- Add bouillon, beer, tomato sauce and tomatoes.
- Add orégano, cumin, chili peppers, sugar and salt. Mix well.
- Cook over low heat for 1 hour. May continue to simmer for up to 2 hours.
- Add masa flour 30 minutes before serving and simmer for 30 minutes.
- Serve with condiments of scallions, cheese and bacon.

Beef Bourguignon

2	pounds lean beef, cut into cubes	*Servings: 6 to 8*
1	bottle Burgundy	*Preparation time: 20 minutes*
3	bay leaves	*Marinating time: overnight*
1/4	teaspoon dried thyme	*Cooking time: 2 hours*
1	cup chopped green onions	
1/2	cup vegetable oil	
1/2	pound fresh mushrooms, sliced	
2	carrots, sliced on the diagonal	
12	small white onions	
1	green onion and tops, thinly sliced	

- Marinate meat overnight in 1/2 bottle Burgundy, bay leaves, thyme and green onions.
- Drain meat and remove excess moisture with paper towels.
- Brown meat in oil in a heavy pot. Add mushrooms, carrots, onions and remaining half bottle Burgundy.
- Cover and let simmer until meat is tender, about 2 hours.

Spicy Beef Stew

2	pounds stew meat
2	onions, sliced
1	pound carrots, sliced lengthwise
1/4	cup soy sauce
1/4	cup Worcestershire sauce
1	cup V-8 juice
3	tablespoons tapioca

Servings: 8
Preparation time: 15 minutes
Baking time: 3-1/2 to 4 hours

- Preheat oven to 250° F.
- Put beef in a buttered deep 2-quart baking dish.
- Layer onions on top of meat and carrots on top of onions.
- Combine soy sauce, Worcestershire, V-8 and tapioca.
- Pour sauce over meat and vegetables.
- Cover tightly and bake for 3-1/2 to 4 hours.

Lazy Day Beef Burgundy

2	pounds stew meat
1-1/2	teaspoons salt
1/2	teaspoon pepper
1/2	cup all-purpose flour
2	medium onions, sliced
1	pound fresh mushrooms
1	cup Burgundy
1	10-ounce can beef bouillon

Servings: 8
Preparation time: 10 minutes
Baking time: 3 hours

- Preheat oven to 300° F.
- Butter a deep 2-quart casserole.
- Put meat in casserole.
- Add salt and pepper.
- Sprinkle flour over meat.
- Stir until well blended.
- Add onions and mushrooms. Mix well.
- Pour Burgundy and bouillon over mixture.
- Cover and bake for 3 hours.

Braised Stuffed Flank Steak

1	2 to 2-1/2-pound flank steak, trimmed of fat
5	tablespoons butter
1/4	cup plus 1 tablespoon vegetable oil
2	cups 1/2-inch bread cubes, crusts removed
1/2	pound ground veal
1/2	pound ground beef
2	eggs, lightly beaten
1-1/2	cups chopped onion
1/2	stalk celery, chopped
1	tablespoon chopped parsley
1	pound fresh mushrooms, sliced
1-1/2	teaspoons salt
1/2	teaspoon pepper
1-1/4	teaspoons dried thyme
	Salt and pepper to taste
3/4	cup finely chopped carrot
2	bay leaves
1	large ripe tomato, skinned and finely chopped
1/2	cup beef broth
1/2	cup dry red wine
3	tablespoons heavy cream
	Parsley for garnish

Servings: 6
Preparation time: 45 minutes
Baking time: 1-1/4 hours

- Make a pocket in steak by cutting meat lengthwise, being careful not to cut through to other side.
- Heat 3 tablespoons butter and 1/4 cup oil in a skillet. Add bread cubes and sauté until golden on all sides.
- In a large bowl, combine veal, beef, eggs, 3/4 cup onion, celery, parsley, 1/4 pound mushrooms, salt, pepper and 1/4 teaspoon thyme.
- Drain sautéed bread cubes and add to veal mixture. Toss to mix well.
- Fill pocket of steak with stuffing. Bring up lower edge of the opening, pressing it against the stuffing. Press top edge of the opening down over it.
- Tie steak every few inches to form a loaf shape. Season with salt and pepper.
- Preheat oven to 350° F.
- In a large deep stove-to-oven casserole, heat 2 tablespoons butter and 1 tablespoon oil. Brown stuffed flank steak on all sides.
- Add carrots, 3/4 cup onion, bay leaves, 1 teaspoon thyme, tomato and 1/4 pound mushrooms.
- Place in oven for 5 minutes. Remove and add broth and wine. Bring to a boil over medium heat on top of stove. Remove from stove.
- Cover and bake in oven for 1-1/4 hours.
- Refrigerate meat for easy slicing.
- Blend heavy cream into cooking liquid and vegetable mixture.

continued...

Braised Stuffed Flank Steak continued...

- When ready to serve, slice cold meat into 1/2-inch thick pieces and heat.
- Add 1/2 pound mushrooms to sauce and reheat.
- Arrange meat slices on a platter and pour sauce over all.
- Garnish with parsley.
- Serve with country French vegetables and wild rice.

Helwig's Salt Steak

1	2-1/2 to 3 inch thick full-cut round steak
1/2	cup olive oil
1/4	cup soy sauce
1/2	cup bourbon
1	medium onion, finely chopped
1	teaspoon garlic salt
1	teaspoon black pepper
1	teaspoon dry mustard
2	tablespoons wine vinegar
1	quart yellow mustard
1	26-ounce box salt

Servings: 18
Preparation time: 30 minutes
Marinating time: 2 days
Cooking time: 1 hour, 20 minutes

- Prick both sides of steak extensively with a fork.
- Make marinade by combining olive oil, soy sauce, bourbon, onion, garlic salt, pepper, dry mustard and wine vinegar.
- Marinate meat for 2 days in the refrigerator, turning meat frequently. Prick meat extensively each time it is turned.
- Remove meat from marinade.
- Thickly cover all sides, top and bottom of meat with mustard and then salt until it looks like an iced cake.
- Make a hot charcoal fire.
- Place meat, top side down, directly on coals, not on grill.
- Cook for 40 minutes, turn and cook another 40 minutes.
- Slice and serve.
- Must be cooked on a hot, thick charcoal fire.

Orange Pork Chops

4	center cut pork chops, 1 inch thick
	Salt, pepper, paprika to taste
1/2	cup water
5	tablespoons sugar
1-1/2	teaspoons cornstarch
1/4	teaspoon salt
1/4	teaspoon ground cinnamon
10	whole cloves
2	teaspoons grated orange rind
1/2	cup orange juice
4	orange slices, halved

Servings: 4
Preparation time: 20 minutes
Cooking time: 45 minutes

- In a large skillet or electric frying pan, heat a piece of fat trimmed from chops over low heat until oil is rendered and then remove.
- Sprinkle chops with salt, pepper and paprika.
- Cook over medium high heat until brown.
- Turn heat to low and add water. Cook, covered, for 45 minutes, turning chops and adding more water if needed.
- Combine next 7 ingredients in small saucepan. Cook until thickened and clear.
- Add orange slices and remove from heat.
- Serve chops with sauce spooned over top and 2 orange slice halves on top of sauce.

Pennsylvania Dutch Apple Pork Chops

4	thick loin pork chops
2	tablespoons vegetable oil
	Salt and pepper to taste
1	cup apple cider
2	large Idaho potatoes, peeled and grated
1	small onion, grated
4	tablespoons butter, softened
	Salt and pepper to taste

Servings: 4
Preparation time: 20 minutes
Cooking time: 1 hour

- Preheat oven to 350° F.
- Brown chops on both sides in oil.
- Salt and pepper chops while browning.
- Arrange chops in a 1-quart baking dish. Pour cider over them.
- Cover and bake for 30 minutes.
- Combine potatoes, onion and butter.
- Mound mixture on chops, shaping lightly with fingers.
- Salt and pepper.
- Continue baking another 30 to 40 minutes or until potatoes are brown and crisp.

Shadydale Pork Chops

6 to 8 pork chops
3/4 cup dry sherry
1/4 cup soy sauce
1/2 cup olive oil
1 large clove garlic, crushed
3-1/2 teaspoons ground ginger
1/2 teaspoon orégano
3 tablespoons maple syrup

Servings: 4
Preparation time: 10 minutes
Baking time: 50 minutes
- Preheat oven to 300° F.
- In large frying pan, lightly brown pork chops over medium high heat.
- Place chops in a 3-quart casserole. Combine remaining ingredients in a jar. Cover and shake well.
- Pour sauce over chops. Cover dish with foil and bake for 50 minutes, basting occasionally.
- When done, serve with sauce ladled over top.

Pork Chops Grand Marnier

1 tablespoon vegetable oil
4 thick pork chops
  Salt and pepper to taste
1 teaspoon salt
1/2 teaspoon dry mustard
1/8 teaspoon pepper
1/4 cup low sugar orange marmalade
4 tablespoons tomato purée
2 tablespoons minced green onions
1/2 cup Grand Marnier

Servings: 4
Preparation time: 10 minutes
Baking time: 1 hour
- Preheat oven to 300° F.
- Heat oil in a heavy skillet.
- Salt and pepper chops. Brown in hot oil.
- Leave chops in skillet if it is ovenproof, or place in an 8 X 8-inch buttered baking dish.
- Combine salt, mustard, pepper, marmalade, tomato purée and onions. Spread on both sides of chops.
- Bake for 1 hour, uncovered, basting occasionally.
- Turn chops halfway through baking. Pour Grand Marnier over chops 20 minutes before end of baking.

Savory Loin of Pork

1	4-pound pork loin, deboned
1-1/2	teaspoons Lawry's seasoned salt
1/2	teaspoon freshly ground black pepper
1/8	teaspoon curry powder
1/8	teaspoon garlic salt
3	tablespoons butter
3	tablespoons chopped onion
3	tablespoons chopped celery
3	tablespoons finely chopped parsley
1	teaspoon Worcestershire sauce
1	tablespoon lemon juice
4	tablespoons red wine
1/2	cup dry bread crumbs

Servings: 12
Preparation time: 30 minutes
Baking time: 2 hours

- Preheat oven to 325° F.
- In a roasting pan, place loin, fat side down and bone cavity up.
- Season with Lawry's salt, pepper, curry powder and garlic salt.
- In a small skillet, melt butter over low heat. Lightly sauté onion, celery and parsley.
- Add Worcestershire, lemon juice and red wine. Stir for 1 minute over low heat.
- Add bread crumbs, stirring lightly to bind.
- Spoon this mixture into cavity of loin, spreading almost to edge.
- Roll up sides toward each other. Tuck in edges and press on ends so all of the dressing is safely inside. Tie with a string.
- Season with salt and pepper.
- Bake, uncovered, in a roasting pan for 35 minutes per pound.
- This dish may be prepared and frozen uncooked. Stuff loin as indicated and cover with plastic wrap.

Sausage Ring

2	eggs, beaten
1/4	cup milk
1-1/2	cups cracker crumbs
1-1/4	cups minced onions
1	cup chopped apples
2	pounds bulk sausage

Servings: 10 to 12
Preparation time: 20 minutes
Baking time: 1 hour

- Preheat oven to 350° F.
- Combine all ingredients.
- Press into a well greased 6-1/2-cup ring mold.
- Place, face down, on a 15 X 10-inch jelly roll pan.
- Bake for 1 hour.
- When done, slide onto serving platter and unmold.
- Fill center with scrambled eggs.
- Garnish with watercress.

Stuffed Roast Pork with Onion Cream

Roast and Stuffing
1	4-pound boned and rolled center cut pork loin roast
	Salt and pepper to taste
6	tablespoons butter
3/4	pound onion, thinly sliced
1	cup pecans, lightly toasted
1/2	cup fresh bread crumbs
2	ounces prosciutto or other good ham
1/2	clove garlic, minced
1	teaspoon salt
1/4	teaspoon cracked black pepper
4	tablespoons chopped fresh parsley

Onion Cream
3/4	pound onion, thinly sliced
2	cups heavy cream
1/2	cup beef stock
	Salt and pepper to taste

Servings: 12
Preparation time: 40 minutes
Roasting time: 1-1/2 hours
Cooking time: 30 minutes

- Untie and unroll roast. Salt and pepper roast.
- Melt butter in a large heavy skillet and sauté onion. (You may also sauté onion for cream sauce at this point and then divide.)
- Combine 3/4 pound onion with remaining ingredients.
- Mince by hand or in food processor using on/off turns.
- Preheat oven to 400° F.
- Spread a fourth of the stuffing over pork loin. Roll up and tie.
- Put remaining stuffing in a 1-quart baking dish. Cover.
- Place roast in hot oven and immediately reduce heat to 350° F.
- Cook roast to 160° F. on a meat thermometer, about 1-1/2 hours.
- Bake stuffing for 30 minutes at 350° F.
- Let roast stand for 15 minutes before carving.
- Sauté onion in a little butter if you have not already done so.
- Combine cream, stock and onion in skillet.
- Simmer over low heat for 30 minutes.
- Purée in a blender or food processor.
- To serve, put a small portion of dressing on each plate, cover with slices of roast and spoon cream to the side.

Ham and Asparagus Casserole

2-1/4	pounds cooked ham
1-1/2	pounds fresh asparagus
3/4	pound pasta
1/2	cup butter
1/2	cup all-purpose flour
3	cups light cream
1-1/2	cups milk
1/2	cup chicken broth
3/4	cup grated sharp Cheddar cheese
1/2	cup grated Parmesan cheese
	Juice of 1 lemon
1-1/2	medium onions, grated
1	tablespoon prepared mustard
2	tablespoons minced fresh parsley
2-1/2	teaspoons salt
1/8	teaspoon dried rosemary
1/8	teaspoon pepper
1	cup mayonnaise

Servings: 12
Preparation time: 1 hour
Baking time: 30 minutes

- Cut ham into 1/2-inch cubes.
- Steam asparagus in salted water until barely tender. Drain and cool. Cut into 1-1/2-inch pieces.
- Cook pasta according to package directions. Rinse and drain.
- Melt butter in a saucepan. Blend in flour. Blend in cream, milk and broth.
- Cook sauce until thickened, stirring constantly. Stir in cheeses.
- Season sauce with lemon juice, onions, mustard, parsley, salt, rosemary and pepper.
- Stir in mayonnaise.
- Preheat oven to 350° F.
- Layer half each of the ham, asparagus, spaghetti and sauce in a buttered 4-quart casserole. Repeat layers.
- Bake, uncovered, for 30 minutes or until bubbly.

Sausage and Apple Bake

1/2	pound bulk sausage
1	package Pork Stove Top Stuffing
1	apple, peeled and cored
6	link sausages, cooked
2	tablespoons butter
2	tablespoons brown sugar
1/8	teaspoon ground cinnamon

Servings: 6 to 8
Preparation time: 25 minutes
Cooking time: 30 minutes

- Brown sausage in a skillet. Drain on paper towels when done and reserve drippings.
- Preheat oven to 350° F.
- In a medium pot, prepare stuffing according to package directions, substituting sausage drippings for butter.

continued...

Sausage and Apple Bake continued...

- Cut half of the apple into slices and reserve. Chop remaining half and combine with sausage and stuffing.
- Put mixture into a round 2-quart casserole.
- Place link sausages on top of casserole like the spokes of a wheel. Place reserved apple slices between spokes.
- Combine remaining ingredients, heat and drizzle on top.
- Bake for 30 minutes.

Pork Tenderloin Casserole

5 to 6   pork tenderloins
1/2   cup butter
      Salt and pepper to taste
6 to 8   medium onions, sliced
1   cup sliced fresh mushrooms
      Salt and pepper to taste
      Paprika to taste
1   cup fresh bread crumbs
1   cup light cream
1   cup grated American cheese

Servings: 12
Preparation time: 30 minutes
Baking time: 30 minutes

- Preheat oven to 350° F.
- Slice tenderloins into small thin pieces.
- In a large heavy skillet, brown pieces in butter. Use butter as needed until meat is just done.
- Salt and pepper meat. Place in the bottom of a buttered 9 X 13-inch casserole.
- Sauté onions and mushrooms in butter until just tender. Season with salt, pepper and paprika.
- Add bread crumbs. Then stir in cream.
- If mixture is too thick, add a little milk or any kind of stock.
- Spoon mixture over meat.
- Top with cheese.
- Bake for 30 minutes.

Lamb Moroccan

2	tablespoons olive oil
2	pounds lamb, cut into 1-inch cubes
1/2	pound fresh mushrooms, sliced
1	medium onion, chopped
1	clove garlic, minced
1	pound tomatoes, peeled and chopped
1/2	cup raisins
1/2	cup slivered almonds, toasted
2	tablespoons sugar
1	teaspoon ground cinnamon
1	teaspoon salt
1	teaspoon ground allspice
1/2	cup chicken broth

Servings: 6
Preparation time: 15 minutes
Cooking time: 30 to 45 minutes

- Heat oil in a large skillet.
- Add lamb and sauté until browned on all sides.
- Add mushrooms, onion and garlic. Continue sautéeing for 2 minutes.
- Add tomatoes, raisins, almonds, sugar, cinnamon, salt and allspice. Simmer, covered, until lamb is tender, about 30 to 45 minutes.
- Add chicken broth as needed for liquid.
- Serve with rice.

Roast Lamb with Herb Mustard

1/2	cup Dijon mustard
2	tablespoons soy sauce
1	clove garlic, mashed
1	teaspoon dried rosemary
1/4	teaspoon ground ginger
2	tablespoons olive oil
1	6-pound leg of lamb

Servings: 6
Preparation time: 15 minutes
Chilling time: 3 hours
Baking time: 1 hour, 20 minutes

- Combine first 5 ingredients.
- Beat in olive oil, one drop at a time, to make a cream the consistency of mayonnaise.
- Paint lamb with mixture. Let sit for several hours in the refrigerator.
- Bake in a roasting pan at 350° F. for 1 to 1-1/4 hours for medium rare or 1-1/4 to 1-1/2 hours for medium well.

Anne Marie's Stuffed Leg of Lamb

1	4 to 5-pound leg of lamb, boned
	Juice of 1 lemon
	Salt and ground pepper to taste
1	clove garlic, pressed
1/2	cup chopped parsley
2	tablespoons bread crumbs
1	teaspoon dried rosemary
1	medium carrot, cut in 1-inch pieces
1	onion, chopped
1	stalk celery, chopped
1/2	teaspoon dried rosemary
1	10-3/4-ounce can chicken broth
1	10-3/4-ounce can beef broth
1	cup dry white wine
1	tablespoon all-purpose flour
3	tablespoons water

Servings: 8 to 10
Preparation time: 30 minutes
Baking time: 1-1/4 hours

- Preheat oven to 450° F.
- Rub lamb with lemon juice, salt and pepper.
- Combine garlic, parsley, bread crumbs and 1 teaspoon rosemary.
- Spread over meat and into pockets left by boning.
- Roll meat into a cylinder to encase stuffing.
- Tie with string and place on rack in a roasting pan.
- Place carrot, onion, celery and 1/2 teaspoon rosemary around meat.
- Bake for 15 minutes. Then baste with a mixture of chicken broth, beef broth and wine.
- Baste again every 10 minutes for another hour.
- Remove roast from oven and let stand for 10 minutes. Remove from pan.
- Mix flour and water and add to pan juices.
- Stir until thickened, strain and serve over lamb.

Devonshire Pie

Pie
1/4	cup butter
2-1/2	pounds boneless lamb, cut in 1-inch pieces
	Salt and pepper to taste
5 to 6	large tart apples, peeled, cored and chopped
2	tablespoons brown sugar
1/2	teaspoon ground cinnamon
1/2	pound fresh mushrooms, sliced
2	large onions, thinly sliced
2	cups brown sauce
1	9-inch deep-dish pie crust or homemade pastry

Brown Sauce
2	tablespoons butter
2	tablespoons all-purpose flour
2	cups beef broth
1	tablespoon tomato paste
	Salt and pepper to taste
2	tablespoons vermouth

Pastry
2-1/2	cups sifted all-purpose flour
1/4	cup Crisco
1	teaspoon salt
1/2	cup butter
2 to 5	tablespoons ice water

Servings: 6
Preparation time: 40 minutes
Baking time: 1-1/2 hours

- In a heavy skillet, heat butter and brown meat.
- Season with salt and pepper.
- Remove meat and drain on paper towels.
- Set skillet aside, reserving drippings.
- In a greased 2-quart ovenproof casserole, place layer of half the meat and cover with half the apples.
- Mix brown sugar and cinnamon. Sprinkle half on apples.
- Next layer half the mushrooms and half the onions.
- Repeat layers of meat, apples, cinnamon mixture, mushrooms and onions.
- Measure 2 tablespoons drippings reserved from meat and return to skillet.
- Add butter and heat until bubbly.
- Add flour and brown 3 to 4 minutes.
- Stir in broth and bring to a boil.
- Reduce heat and simmer 20 to 25 minutes or until thick.
- Stir in tomato paste, salt, pepper and vermouth.
- Pour over lamb.
- Preheat oven to 425° F.
- Mix flour, Crisco, salt and butter. Cut with a pastry blender until well mixed.
- Add water as needed to knead pastry. Knead and roll out.
- Cover lamb with pastry and prick with a fork.
- Bake, covered with foil, for 10 minutes.
- Reduce heat to 350° F. and bake for 1 hour and 20 minutes.
- Remove foil for last 10 minutes of cooking.

Marinated Leg of Lamb

1-1/4	cups red wine
1/3	cup olive oil
2	tablespoons red currant jelly
3	bay leaves
3	peppercorns
1	clove garlic, crushed and minced
1	teaspoon salt
1/2	teaspoon pepper
1	4 to 5-pound boned and rolled leg of lamb

Servings: 8
Preparation time: 15 minutes
Baking time: 50 to 60 minutes
Marinating time: 1 hour or overnight

- Combine first 8 ingredients to make marinade. Warm until jelly melts. Then remove from heat.
- Marinate lamb for at least 1 hour or overnight.
- Preheat oven to 425° F.
- Roast lamb for 25 to 30 minutes on each side.
- Let stand for 10 minutes before carving.

Veal Marsala

1-1/2	pounds veal scaloppine
	Salt and pepper to taste
	Flour
4	tablespoons vegetable oil
5	tablespoons butter
1/4	cup Marsala wine
3	tablespoons chicken broth
1	tablespoon lemon juice
1	tablespoon chopped parsley
	Parsley for garnish

Servings: 4 to 6
Preparation time: 15 minutes
Cooking time: 5 minutes

- Pound veal with mallet.
- Salt and pepper veal. Dredge in flour.
- Heat half each of the oil and butter in a large skillet. Brown half the veal slices for 2 minutes on each side.
- Repeat the process using the other half of the veal, butter and oil.
- Remove veal to a warm platter.
- Add wine, broth and lemon juice to skillet. Cook briefly over high heat.
- Return veal to skillet and cover with sauce.
- Sprinkle with parsley.
- Serve on warm platter and garnish with parsley.

Veal Malagasy

1-1/2	pounds veal scaloppine
	Salt and pepper to taste
2	tablespoons all-purpose flour
3	tablespoons butter
1/4	cup minced onion
1/4	pound fresh mushrooms, sliced
1	teaspoon crushed green peppercorns
1/4	cup dry white wine
1/2	cup light cream
	Juice of 1/2 lemon
1/2	teaspoon Worcestershire sauce

Servings: 4
Preparation time: 10 minutes
Cooking time: 10 minutes

- Salt and pepper veal. Dust with flour.
- In a large skillet, brown veal slices in butter for 2 minutes or less on each side. Remove veal to a warm platter.
- Briefly sauté onion, mushrooms and green peppercorns.
- Add wine and simmer to reduce mixture by half.
- Stir in cream, lemon juice and Worcestershire.
- Correct seasonings.
- Return veal to skillet and heat through.
- Serve with buttered noodles.

Veal Piccata

8	slices veal scaloppine
	Salt and pepper to taste
	Flour
1/4	cup olive oil
4	tablespoons butter
1/2	cup dry white wine
1/2	cup chicken broth
	Juice of 1 lemon
2	tablespoons finely chopped fresh parsley
	Chopped fresh parsley for garnish

Servings: 4
Preparation time: 20 minutes
Cooking time: 10 minutes

- Pound veal with a mallet.
- Salt and pepper veal.
- Dredge in flour.
- Heat oil and butter in a large skillet.
- Brown veal for 2 minutes on each side.
- Remove to a heated platter.
- Add wine, broth, lemon juice and parsley to skillet.
- Cook, scraping brown pieces from bottom and sides of skillet.
- Return veal to skillet and coat in sauce.
- Serve on warm platter, garnished with chopped parsley.

Veal Lassere

1	tablespoon butter
1-1/2	cups sliced fresh mushrooms
2	pounds veal scaloppine or 6 good size cutlets
1	cup all-purpose flour
1	teaspoon dried thyme
1	teaspoon Lawry's seasoned salt
1/4	teaspoon pepper
4	tablespoons butter
	Juice of 1 lemon
1/2	cup dry sherry
1	14-ounce can artichoke hearts, halved
2	cups consommé

Servings: 6
Preparation time: 30 minutes
Cooking time: 20 minutes

- Melt butter in a heavy 10-inch skillet.
- Sauté mushrooms. Remove and set aside.
- Pound veal between sheets of waxed paper until paper thin.
- Combine flour, thyme, seasoned salt and pepper.
- Dust veal pieces with flour mixture.
- Melt 2 tablespoons butter in same heavy skillet.
- Brown veal in butter, adding more butter as needed.
- Remove veal to a hot platter, sprinkle with lemon juice and keep warm.
- Add sherry to skillet and boil until reduced by half.
- Add artichokes and reserved mushrooms.
- Add consommé and simmer for 5 minutes.
- Spoon vegetables and sauce over veal before serving.

Veal with Vermouth

6	tablespoons butter
6	shallots or large green onions, finely chopped
1	pound fresh mushrooms
2	pounds veal scaloppine
1/2	cup flour
	Salt and pepper to taste
3/4	cup beef broth
1/3	cup dry vermouth
	Salt and pepper to taste
1	teaspoon dried tarragon

Servings: 6
Preparation time: 30 minutes
Cooking time: 10 to 15 minutes

- In a large heavy skillet, melt 1 tablespoon butter. Sauté shallots.
- Remove shallots and set aside.
- Using more butter, sauté mushrooms for a few minutes. Set aside.
- Dredge veal lightly in flour. Salt and pepper veal.
- In same skillet, add remaining butter and quickly brown veal.
- Layer shallots, then mushrooms, over top of veal.
- Pour beef broth and vermouth over all.
- Sprinkle with salt, pepper and tarragon.
- Cover and simmer for 10 minutes.
- Serve with rice.

Vegetables

Artichoke and Spinach Casserole

1	10-ounce package frozen chopped spinach
1	8-1/2-ounce can artichoke hearts or bottoms
1	clove garlic, minced
1/4	cup salad oil
1/4	cup red wine vinegar
2	tablespoons butter
2	tablespoons all-purpose flour
1	cup Half and Half
1/2	cup freshly grated Parmesan cheese
	Salt and pepper to taste
1/8	cup freshly grated Parmesan cheese

Servings: 6
Preparation time: 20 minutes
Baking time: 20 minutes

- Preheat oven to 350° F.
- Cook spinach according to package directions. Drain and set aside.
- Drain artichoke hearts.
- Combine garlic, oil and vinegar. Pour over artichokes.
- Melt butter and stir in flour. Gradually add Half and Half, stirring constantly with a wire whisk.
- Add 1/2 cup Parmesan cheese.
- Add spinach, salt and pepper.
- Remove artichokes from marinade and place in bottom of a small buttered casserole.
- Cover with spinach mixture.
- Sprinkle with 1/8 cup Parmesan cheese.
- Bake, uncovered, for 20 minutes.

Sautéed Cherry Tomatoes

6	tablespoons butter
2	pints cherry tomatoes
2	tablespoons freshly chopped chives
1	tablespoon freshly chopped parsley
	Salt to taste
	Freshly ground black pepper to taste

Servings: 8
Preparation time: 10 minutes
Cooking time: 3 minutes

- Melt butter in a large sauté pan over medium heat.
- Add tomatoes and sauté for 3 minutes.
- Add herbs, stirring to blend well.
- Correct seasoning. Add salt and pepper.
- Tomatoes should be just warmed through. Do not overcook or skins will split and tomatoes will turn mushy.

Fancy Baked Tomatoes

4	large firm ripe tomatoes
1/4	cup all-purpose flour
1/2	teaspoon salt
1/2	teaspoon dry mustard
1/4	teaspoon paprika
2	tablespoons finely chopped onion
2	tablespoons finely chopped green bell pepper
1	teaspoon Worcestershire sauce
4	strips lean bacon, cut in half
1/3	cup grated sharp Cheddar cheese
	Parsley for garnish

Servings: 8
Preparation time: 15 minutes
Baking time: 25 to 30 minutes
- Preheat oven to 350° F.
- Wash tomatoes and cut in half.
- Arrange, cut side up, in a shallow baking dish.
- Combine next 7 ingredients.
- Spread equal portions of mixture on each tomato half.
- Lay 1 strip of bacon on each tomato.
- Sprinkle with grated cheese.
- Bake for 25 to 30 minutes.

Spinach and Tomatoes

2	10-ounce packages frozen chopped spinach
1	tablespoon vegetable oil
6	green onions, chopped
3/4	cup bread crumbs
3	eggs, beaten
1/3	cup butter, melted
1/2	cup grated Parmesan cheese
2	teaspoons Accent
1/2	teaspoon dried thyme
1	teaspoon coarsely ground black pepper
1/2	teaspoon cayenne pepper
	Salt to taste
8	slices of tomato *or* cherry tomatoes with seeds scooped out

Servings: 6 to 8
Preparation time: 20 minutes
Baking time: 15 to 20 minutes
- Preheat oven to 350° F.
- Cook and drain spinach.
- Sauté onions in oil. Combine all ingredients, except tomatoes.
- Arrange tomatoes in the bottom of a buttered baking dish.
- Top with mounds of spinach mixture.
- Bake for 15 to 20 minutes, until thoroughly heated.

Tomatoes Stuffed with Summer Squash

1	pound yellow squash, grated
1	pound zucchini, grated
2	teaspoons salt
8	small tomatoes
	Salt and pepper to taste
	Olive oil as needed
1	onion, chopped
2	tablespoons butter
2	tablespoons olive oil
1	cup heavy cream
	Salt and pepper to taste
1/2	cup grated Swiss cheese
1/4	cup grated Parmesan cheese
4	tablespoons grated Parmesan cheese

Servings: 8
Preparation time: 45 minutes
Baking time: 15 minutes

- Spread squash and zucchini in a large colander. Sprinkle with salt, toss and let drain for 30 minutes.
- Transfer vegetables to a tea towel and squeeze out remaining moisture.
- Preheat oven to 325° F.
- Slice tops off tomatoes and scoop out seeds.
- Sprinkle insides with salt and pepper. Brush with olive oil.
- Bake, cut side up, on a baking sheet for 10 minutes.
- When done, remove tomatoes and invert on a rack to drain for 30 minutes.
- Sauté onion in butter and olive oil until soft.
- Add squash and zucchini. Cook for 2 minutes.
- Stir in cream, salt and pepper. Cook until cream is absorbed.
- Remove pan from heat. Stir in Swiss cheese and 1/4 cup Parmesan cheese.
- Stuff tomatoes with mixture and sprinkle tops with 4 tablespoons Parmesan cheese.
- Broil for 3 to 4 minutes until tops are bubbly and golden.
- If prepared ahead and refrigerated, cook, covered, at 300° F. for 15 minutes before putting under broiler.
- For a variation, line bottom of a casserole with sliced tomatoes, cover with squash mixture, sprinkle with Parmesan and proceed as usual.

Spinach Stuffed Onions

8	Spanish onions
3	bunches fresh spinach, washed and stemmed, or 2 packages frozen chopped spinach
1/2	teaspoon salt
1/4	teaspoon pepper
1/4	teaspoon ground nutmeg
1	teaspoon fresh lemon juice
3	tablespoons freshly grated Parmesan cheese
2	tablespoons butter
2	tablespoons all-purpose flour
1/4	cup sour cream
2	eggs, beaten

Servings: 8
Preparation time: 35 minutes
Baking time: 20 minutes

- Peel onions and place in boiling water. Cook for 15 minutes.
- Cool and hollow out centers, leaving 1/3-inch thick shell.
- Cook spinach until soft, drain on paper towels and chop finely.
- Preheat oven to 375° F.
- Place spinach in a bowl. Add salt, pepper, nutmeg, lemon juice and cheese.
- Melt butter in a large skillet. Slowly add flour, stirring constantly, to make a roux. Allow to cool. Then add sour cream and eggs.
- Add sour cream mixture to spinach and mix well.
- Fill onion cups with spinach mixture and place in shallow baking pan. Bake, uncovered, for 20 minutes.

Gingered Carrots

1	16-ounce package tiny carrots
1	teaspoon sugar
	Salt and white pepper to taste
2	tablespoons butter
1	tablespoon finely chopped crystallized ginger

Servings: 4
Preparation time: 5 minutes
Cooking time: 5 to 10 minutes

- Scrape carrots and cut into julienne slices.
- Boil with sugar until fork tender. Drain.
- Add salt and white pepper.
- Toss with butter and ginger.

Festive Onions

4	cups sliced onions, cut 1/8-inch thick
5	tablespoons butter
	Salt and pepper to taste
2	eggs
1	cup light cream
2/3	cup freshly grated Parmesan cheese
	Parsley for garnish

Servings: 4
Preparation time: 15 minutes
Baking time: 15 minutes

- Preheat oven to 425° F.
- Butter a 1-quart casserole.
- Place onions in casserole and dot with butter.
- Generously add salt and pepper.
- Mix eggs and cream. Pour over onions.
- Top with Parmesan cheese and bake for 15 minutes.
- Garnish with parsley.

Onion Pie

4	medium onions, sliced
4	tablespoons butter
2	large eggs
1	cup evaporated milk
1	teaspoon salt
1/4	teaspoon pepper
1/8	teaspoon dried thyme
1/8	teaspoon Tabasco sauce
3/4	cup fresh bread crumbs
1/4	cup grated Parmesan cheese
4	tablespoons butter
4	slices bacon, slightly cooked and crumbled
1	tablespoon poppy seeds

Servings: 8
Preparation time: 20 minutes
Baking time: 40 minutes

- Preheat oven to 375° F.
- Sauté onions in 4 tablespoons butter.
- Place onions in a greased 2-quart casserole or in a deep 9-inch pie pan.
- Beat eggs. Add next 5 ingredients. Pour mixture over onions.
- Mix bread crumbs and cheese and spread over onions.
- Dot with 4 tablespoons butter.
- Top with bacon and poppy seeds.
- Bake for 35 to 40 minutes.

Souffléed Corn

Corn
- 1/2 cup butter
- 1/2 cup sugar
- 1 tablespoon all-purpose flour
- 2/3 cup evaporated milk
- 2 eggs, beaten
- 1/2 tablespoon baking powder
- Fresh corn cut from 8 ears or 2 12-ounce cans whole kernel corn

Topping
- 1 tablespoon butter, melted
- 1/3 cup sugar
- 1/2 teaspoon ground cinnamon

Servings: 8
Preparation time: 15 minutes
Baking time: 45 minutes

- Preheat oven to 350° F.
- Melt butter in a heavy saucepan. Stir in sugar.
- Stir in flour until well blended and remove from heat.
- Gradually stir in milk. Add eggs and baking powder.
- Fold in corn and turn into a buttered 9-inch square pan. Bake for 45 minutes or until a knife inserted in middle comes out clean.
- After cooking is completed, pour melted butter on top of corn and sprinkle with sugar and cinnamon.

Fresh Corn Pudding

- 8 to 10 ears fresh corn
- 1 teaspoon salt
- 1 tablespoon sugar
- 4 eggs, beaten
- 2 cups milk, scalded
- 3 tablespoons butter, melted

Servings: 6 to 8
Preparation time: 20 minutes
Baking time: 1 hour

- Preheat oven to 350° F.
- Split kernels of corn lengthwise with a knife.
- Scrape corn off cob. Measure to yield 2-1/2 cups.
- Mix in salt, sugar and eggs.
- Combine milk and butter. Add to corn mixture.
- Pour into a 2-quart baking dish and bake, uncovered, for 1 hour.

Zucchini Pie

4	cups thinly sliced unpeeled zucchini
1	cup chopped onion
1/2	cup butter
1/2	cup chopped parsley
1/2	teaspoon salt
1/2	teaspoon pepper
1/4	teaspoon garlic powder
1/4	teaspoon dried basil
1/4	teaspoon dried orégano
2	eggs, beaten
2	cups (8 ounces) grated Muenster or mozzarella cheese
1	8-ounce can refrigerated quick crescent dinner rolls
2	teaspoons Dijon mustard

Servings: 6
Preparation time: 15 minutes
Baking time: 20 minutes

- Preheat oven to 375° F.
- In a 10-inch skillet, cook zucchini and onion in butter until tender, about 10 minutes.
- Stir in parsley and seasonings.
- In a large bowl, blend eggs and cheese. Stir in vegetable mixture. Set aside.
- Separate dough into 8 triangles.
- Place triangles in an ungreased 8 X 12-inch baking dish, forming a crust on bottom and up sides of dish.
- Spread mustard over crust.
- Pour vegetable mixture evenly onto crust.
- Bake for 20 minutes or until knife comes out clean when inserted in center.
- Let stand for 10 minutes before serving.
- When ready to serve, cut in wedges.

Zucchini Frittata

2	cups thinly sliced zucchini
1	clove garlic, mashed
1/2	cup chopped onion
3	tablespoons chopped fresh parsley
2 to 3	tablespoons butter
8	eggs, beaten
3/4	cup freshly grated Parmesan cheese
1/4	teaspoon salt
1/4	teaspoon pepper

Servings: 8
Preparation time: 10 minutes
Baking time: 20 minutes

- Preheat oven to 350° F.
- In a large skillet, sauté zucchini, garlic, onion and parsley in butter for 2 to 3 minutes.
- Remove skillet from heat. Add eggs, cheese, salt and pepper.
- Pour into a greased 9-inch square baking dish.
- Bake for 20 to 25 minutes.
- Cut in squares and serve at once.

Zucchini Rounds

1/3	cup Bisquick
1/4	cup grated Parmesan cheese
1/8	teaspoon pepper
2	large eggs, slightly beaten
2	cups shredded zucchini
2	tablespoons butter

Servings: 4 to 6
Preparation time: 20 to 25 minutes
Cooking time: 15 minutes

- Combine Bisquick, Parmesan cheese and pepper.
- Add eggs and stir until well moistened.
- Fold zucchini into egg mixture.
- Melt butter in a 10-inch skillet. Place 2 to 3 tablespoons of vegetable mixture for each "round" in skillet. Brown on each side.
- Serve immediately.
- These may be transferred to a warm platter and held for 1 hour.
- Excellent with a steak or roast.

Zucchini Tarragon

3	pounds zucchini, washed and trimmed
4	cups chicken broth
8	tablespoons butter
1-1/2	teaspoons salt
	Freshly ground pepper to taste
1	teaspoon dried tarragon

Servings: 6
Preparation time: 10 minutes
Cooking time: 8 minutes

- Slice zucchini into strips 2 inches long and 1/8-inch thick.
- Bring chicken broth to a rapid boil in a large skillet.
- Cook zucchini in chicken broth in separate batches for 3 to 4 minutes each time. Remove zucchini.
- Pour broth in a storage container for use at another time.
- Melt butter in skillet.
- Add zucchini, salt, pepper and tarragon.
- Toss over high heat for 3 to 4 minutes.
- Serve at once.

Zucchini Soufflé

2/3	cup butter
1/4	cup chopped onion
2/3	cup all-purpose flour
1	teaspoon salt
1-1/3	cups milk
1-1/3	cups chicken stock
8	egg yolks, lightly beaten
8	ounces Swiss cheese, grated
6	cups finely grated unpeeled zucchini
8	egg whites, stiffly beaten
	White pepper and salt to taste
	Worcestershire sauce to taste

Servings: 16
Preparation time: 30 minutes
Baking time: 1 hour

- Preheat oven to 325° F.
- Melt butter in a large saucepan.
- Sauté onion until soft.
- Add flour and salt, stirring to form a paste.
- Slowly add milk and stock, stirring until a smooth sauce is obtained.
- Cook until sauce is quite thick.
- Add egg yolks and cheese.
- Remove from heat and allow sauce to cool.
- Add zucchini.
- Fold in egg whites.
- Add pepper, salt and Worcestershire.
- Pour into 2 greased 1-1/2-quart soufflé dishes.
- Place dishes in a shallow pan of hot water in the oven and bake for 1 hour.

Snow Peas with Water Chestnuts

1/2	6-ounce can water chestnuts, thinly sliced
2	tablespoons butter
2	7-ounce packages frozen snow peas, thawed to room temperature

Servings: 4
Preparation time: 10 minutes
Cooking time: 5 minutes

- Slightly heat water chestnuts in butter.
- Boil peas in lightly salted water to cover for 1 minute.
- Drain peas and toss with water chestnuts in butter.

Green Beans Tarragon

1	pound green beans
1	tablespoon olive oil
1	tablespoon butter
1	clove garlic, minced
1	onion, minced
1	medium tomato, peeled and chopped
2	tablespoons tarragon vinegar
1/2	teaspoon brown sugar
	Salt to taste
	Freshly ground black pepper to taste

Servings: 4
Preparation time: 40 minutes
Cooking time: 40 minutes

- Cut beans in quarters or thirds.
- Steam until almost tender. Drain.
- Run cold water over beans to prevent further cooking.
- Heat oil and butter in a heavy skillet.
- Add garlic and onion. Sauté for 10 minutes.
- Add tomato. Blend well.
- Add vinegar, sugar, salt and pepper.
- Cook sauce slowly for 5 minutes.
- Add beans. Toss to mix well.
- Cover and simmer for 15 to 20 minutes.

Dilled Green Beans

2-1/2	pounds fresh green beans
1/2	cup butter
1	teaspoon dried dill weed
1	teaspoon dried tarragon
	Parsley for garnish

Servings: 6
Preparation time: 15 minutes
Cooking time: 7 to 10 minutes

- Cook green beans in a small amount of boiling water for 7 to 10 minutes. Drain.
- Toss in butter and herbs.
- Garnish with fresh parsley and serve.
- Do not overcook beans—they are best when crunchy.

Beans with Dill Sauce

1	pound green beans
1/2	cup sour cream
1	cup mayonnaise
2	tablespoons dill weed
3 to 6	tablespoons cider vinegar
1/4	cup chopped onions
1	tablespoon onion salt
4	slices bacon, cooked and crumbled

Servings: 6
Preparation time: 15 minutes
Refrigeration time: overnight

- Blanch beans for 2 minutes in boiling water. Drain.
- Combine sour cream, mayonnaise, dill weed, vinegar, onions and onion salt. Mix well.
- Add beans. Toss well and refrigerate overnight.
- Serve cold with bacon on top.

Fresh Green Beans with Sour Cream Sauce

2	pounds fresh green beans
1	tablespoon granulated chicken bouillon
3	tablespoons butter
1	8-1/2-ounce can sliced water chestnuts
1/2	cup finely chopped onion
1	cup sour cream
1	teaspoon vinegar
1	teaspoon sugar
1/2	teaspoon salt
1/4	teaspoon pepper
1	pimento, sliced
1/4	cup chopped parsley

Servings: 8
Preparation time: 15 minutes
Cooking time: 10 minutes

- Cover beans with salted water and simmer with chicken bouillon until just done, about 10 minutes. Drain.
- Melt butter in a large skillet.
- Sauté water chestnuts and onion.
- Stir in sour cream and seasonings.
- Add beans and pimento. Just heat through.
- Sprinkle top with parsley before serving.

Autumn Acorn Squash

2	small acorn squash
2	tablespoons butter
	Salt and pepper to taste
	Ground nutmeg to taste
	Curry powder to taste (optional)
6	teaspoons water

Servings: 4
Preparation time: 10 minutes
Baking time: 45 minutes

- Preheat oven to 350° F.
- Wash and dry squash. Cut in half lengthwise.
- Scoop out seeds. Remove a small slice from the bottom of each half so it will rest firmly in pan.
- Butter the flat rim of each cut side and divide remaining butter among the four hollows.
- Season each hollow with salt, pepper, nutmeg and curry powder.
- Place squash in a small baking dish with 1/4-inch of water in bottom of pan.
- Spoon 1-1/2 teaspoons of water in each hollow.
- Bake, uncovered, for 45 minutes or until pierced easily with a fork.
- Serve with extra butter.
- May be done ahead and baked before serving.

Mushrooms Polonaise

1/4	cup butter	
1/2	pound fresh mushrooms, sliced	
1	medium onion, finely chopped	
2	tablespoons all-purpose flour	
1	cup sour cream	
1/4	cup heavy cream	
	Salt and pepper to taste	
1/4	teaspoon ground nutmeg	
4	tablespoons chopped fresh parsley	
	Parsley for garnish	

Servings: 6
Preparation time: 15 minutes
Baking time: 35 to 40 minutes

- Preheat oven to 325° F.
- Butter a shallow baking dish.
- Melt butter. Add mushrooms and onions. Sauté until mushrooms are brown and onions are soft.
- Slowly stir in flour. Cook over low heat for 5 minutes.
- Combine sour cream, cream, salt, pepper and nutmeg. Add to onion mixture.
- Cook until thickened.
- Stir in parsley and pour into casserole.
- Bake for 35 minutes.
- Garnish with parsley.

Spinach Flexibility

1	10-ounce package frozen chopped spinach, thawed and well drained
1	cup sour cream
1	tablespoon mayonnaise
1	green onion, chopped
1	4-ounce package ranch style buttermilk dressing
1	teaspoon garlic salt (optional)

Servings: 4 as a vegetable or 10 to 12 as an appetizer
Preparation time: 5 minutes
Cooking time: 15 to 20 minutes

- Combine all ingredients and chill.
- This may be served in a number of ways:
  (1) Serve cold as a dip with corn chips or raw vegetables.
  (2) Serve heated over pasta.
  (3) Stuff tomatoes or top baked potatoes with this mixture and heat in a 350° F. oven.
  (4) Double recipe and bake in 350° F. oven until warm and serve as a vegetable dish.

Spinach and Potato Casserole

1	10-ounce package frozen chopped spinach
8	medium potatoes, peeled and quartered
1/2	cup margarine, softened
1	cup sour cream
1	8-ounce package cream cheese, softened
1	teaspoon dried dill weed
	Salt and pepper to taste
1/4	cup grated Parmesan cheese

Servings: 8
Preparation time: 30 minutes
Baking time: 20 minutes
- Preheat oven to 325° F.
- Cook spinach according to package directions. Squeeze dry.
- Boil potatoes until tender. Drain.
- In a large mixing bowl, combine potatoes, margarine, sour cream, cream cheese, dill, salt and pepper.
- Stir in spinach.
- Pour in a greased 2-quart casserole. Sprinkle with Parmesan cheese.
- Bake, uncovered, for 20 minutes.

Sour Cream Potato Casserole

6	medium potatoes
1/2	cup butter, melted
2	cups grated Cheddar cheese
2	cups sour cream
1/2	cup chopped green onions
	Salt and pepper to taste
2	tablespoons butter
	Parsley or paprika for garnish

Servings: 6 to 8
Preparation time: 25 minutes
Baking time: 25 minutes
- Preheat oven to 350° F.
- Boil potatoes for 8 minutes. Then finely dice.
- Combine potatoes, 1/2 cup butter, cheese, sour cream, onions, salt and pepper.
- Pour into a greased casserole.
- Dot with butter.
- Bake for 25 minutes.
- Garnish with fresh parsley or paprika.

Italian Scalloped Potatoes

3	cups thinly sliced onions
2	cloves garlic, crushed and minced
2	tablespoons olive oil
4	tablespoons butter
4	tomatoes
8 to 10	potatoes
1-1/2	teaspoons salt
	Pepper to taste
2	tablespoons chopped parsley
1/2	teaspoon dried basil
1/4	teaspoon dried orégano
1	cup grated Swiss cheese
2	tablespoons grated Parmesan cheese
	Salt and pepper to taste
2	tablespoons butter

Servings: 8
Preparation time: 45 minutes
Baking time: 1 hour

- Sauté onion and garlic in olive oil and butter until just tender.
- Peel tomatoes and cut in half. Squeeze out seeds and drain, upside down, on paper towels.
- Peel potatoes and slice very thin.
- Dice tomatoes. Add tomatoes, salt, pepper, parsley, basil and orégano to onion. Mix well.
- Butter a 3-quart casserole.
- Preheat oven to 325° F.
- Spoon a third of the tomato mixture into casserole.
- Add half each of the potatoes, Swiss cheese, Parmesan, salt and pepper.
- Repeat once and top with remaining third of the tomato mixture.
- Dot with butter.
- Bake for 1 hour or until potatoes are tender.

New Potatoes au Caviar

8	new potatoes
1	8-ounce carton sour cream
1	2-ounce jar caviar, the best you can find

Servings: 4
Preparation time: 5 minutes
Cooking time: 20 minutes

- Peel potatoes. Boil in lightly salted water until done. Drain.
- Slice a thin piece off the bottom of each so potatoes will sit nicely on a plate.
- Using a melon scoop, remove a small portion from the top of each potato.
- Fill with a dollop of sour cream and top with a sprinkling of caviar.

Broccoli Extraordinaire

8	ounces vermicelli
6	cups chicken broth
1	pound fresh broccoli
8	scallions, chopped
2	tablespoons butter
3/4	teaspoon salt
1/4	teaspoon pepper
10	ounces mild Cheddar cheese, sliced thin
3/4	cup light cream

Servings: 6 to 8
Preparation time: 30 minutes
Baking time: 30 minutes

- Preheat oven to 375° F.
- Butter a 2-quart oblong ovenproof casserole.
- Cook vermicelli in chicken broth, drain and set aside.
- Cook broccoli until just tender, drain and cut in 2-inch pieces.
- Sauté scallions in butter until transparent.
- Add broccoli, salt and pepper. Cook for 5 minutes over low heat.
- Put vermicelli in casserole. Cover with half the cheese slices.
- Pour cream over cheese, add broccoli mixture and cover with remaining cheese.
- Bake for 30 minutes.
- May be prepared and frozen before baking, however, cooking time should be increased by 15 minutes.

Broccoli Soufflé

1	large bunch fresh broccoli, about 6 cups when chopped
2	tablespoons butter
2	tablespoons all-purpose flour
1	teaspoon salt
1/4	teaspoon pepper
1/2	cup milk
1/3	cup freshly grated Parmesan cheese
4	eggs, separated

Servings: 6
Preparation time: 30 minutes
Baking time: 35 minutes

- Preheat oven to 350° F.
- Steam broccoli until just tender. Drain well and chop fine.
- Add butter to broccoli.
- Blend in flour, salt and pepper. Stir in milk.
- Cook over medium heat until mixture thickens and bubbles.
- Remove from heat and stir in cheese.
- Beat egg yolks until thick and lemon colored. Add to broccoli mixture.
- Beat egg whites until stiff.
- Fold broccoli mixture into egg whites.
- Pour into an ungreased 1-quart soufflé dish.
- Bake for 35 minutes.
- Serve immediately.

California Cabbage

2	tablespoons butter or margarine
8	cups chopped or finely shredded cabbage
1	clove garlic
1/4	cup water
1-1/2	teaspoons salt
1/2	teaspoon Accent
1/4	teaspoon pepper
1/2	cup sour cream
1	tablespoon sugar
2	tablespoons vinegar
1	teaspoon caraway seed

Servings: 6
Preparation time: 10 minutes
Cooking time: 10 to 12 minutes

- Melt butter in a large heavy skillet.
- Add next 6 ingredients.
- Cover tightly and steam for 10 to 12 minutes.
- Remove garlic clove.
- Blend sour cream, sugar and vinegar. Add to cabbage.
- Correct seasonings and sprinkle with caraway.

Chinese Celery

4	cups chopped celery, cut in 1/2-inch diagonal pieces
1	10-ounce can chicken broth
1	8-ounce can water chestnuts, sliced
1/2	pound fresh mushrooms, sliced
5	tablespoons butter
	Salt and pepper to taste
1/2	cup slivered almonds
	Parmesan cheese to taste

Servings: 6 to 8
Preparation time: 15 minutes
Cooking time: 5 to 8 minutes

- Bring chicken broth to a boil.
- Add celery and cook for 5 minutes. Celery should still be crisp.
- Add water chestnuts, mushrooms and butter.
- Cook only until all ingredients are thoroughly heated. Drain.
- Season with salt and pepper.
- Sprinkle with almonds and Parmesan cheese.
- Serve immediately.
- Excellent over rice.
- For variation, add 1 cup of diced cooked chicken.

Gourmet Braised Turnips

2	pounds turnips
1/4	pound sliced bacon
2	tablespoons butter
1/2	cup finely chopped onion
1/2	cup chicken stock
3/4	teaspoon sugar
3/4	teaspoon salt
2	tablespoons minced parsley
	Lemon juice to taste
	Salt and pepper to taste

Servings: 6
Preparation time: 30 minutes
Cooking time: 15 minutes

- Peel and dice turnips into 1/2-inch cubes.
- Cook in boiling water for 1 minute.
- Drain in a colander, pat dry and set aside.
- Sauté bacon until crisp. Drain on a paper towel.
- Melt butter. Add onion and sauté until translucent.
- Add turnips, stock, sugar and salt.
- Cook, covered, over low heat for 15 minutes.
- Add crumbled bacon, parsley, lemon juice, salt and pepper.
- Toss well and transfer to a heated serving dish.

Ratatouille

1	green bell pepper, coarsely chopped
1/2	cup coarsely chopped onion
1/2	pound fresh mushrooms, sliced
1	clove garlic, minced
1/4	cup olive oil
2/3	pound zucchini, sliced
2/3	pound cubed eggplant
1	pound or 2 cups firm ripe tomatoes, peeled and seeded
1/4	cup fresh chopped parsley
1	teaspoon dried basil
1	teaspoon dried orégano
	Salt and pepper to taste
	Watercress for garnish
	Parsley for garnish

Servings: 8
Preparation time: 30 minutes
Baking time: 30 minutes
Chilling time: 2 hours

- Preheat oven to 350° F.
- In a heavy frying pan, sauté green pepper, onion, mushrooms and garlic in olive oil for 5 minutes. Remove to a large bowl with a slotted spoon.
- Sauté zucchini until tender and remove to bowl.
- Sauté eggplant until tender, adding more oil if necessary. Add to other vegetables.
- Stir in tomatoes and parsley. Season with basil, orégano, salt and pepper.
- Pour mixture into a 9 X 13-inch baking dish. Bake for 30 minutes.
- Dish may be served hot or cold. If cold, chill for 2 hours. Garnish with watercress and parsley.

Black Beans and Rice

1	12-ounce package black beans
7	cups water
8	cloves garlic, minced
2	large onions, chopped
2	green bell peppers, chopped
1/3	cup olive oil
	Ham bone
4	teaspoons salt
1	teaspoon black pepper
3	tablespoons vinegar
1/2	cup chopped onion and scallions

Servings: 8
Soaking time: overnight
Preparation time: 30 minutes
Cooking time: 3 to 4 hours

- Soak beans overnight in water to cover.
- Drain beans.
- Combine black beans with next 8 ingredients in a soup pot.
- Simmer for 3 to 4 hours or until beans are tender and liquid is thick.
- Add vinegar just before serving.
- Serve over rice and garnish with chopped onion.

Red Beans and Rice

1	pound dried red beans
2	pounds smoked sausage
2	large onions, chopped
3	stalks celery with tops, chopped
1	large green bell pepper, chopped
2	cloves garlic, minced
2	teaspoons salt
1	teaspoon pepper
1/2	cup chopped fresh parsley
	Tabasco sauce to taste
1	teaspoon dried orégano
2	bay leaves
1	tablespoon sugar

Servings: 8
Soaking time: overnight
Preparation time: 30 minutes
Cooking time: 3 to 4 hours

- Soak beans overnight in water to cover. Sort, wash and drain beans.
- Brown sausage in small amount of water.
- Combine all ingredients in a large pot. Add water to cover.
- Bring to boil. Then reduce heat. Simmer 3 to 4 hours, stirring occasionally.
- If necessary, add more water.
- Serve over hot rice.

Escalloped Green Peppers

6	medium green bell peppers
1/4	cup butter
2	tablespoons all-purpose flour
1/2	teaspoon salt
2	cups milk, scalded
5	ounces Cheddar cheese, grated
1	teaspoon Worcestershire sauce
1/2 to 3/4 cup dry bread crumbs	

Servings: 8
Preparation time: 15 minutes
Baking time: 30 to 40 minutes

- Preheat oven to 375° F.
- Cut peppers in half lengthwise and remove seeds.
- Boil peppers in a small amount of lightly salted water for 3 to 4 minutes.
- Drain peppers and cut into strips.
- Melt butter in a saucepan. Stir in flour and salt.
- Add milk and stir with a wire whisk. Cook until thick.
- Add cheese and Worcestershire.
- In a buttered 1-quart baking dish, put layers of peppers, cheese sauce and bread crumbs, ending with bread crumbs.
- Bake for 30 to 40 minutes.

Hot Pineapple Casserole

1	20-ounce can pineapple chunks
3	tablespoons pineapple juice
1/2	cup sugar
3	tablespoons all-purpose flour
1	cup grated Cheddar cheese
1/4	cup butter, melted
1/2	cup butter cracker crumbs (Townhouse or Ritz crackers)

Servings: 4
Preparation time: 20 minutes
Baking time: 30 minutes

- Preheat oven to 350° F.
- Drain pineapple, reserving 3 tablespoons of juice.
- Combine sugar, flour and reserved pineapple juice.
- Add cheese and pineapple chunks. Mix well.
- Spoon into a greased 1-quart casserole.
- Combine butter and cracker crumbs. Stir well.
- Sprinkle over pineapple mixture.
- Bake for 30 minutes.
- This is easy to double and may be prepared ahead of time.

Baked Apricots

2	16-ounce cans pitted and halved apricots, drained
1	cup dark brown sugar
8	ounces Ritz crackers, crushed
1/2	cup butter

Servings: 8
Preparation time: 15 minutes
Baking time: 1 hour

- Preheat oven to 300° F.
- Place half the apricots in a greased 2-quart baking dish.
- Cover with half the sugar, then half the crumbs.
- Dot thickly with half the butter.
- Repeat layers, ending with butter.
- Bake for 1 hour or until thick and crusty on top.
- A wonderful accompaniment to chicken or pork.
- Baked apricots also make a delicious dessert served with ice cream or whipped cream.

French Peas

2	cups water
1	teaspoon sugar
1/2	teaspoon salt
2	10-ounce packages frozen peas
3	tablespoons butter
1	cup sliced green onions, use tops
1/3	pound fresh mushrooms, sliced
1	cup shredded lettuce
	Salt and freshly ground pepper to taste
2	tablespoons sliced pimento

Servings: 8
Preparation time: 15 minutes
Cooking time: 15 minutes

- Bring water, sugar and salt to a boil.
- Add peas and return to boil, separating peas with a fork to break up chunks if necessary.
- As soon as mixture returns to a rolling boil, drain in a colander and run under cold water to stop cooking process. Set aside.
- In a heavy skillet over medium heat, melt butter. Sauté onions and mushrooms for 3 minutes.
- Stir lettuce into onion mixture and sauté for another 3 minutes.
- Add peas and continue to cook until peas are thoroughly heated and lettuce is just transparent.
- Add salt and pepper.
- Turn into serving dishes and garnish with pimento.

Grains & Breads

Orange Sugar Biscuits

2	cups self-rising flour, sift before measuring
3	tablespoons Crisco
2-1/2	cups milk
16	sugar cubes
1/3	cup orange juice

Servings: 12 to 16
Preparation time: 20 minutes
Baking time: 12 minutes

- Preheat oven to 450° F.
- Cut Crisco into flour with a knife and fork until texture resembles coarse cornmeal.
- Add just enough milk to make a soft dough.
- Knead lightly on a floured surface. Then pat out to 1-inch thickness.
- Cut with a biscuit cutter and place on an ungreased baking sheet.
- Dip each sugar cube in orange juice. Then press one into each biscuit.
- Bake for 12 minutes. Serve immediately.

Southern Biscuits

2	cups all-purpose flour
4	teaspoons baking powder
1/2	teaspoon salt
1/2	teaspoon cream of tartar
2	teaspoons sugar
1/2	cup Crisco
2/3	cup milk

Servings: 15 biscuits
Preparation time: 10 minutes
Baking time: 10 minutes

- Preheat oven to 450° F.
- Sift together all dry ingredients.
- Cut in Crisco with a knife and fork or pastry blender, until mixture resembles fine gravel.
- Sprinkle in milk until mixture forms a ball.
- On a floured surface, gently pat out dough. Then roll to desired thickness. Thin biscuits will be crunchy, thick biscuits will be light and fluffy.
- Cut biscuits to desired size.
- Bake on an ungreased cookie sheet for 10 minutes or until golden brown.

Poppy Seed Pastries

1	cup butter, softened
2	3-ounce packages cream cheese
1	cup firmly packed finely grated extra sharp Cheddar cheese
1/2	teaspoon cayenne pepper
4	teaspoons mixed Italian seasonings
2	cups Wondra flour
	Poppy seeds

Yield: 88 to 96 pastries
Preparation time: 15 to 20 minutes
Chilling time: 3 hours
Baking time: 8 to 10 minutes

- Cream butter and cream cheese.
- Add Cheddar cheese, pepper and seasonings.
- Add flour and work in well.
- Cover and chill for several hours or overnight.
- Preheat oven to 400° F.
- Remove dough from refrigerator an eighth at a time.
- Roll out on a lightly floured pastry cloth.
- Dough should be rolled thin enough to get 11 to 12 circles from each portion, using a 2-1/2-inch round cutter.
- Fold each round over to make a half circle. Crimp edges with a fork.
- Place on an ungreased cookie sheet.
- Sprinkle with poppy seeds.
- Proceed with each portion of dough.
- Bake for 8 to 10 minutes.

Quick Mayonnaise Rolls

2	cups self-rising flour
1	cup milk
4	tablespoons Hellmann's mayonnaise

Servings: 12 rolls
Preparation time: 5 minutes
Baking time: 12 to 15 minutes

- Preheat oven to 350° F.
- Combine all ingredients.
- Spoon into greased muffin tins.
- Bake 12 to 15 minutes until light brown.

One Hour Rolls

1	envelope yeast
1/4	cup warm water
2	tablespoons sugar
2	cups all-purpose flour, sifted
1/2	teaspoon salt
1/2	teaspoon baking powder
1/4	teaspoon baking soda
1/4	cup butter, melted
1/2	cup buttermilk or 1 tablespoon vinegar and fill to 1/2 cup with milk
1	tablespoon butter, melted

Servings: 12 rolls
Preparation time: 20 minutes
Rising time: 1 hour
Baking time: 15 minutes

- Dissolve yeast in warm water.
- Add sugar.
- Sift together flour, salt, baking powder and baking soda.
- Mix 1/4 cup butter and buttermilk in a large bowl.
- Add yeast mixture.
- Sift in dry ingredients and stir well.
- Turn onto a lightly floured board and knead well, about 10 to 20 minutes.
- Roll out 1/2-inch thick and cut into 1 to 1-1/2-inch rounds.
- Brush each roll with melted butter and fold over.
- Place in a buttered biscuit pan and let rise for 1 hour.
- Bake in a preheated 425° F. oven for 15 minutes.

Spring Crest Cornbread

1	7-ounce box Jiffy corn muffin mix
1	cup sour cream
1	8-ounce can creamed corn
1/3	cup vegetable oil
3	large eggs

Servings: 8
Preparation time: 5 minutes
Baking time: 35 minutes

- Preheat oven to 350° F.
- Mix all ingredients and pour into a greased 8 X 8-inch pan.
- Bake for 35 minutes.
- Serve immediately.

Fluffy Rolls

1	cup boiling water
1-3/4	teaspoons salt
1	cup Crisco
3/4	cup sugar
2	eggs, slightly beaten
2	envelopes yeast
1	cup lukewarm water
6	cups all-purpose flour

Servings: 36 rolls
Preparation time: 30 minutes
Baking time: 15 minutes
Rising time: 3 hours

- Preheat oven to 400° F.
- Blend boiling water, salt, Crisco and sugar.
- Add eggs.
- Dissolve yeast in water. Then add to mixture.
- Add flour and mix.
- Put mixture in refrigerator and let rise for at least 3 hours or until it does not stick to the hand.
- Roll out and cut with a small round cutter.
- Brush each roll with melted butter and fold over.
- Place on a greased cookie sheet and bake until brown, about 15 minutes.

Swiss Cheese Cornbread

2	eggs, beaten
1	7-1/2-ounce package corn muffin mix
1	8-ounce can cream style corn
1	7-ounce can whole kernel corn, drained
1	8-ounce carton sour cream
1/2	cup butter or margarine, melted
1	cup (1/4 pound) shredded Swiss cheese

Servings: 9 to 12
Preparation time: 15 minutes
Baking time: 45 minutes

- Preheat oven to 350° F.
- Combine first 6 ingredients in a medium mixing bowl.
- Mix well.
- Pour into a lightly greased 12 X 7-1/2 X 1-1/2-inch baking pan.
- Bake for 35 minutes.
- Remove from oven.
- Sprinkle with cheese. Bake an additional 10 minutes.
- May be made ahead and stored in refrigerator.
- Reheat covered with foil.
- May be frozen 2 or 3 weeks.

Cranberry Bread

2	cups sifted all-purpose flour
1	teaspoon salt
1-1/2	teaspoons baking powder
1/2	teaspoon baking soda
1	cup sugar
1	egg, slightly beaten
4	tablespoons butter, melted
3/4	cup orange juice
	Juice of 1 lemon
1	tablespoon grated orange rind
1	tablespoon grated lemon rind
2	cups cranberries, coarsely chopped
1/2	cup broken pecans

Servings: 1 loaf
Preparation time: 15 minutes
Baking time: 1 hour

- Preheat oven to 350° F.
- Combine all ingredients in order given.
- Pour into a greased 9 X 5 X 3-inch loaf pan.
- Bake for 1 hour.
- If top of bread gets too brown while baking, cover with foil.

Herb Roll-Ups

1	cup butter, softened
1	teaspoon dried savory
1	teaspoon dried basil
4	tablespoons chopped chives
	Beau-Monde seasoning to taste
1	loaf white thin sliced soft sandwich bread
	Plain wooden toothpicks

Servings: 20
Preparation time: 40 minutes
Baking time: 25 minutes

- Preheat oven to 350° F.
- Combine butter and herbs. Mix well.
- Trim all crusts from bread slices.
- Roll bread lightly with a rolling pin until flat.
- Spread slices with butter mixture.
- Roll up bread slices and fasten with toothpicks.
- Place on a baking sheet and bake for 25 minutes or until browned.
- Slices may be cut in thirds and used as hors d'oeuvres.

Sweet Lemon Bread

1	cup butter, softened
2	cups sugar
4	eggs
1/2	teaspoon salt
1/2	teaspoon baking soda
3	cups all-purpose flour
1	cup buttermilk
1	lemon rind, grated
1	cup chopped pecans
	Juice of 3 lemons
1	cup sugar

Servings: 2 loaves
Preparation time: 30 minutes
Baking time: 1 hour

- Preheat oven to 325° F.
- Cream butter and sugar.
- Add eggs, one at a time, beating after each addition.
- Sift together salt, soda and flour. Add to sugar mixture alternating with buttermilk.
- Stir in lemon rind and pecans.
- Pour into 2 greased and floured loaf pans.
- Bake for 1 hour.
- While bread bakes, mix lemon juice and sugar. Stir until sugar is dissolved, making a glaze.
- After bread has baked, turn onto waxed paper and spoon glaze over top while bread is still hot.

Apple Cheddar Bread

2/3	cup sugar
2	cups self-rising flour
1	teaspoon ground cinnamon
1/2	cup chopped nuts
2	eggs, slightly beaten
1/2	cup melted butter or vegetable oil
1-1/2	cups finely chopped peeled apples
1/2	cup grated sharp Cheddar cheese
1/4	cup milk

Servings: 1 loaf
Preparation time: 20 minutes
Baking time: 60 minutes

- Preheat oven to 350° F.
- Grease well a 9 X 5 X 3-inch loaf pan.
- Mix sugar, flour, cinnamon and nuts.
- Combine eggs, butter, apples, cheese and milk.
- Add to sugar mixture.
- Stir just until blended. Batter will be lumpy.
- Pour batter into prepared loaf pan.
- Bake for 60 to 70 minutes.
- Cover with foil during baking if top gets too brown.

Oatmeal Bread

1	cup quick cooking oats
2	cups boiling water
1/2	cup lukewarm water
1	envelope yeast
1/2	cup molasses
2 to 3	tablespoons vegetable oil
2 to 3	cups unbleached flour
1	tablespoon salt
2 to 3	cups unbleached flour

Servings: 2 loaves
Preparation time: 30 minutes
Rising time: 4 hours
Baking time: 35 minutes

- Combine oats and boiling water. Let cool.
- Dissolve yeast in lukewarm water. Add to cooled oatmeal.
- Add molasses, oil, 2 to 3 cups flour and salt so that a sticky dough is made.
- Knead dough on a floured board and add 2 to 3 more cups of flour.
- Knead until smooth.
- Roll dough into a large ball. Place in an oiled bowl.
- Cover and let rise in a warm place for 2 hours.
- Punch down and knead again.
- Shape into 2 loaves and put into French bread or regular bread pans.
- Let rise again until double in bulk, about 2 hours.
- Bake in a preheated 350° F. oven for 35 minutes.
- Serve with a hearty soup or stew.

Hush Puppies

1	cup white corn meal
1 to 1-1/2	teaspoons baking powder
1/3	cup all-purpose flour
1	teaspoon salt
2	tablespoons sugar
1	egg, beaten
1	small onion, minced
1/4	green bell pepper, minced
2	stalks celery, minced
3/8	cup milk <u>and</u>
3/8	cup water, combined
	Oil for deep fat frying

Servings: 8
Preparation time: 10 minutes
Refrigeration time: 30 minutes
Cooking time: 5 minutes

- Combine first 11 ingredients in order given.
- Stir only until moistened.
- Refrigerate for 30 minutes, until mixture becomes slightly firm.
- Gently drop by spoonfuls into hot oil, frying until golden brown.

Unbelievable Garlic Bread

1	cup mayonnaise
6	cloves garlic, minced
3/4	cup grated Parmesan cheese
1/2	cup grated Cheddar cheese
1	tablespoon light cream
1/4	teaspoon paprika
1	loaf French bread

Servings: 8
Preparation time: 20 minutes
Broiling time: 2 to 3 minutes

- Mix mayonnaise, garlic and Parmesan cheese in a small bowl.
- In a saucepan, melt Cheddar cheese, cream and paprika, stirring constantly.
- Blend mayonnaise mixture into cheese mixture.
- Cut French bread in half, lengthwise. Toast lightly.
- Spread cheese on French bread.
- Broil in oven for 2 to 3 minutes.
- This mixture will keep indefinitely in the refrigerator in an airtight container.

Sister's Sally Lunn

2	eggs
3/4	cup sugar
2	cups all-purpose flour
2	teaspoons baking powder
1/8	teaspoon salt
1	cup milk
3	tablespoons butter, melted
	Butter

Servings: 12
Preparation time: 20 minutes
Baking time: 25 minutes

- Preheat oven to 400° F.
- Beat eggs. Add sugar gradually.
- Sift dry ingredients together.
- Add alternately with milk to eggs.
- Add butter.
- Pour into a greased 9 X 13-inch baking dish.
- Bake for 25 minutes.
- Cut into squares, spread with butter and serve immediately.

Scottish Scones

2-1/2	cups all-purpose flour
4	tablespoons sugar
1/2	teaspoon baking soda
1/2	teaspoon cream of tartar
1/4	pound butter
1/2	cup raisins
3/4	cup milk
1/3	cup sugar

Servings: 10 to 12
Preparation time: 15 minutes
Baking time: 10 to 12 minutes

- Preheat oven to 425° F.
- Mix flour, 4 tablespoons sugar, baking soda and cream of tartar.
- Cut in butter.
- Add raisins and milk.
- Pour mixture onto a floured board and roll lightly to 1-inch thickness.
- Cut out with cookie cutter.
- Put on an ungreased cookie sheet.
- Dust with 1/3 cup sugar.
- Bake for 10 to 12 minutes.

Spice Muffins

1	cup butter, softened
2	cups sugar
2	eggs
2	cups applesauce
3	teaspoons ground cinnamon
2	teaspoons ground allspice
1/2	teaspoon ground cloves
1	teaspoon salt
2	teaspoons baking soda
4	cups all-purpose flour
1	cup chopped pecans
	Powdered sugar

Servings: 2 dozen regular size or 72 small muffins
Preparation time: 25 minutes
Baking time: 10 minutes

- Preheat oven to 350° F.
- Cream butter and sugar with an electric mixer.
- Add eggs, one at a time.
- Mix in applesauce and spices.
- Sift together salt, soda and flour. Add to batter and beat well.
- Stir in nuts.
- Bake in lightly greased muffin tins for 8 to 10 minutes.
- Sprinkle with powdered sugar.
- Batter will keep covered in the refrigerator for 3 weeks.

Apple Carrot Muffins

1/2	cup powdered milk
3	teaspoons baking powder
1/2	teaspoon salt
1	teaspoon ground cinnamon
1/2	teaspoon ground nutmeg
1/2	teaspoon ground allspice
2	cups whole wheat flour
1/2	cup all-purpose flour
1	cup honey
1	cup vegetable oil
4	eggs
1	teaspoon vanilla extract
1	cup grated apple
1	cup grated carrots

Servings: 24 muffins
Preparation time: 20 minutes
Baking time: 15 minutes

- Preheat oven to 400° F.
- Combine milk, baking powder, salt, spices and flours.
- Combine honey, oil, eggs and vanilla.
- Stir into dry ingredients.
- Fold in apples and carrots.
- Spoon into greased medium muffin tins or muffin papers.
- Bake for 15 minutes.
- May use food processor to grate apples and carrots.
- May halve recipe.
- Serve with cream cheese.

Oatmeal Muffins

1	cup rolled oats
1	cup buttermilk
1	egg, beaten
1/2	cup vegetable oil
1/2	cup brown sugar
1	cup all-purpose flour
1/2	teaspoon salt
1/2	teaspoon baking soda
1-1/2	teaspoons baking powder
1/2	cup raisins (optional)
1/2	cup chopped pecans (optional)

Servings: 12 large muffins
Preparation time: 10 minutes
Standing time: 30 minutes
Baking time: 25 minutes

- Combine oats and buttermilk. Let stand for 30 minutes.
- Preheat oven to 350° F.
- Stir egg, oil and brown sugar into oatmeal mixture. Blend thoroughly.
- Stir in dry ingredients and mix only enough to moisten. Batter will be lumpy.
- Stir in raisins and nuts.
- Spoon into greased muffin tins.
- Bake for 25 minutes.

Dill Muffins

1/2	cup margarine
1	cup self-rising flour
1	teaspoon dill seed
1/2	cup sour cream

Servings: 18
Preparation time: 15 minutes
Baking time: 20 to 25 minutes

- Preheat oven to 350° F.
- Melt margarine in a small saucepan.
- Combine margarine, flour and dill seed.
- Stir in sour cream.
- Spoon into greased muffin tins, filling 2/3 full.
- Bake for 20 to 25 minutes.

Crisp Miniature Cinnamon Muffins

1/2	cup sugar
1/3	cup Crisco
1	egg
1/2	cup milk
1-1/2	cups all-purpose flour
1-1/2	teaspoons baking powder
1/2	teaspoon salt
1/2	teaspoon ground nutmeg
6	tablespoons butter, melted
1	teaspoon ground cinnamon
1/2	cup sugar

Servings: 36 muffins
Preparation time: 20 minutes
Baking time: 20 to 25 minutes

- Preheat oven to 350° F.
- Cream sugar and Crisco.
- Add egg and milk.
- Combine flour, baking powder, salt and nutmeg.
- Add flour mixture to batter. Stir until just combined.
- Spoon into well-greased miniature muffin tins, filling cups 2/3 full.
- Bake for 20 to 25 minutes.
- Combine cinnamon and sugar.
- When muffins are done, remove from tins. Roll in melted butter, then in cinnamon and sugar mixture.
- To reheat, wrap partially open in foil.
- May be made ahead.
- May be frozen.

Strawberry Preserve Coffeecake

1-1/4 cups all-purpose flour
1/2 cup sugar
1 teaspoon baking powder
1/4 teaspoon baking soda
1/4 teaspoon salt
1 egg, beaten
1/2 cup butter, melted
1/2 cup buttermilk
1 teaspoon vanilla extract
2/3 cup strawberry preserves
3 tablespoons sugar
2 tablespoons all-purpose flour
1 tablespoon butter

Servings: 12
Preparation time: 15 minutes
Baking time: 40 minutes

- Preheat oven to 325° F.
- Stir together 1-1/4 cups flour, 1/2 cup sugar, baking powder, baking soda and salt.
- Make a "well" in the center of dry ingredients.
- Combine egg, butter, buttermilk and vanilla.
- Add to dry ingredients, mixing well.
- Turn batter into a greased 10 X 6 X 2-inch baking dish.
- Cut up any large berries in preserves.
- Drop preserves by teaspoonfuls on top of batter.
- Swirl batter up and over preserves with a spatula.
- In a small bowl, combine 3 tablespoons sugar and 2 tablespoons flour.
- Cut in butter until mixture is crumbly. Sprinkle over batter.
- Bake for 40 minutes.
- Cut into squares and serve warm.
- This cake is so moist it needs a plate and fork.

Club Waffles and Pancakes

2 cups Bisquick
1 egg
1/2 cup salad oil
1-1/3 cups club soda

Servings: 8
Preparation time: 5 minutes
Cooking time: 10 minutes

- Mix all ingredients.
- Pour on a griddle for pancakes or into a waffle iron for waffles.
- Cook until brown on both sides.

Gram's Pancake and Waffle Batter

2	cups Wondra flour
2	teaspoons baking powder
1	teaspoon salt
3	tablespoons sugar
3	egg whites
2	egg yolks
2	cups milk
4	tablespoons butter, melted
	Bacon grease to coat

Servings: 6 waffles or 24 pancakes
Preparation time: 15 minutes
Cooking time: 10 minutes

- Measure first 3 ingredients into a large mixing bowl. Combine with a wire whisk.
- Beat egg whites and sugar until stiff.
- Add egg yolks and milk to dry ingredients. Blend well.
- Add melted butter.
- Fold in egg whites.
- Grill cakes on a hot griddle that has been lightly greased with bacon grease or on an electric skillet set at 375° F. Cook until golden brown, turn and cook other side. If waffle iron is used, follow directions of manufacturer.
- Serve with fresh berries and hot syrup.
- All-purpose flour may be substituted for Wondra.

Breakfast Puff

1	tablespoon vegetable oil
1	cup all-purpose flour
1	teaspoon salt
1	cup milk
2	eggs
1	tablespoon vegetable oil
3	tablespoons lemon juice
3	tablespoons powdered sugar

Servings: 8
Preparation time: 5 minutes
Baking time: 30 minutes

- Preheat oven to 425° F.
- Grease a heavy iron 10-inch skillet with 1 tablespoon oil.
- Heat skillet in oven.
- Mix flour, salt, milk, eggs and 1 tablespoon oil. Beat with a rotary beater until batter is smooth.
- Pour batter into hot skillet.
- Bake for 30 minutes without peeking.
- Sprinkle with lemon juice and powdered sugar while still warm.
- A variation would be to spread with butter and any good preserves.

Butterscotch Breakfast Ring

2	tablespoons butter
1	6-ounce package butterscotch morsels
2	tablespoons all-purpose flour
1/8	teaspoon salt
1/2	cup chopped pecans
1	10-ounce package refrigerator quick crescent dinner rolls
7	teaspoons light corn syrup

Servings: 8
Preparation time: 15 minutes
Baking time: 15 minutes

- Preheat oven to 375° F.
- In the top of a double boiler over hot (not boiling) water, melt butter and half of the butterscotch morsels. Remove from heat.
- With a fork, mix in flour, salt and pecans. Set aside.
- Separate crescent roll triangles.
- On a greased cookie sheet, arrange triangles, with edges overlapping, to form a circle with a 4-inch diameter. Long pointed ends should point out.
- Spread 2 rounded teaspoonfuls of butterscotch mixture on each triangle.
- Roll up triangles, jelly roll fashion, towards center. Slash each triangle in the middle.
- Bake for 15 minutes.
- Cool.
- In the top of a double boiler over hot water, melt corn syrup and remaining half of the butterscotch morsels. Mix well.
- Drizzle over top of ring.

Granola

4	cups rolled oats
1/2	cup sesame seeds
1/2	cup wheat germ
1/2	cup sunflower seeds
1/2	cup sliced almonds
1	teaspoon salt
1	teaspoon vanilla extract
1/4	cup honey
1/4	cup vegetable oil
1/2	cup grated coconut (optional)
1/2	cup raisins

Servings: 7 cups
Preparation time: 10 minutes
Baking time: 40 minutes

- Preheat oven to 325° F.
- Thoroughly mix first 10 ingredients.
- Bake for 40 minutes, stirring every 10 minutes.
- Stir in raisins.
- Store in an airtight container.

Cinnamon Bread

Bread

1	envelope yeast
1/4	cup lukewarm milk
1	teaspoon sugar
1-3/4	cups milk
1/2	cup butter
1/2	cup sugar
1	teaspoon salt
3	eggs
6 to 7	cups all-purpose flour

Filling

1/2	cup butter, softened
9	tablespoons dark brown sugar
9	tablespoons ground cinnamon
	Raisins (optional)
1	egg, beaten

Servings: 3 loaves
Preparation time: 40 minutes
Rising time: 1 hour, 40 minutes
Baking time: 30 minutes

- Proof yeast in 1/4 cup milk with 1 teaspoon sugar.
- Scald 1-3/4 cups milk. Add butter, allowing it to melt. Cool.
- In a large mixing bowl, blend yeast with milk mixture.
- Add 1/2 cup sugar and salt.
- Beat in eggs, one at a time.
- Stir in flour, 1 cup at a time.
- Turn dough onto a lightly floured surface. Knead until smooth, elastic and shiny.
- Work in more flour if dough is sticky.
- Put dough in a large buttered bowl, cover and let rise in a warm place until doubled in bulk, about 1 hour.
- Punch down dough. Turn onto a floured work surface and knead for 10 minutes.
- Divide dough into 3 equal parts.
- Roll each piece of dough into a rectangle 1/4-inch thick.
- Spread rectangles with butter.
- Sprinkle with sugar, cinnamon and raisins.
- Roll up, like a jellyroll, lengthwise.
- Place rolls in 3 large buttered loaf pans.
- Cover and let rise in a warm place for 40 to 45 minutes.
- Preheat oven to 350° F.
- Brush tops of loaves with egg. Bake for 30 to 35 minutes or until light brown and loaves sound hollow when tapped.

Apple Popover Pancake

3	tablespoons butter, divided
3	eggs
1/2	cup milk
1/4	cup all-purpose flour
3	tablespoons sugar, divided
1/2	teaspoon salt
1	large cooking apple, peeled, cored and sliced
1/4	teaspoon dried mace or ground cinnamon

Servings: 4
Preparation time: 15 minutes
Cooking time: 10 minutes
Baking time: 20 minutes

- Preheat oven to 450° F.
- Melt 1 tablespoon butter in a 9-inch pie plate in oven.
- Tilt plate so butter completely covers bottom.
- Combine eggs, milk, flour, 1 tablespoon sugar and salt. Beat until smooth.
- Pour batter into hot pie plate.
- Bake for 8 minutes.
- Reduce heat to 375° F. and bake until golden brown and sides are puffy, about 8 to 10 minutes longer.
- While popover bakes, combine apple slices, remaining 2 tablespoons butter, 2 tablespoons sugar and mace in a saucepan.
- Cook over low heat until apple slices are tender, about 10 minutes.
- Spoon apple mixture over pancake immediately upon removing from oven. Serve at once.

Croissants

2	envelopes yeast
1/2	cup warm water
2	tablespoons sugar
1-1/2	cups warm milk
1	teaspoon salt
4-1/2 to 5	cups all-purpose flour
1	pound sweet butter
2	egg yolks, beaten

Servings: 48 croissants
Preparation and chilling time: 5 hours
Baking time: 25 minutes

- Dissolve yeast in warm water and proof with sugar until bubbly.
- Combine milk and salt in a large mixing bowl. Add yeast mixture.
- Stir in flour, 1 cup at a time, and beat until a soft dough is formed.
- Remove dough to a floured board. Knead for 5 to 8 minutes. If a dough hook is used, knead for 3 minutes.

continued...

Croissants continued...

- Place dough in a buttered bowl and grease all sides.
- Cover with a damp towel and let rise in a warm place for 1-1/2 hours or until doubled in bulk.
- Punch dough down, wrap in waxed paper and chill for 20 minutes.
- Cut butter in slices lengthwise. Sprinkle slices with flour and roll out, side by side, with a rolling pin. It must be cold and malleable.
- Roll cold dough into a rectangle 1/4-inch thick. Place square of cold butter in center.
- Fold top edge of dough down and bottom edge up, pinching edges together.
- Flour package of dough lightly and roll into a rectangle about 18 X 6-inches.
- Fold the dough in thirds again by folding top third down and bottom third up like a business letter, using enough flour to prevent sticking.
- Turn dough around so top flap is to your right and roll again into a rectangle and fold again into 3 layers.
- Flour lightly, wrap in waxed paper and chill for 1 hour.
- Repeat previous 2 steps three more times.
- After final hour of chilling, roll dough 1/8-inch thick, cut into triangles, roll and shape like a crescent.
- Place on a lightly greased baking sheet.
- Cover and let rise until almost double. May be frozen at this point.
- Preheat oven to 375° F.
- Brush with egg yolks and bake for 25 minutes. If frozen, bake for 30 minutes.

Sour Cream Crescent Rolls

1-1/2	envelopes yeast
1/3	cup warm water, approximately 105° F.
1	cup sour cream
1	cup butter, softened
1/2	cup sugar
1/2	teaspoon salt
4	cups all-purpose flour,
2	eggs, beaten

Servings: 48 rolls
Preparation time: 30 minutes
Baking time: 15 minutes
Chilling time: 6 hours
Rising time: 1 hour

- Dissolve yeast in warm water. Let stand 5 to 10 minutes to proof.
- Heat sour cream in the top of a double boiler over simmering water until it becomes slightly yellow around the edges. Do not worry if sour cream seems to separate.
- Put butter, sugar and salt in a large mixing bowl. Immediately add sour cream.
- Stir mixture until butter is melted. Then cool to lukewarm.
- Blend 1 cup flour into sour cream, beating until smooth.
- Add dissolved yeast to flour mixture, beating well.
- Beat in 1 more cup of flour. Then thoroughly beat in eggs.
- Add remaining 2 cups flour and beat well.
- Cover bowl and refrigerate for 6 hours or overnight.
- Divide dough into fourths.
- On a lightly floured surface, roll each fourth into a circle 1/4-inch thick.
- Divide each circle into 12 pie-shaped pieces.
- Roll up each piece of dough beginning at wide end.
- Place rolls on greased cookie sheets with points underneath.
- Curve into crescents.
- Let rise in a warm place, covered, for 1 hour or until light.
- Bake at 375° F. for 15 minutes.

For wonderful sweetrolls, roll fourths of dough into rectangles and brush with butter. Use one of the following as a filling: sprinkle with cinnamon, sugar and finely chopped nuts; sprinkle with grated orange or lemon rind and sugar; spread with honey and nuts. Roll dough up lengthwise like a jelly roll. Slice crosswise into 12 pieces. Let rise. Then bake in cake pans.

Butterflake Treats

Rolls
4	cups all-purpose flour
1	teaspoon salt
1	envelope yeast
1/2	cup butter
3/4	cup shortening
3	egg yolks
1	cup sour cream
1	teaspoon vanilla extract

Filling
3	egg whites
1	cup sugar
1	teaspoon vanilla extract
1	cup finely chopped pecans or walnuts
	Powdered sugar

Butter Frosting
2	cups powdered sugar
1/4	cup butter, melted
1/4	cup milk
1/4	teaspoon salt
1/2	teaspoon almond extract
1	3-ounce package cream cheese, softened

Servings: 35 treats
Preparation time: 1 hour
Baking time: 12 minutes
Chilling time: overnight

- Sift together flour and salt.
- Add yeast and combine thoroughly.
- Cut in butter and shortening with a pastry blender or 2 knives.
- Beat egg yolks slightly.
- Add sour cream and vanilla.
- Mix with dry ingredients. Wrap in plastic wrap or waxed paper and refrigerate overnight.

- Preheat oven to 375° F.
- Separate dough into 4 equal balls.
- Beat egg whites until foamy. Add sugar, 1 tablespoon at a time, until whites hold peaks.
- Beat in vanilla. Fold in nuts.
- Work with 1 pastry ball at a time.
- Roll each ball out on waxed paper sprinkled with powdered sugar.
- Roll ball into a 12-inch circle.
- Spread dough with a fourth of the meringue filling.
- Cut each circle of dough into 8 or 12 wedges.
- Roll each wedge up tightly and place, point down, on a greased baking sheet.
- Bake for 12 minutes or until slightly browned.

- Combine all ingredients and beat until smooth. Spread on all of the baked rolls.

Onion Rolls

Rolls
1	envelope yeast
1	cup lukewarm water
2	tablespoons sugar
1-1/2	teaspoons salt
3	large eggs
6	tablespoons vegetable oil
4-1/2 to 5 cups all-purpose flour	

Servings: 24 rolls
Preparation time: 30 minutes
Rising time: 1-1/4 hours
Baking time: 15 to 20 minutes

- Soften yeast in warm water in a large mixing bowl.
- Add sugar and allow to proof, about 4 minutes.
- Stir in salt, eggs, oil and enough flour to make a dough. Mix well until dough pulls away from sides of bowl.
- Turn dough onto a floured board and knead for 5 to 8 minutes, until elastic and smooth. Add flour, 1 tablespoon at a time, if needed.
- Place in a greased bowl and let rise for 45 minutes or until doubled in bulk.
- Punch down and roll out on a floured board into an 18 X 24-inch rectangle.
- Cut rectangle into twenty-four 6 X 3-inch pieces.

Filling
1	cup finely chopped onion
1	teaspoon salt
1	tablespoon poppy seeds
1-1/2	teaspoons carraway seeds
1	cup day old bread crumbs

- Combine all ingredients.
- Using 3/4 of the filling, spoon it evenly across centers of the twenty-four pieces of dough.
- Folding lengthwise, fold a third of the dough over filling and remaining third over from other side.
- Place, seam side down, on a greased cookie sheet.
- Flatten rolls with rolling pin until they are 5 inches long.
- Cut in half and seal edges with moistened fingertips.

Glaze
1	egg
2	tablespoons milk

- Combine all ingredients.
- Brush rolls with glaze and sprinkle with remaining filling.
- Let rise, covered, for 30 minutes.
- Bake in a preheated oven at 375° F. for 15 to 20 minutes.

Cheese, Eggs, Rice & Pasta

Cheese Savory

6	eggs, beaten
1	cup heavy cream
1	cup Half and Half
1-1/2	cups grated Swiss cheese
1-1/2	cups grated fresh Parmesan cheese
1/4	teaspoon cayenne pepper
1/4	teaspoon ground nutmeg

Servings: 6
Preparation time: 20 minutes
Baking time: 30 minutes

- Preheat oven to 375° F.
- Mix all ingredients together and blend well.
- Pour into a greased 9 X 13 X 2-inch casserole.
- Bake for 30 minutes.
- Leftover meat or vegetables may be lined in bottom of casserole before pouring in mixture.

Olive Cheese Strata

5	slices white bread
2	tablespoons butter, softened
1	cup grated sharp Cheddar cheese
1/2	cup sliced pimento-stuffed green olives
2	tablespoons butter
3	eggs, beaten
1/8	teaspoon dry mustard
1/3	cup liquid from olives
2	cups hot milk

Servings: 6
Preparation time: 20 minutes
Baking time: 1 hour

- Preheat oven to 350° F.
- Cut crusts from bread.
- Spread 2 tablespoons butter on bread and cut into 1/2-inch cubes.
- Cover bottom of a greased 9 X 13-inch casserole with a third of the bread cubes.
- Sprinkle a third of the cheese over bread. Then layer 1/4 cup olives.
- Repeat another layer. Then end with last third of bread and cheese.
- Dot with 2 tablespoons butter.
- Combine eggs, mustard and liquid from olives.
- Gradually stir in hot milk.
- Pour mixture over casserole.
- Bake for 1 hour.

Sausage Grits Casserole

1	pound hot bulk sausage
1/2	cup chopped onion
1	cup raw grits
8	ounces sharp Cheddar cheese, grated
2	eggs, beaten
1/2	teaspoon salt
	Pepper to taste
1/4	cup grated sharp Cheddar cheese

Servings: 8
Preparation time: 30 minutes
Baking time: 1 hour

- Preheat oven to 350° F.
- Brown sausage and onion. Drain well on paper towels.
- Cook grits according to package directions.
- Combine onion, sausage, grits, 8-ounces Cheddar cheese, eggs, salt and pepper.
- Pour into 9 X 13-inch buttered baking dish.
- Top with remaining 1/4 cup cheese.
- Bake for 1 hour.

Eggs in Cheese and Sherry Sauce

10	hard-boiled eggs
1/2	cup butter
1/2	cup all-purpose flour
1	teaspoon salt
	Pepper to taste
2-1/3	cups milk
1	teaspoon Worcestershire sauce
1/3	cup dry sherry
4	ounces sharp Cheddar cheese, grated
	Hot toast points

Servings: 8
Preparation time: 30 minutes
Cooking time: 10 minutes

- Peel and quarter eggs.
- In a large saucepan, melt butter. Mix in flour.
- Add salt, pepper, milk and Worcestershire sauce. Blend and cook over low heat until thick.
- Add sherry and cheese. Simmer only until blended.
- When ready to serve, add eggs and serve on hot toast points.
- May add cooked shrimp.

John Wayne Pie

4	4-ounce cans Old El Paso Green Chilies, veined and chopped
1	pound Monterey Jack cheese, grated
1	pound Cheddar cheese, grated
4	egg whites
4	egg yolks
2/3	cup evaporated milk
1	tablespoon all-purpose flour
1	teaspoon salt
1/8	teaspoon pepper
2	medium tomatoes, sliced

Servings: 6
Preparation time: 15 minutes
Baking time: 1 hour

- Preheat oven to 325° F.
- Combine chilies and cheeses in a well buttered 1-quart casserole.
- Beat egg yolks. Beat whites until stiff. Fold together.
- Add milk, flour, salt and pepper.
- Pour over cheese and chili mixture.
- Bake for 30 minutes.
- Remove and arrange tomatoes on top.
- Bake for another 30 minutes or until knife comes out clean.

Egg and Artichoke Casserole

2	6-1/2-ounce jars marinated artichoke hearts
3/4	cup chopped green onion
1	clove garlic, minced
4	eggs, beaten
8	ounces medium Cheddar cheese, grated
6	soda crackers, crushed

Servings: 6
Preparation time: 15 minutes
Baking time: 40 minutes

- Preheat oven to 350° F.
- Drain artichoke hearts, reserving marinade.
- Cut artichokes into thirds.
- Sauté onion and garlic in a little of the reserved marinade.
- Grease a 9 X 9-inch baking dish with artichoke marinade.
- Combine artichokes, onion, garlic, eggs, cheese and crackers. Pour into prepared dish.
- Bake for 40 minutes.

Baked Deviled Eggs

8	large hard-boiled eggs
1	8-ounce carton sour cream
2	tablespoons prepared mustard
	Salt and pepper to taste
2	tablespoons butter
1/2	cup chopped onion
1/2	cup chopped green bell pepper
1/2	cup chopped fresh mushrooms
1	cup heavy cream
1/4	cup pimentos, chopped
1	cup grated sharp Cheddar cheese

Servings: 8
Preparation time: 45 minutes
Baking time: 25 minutes

- Split eggs and remove yolks.
- Make a filling by combining 3 tablespoons sour cream, mustard, salt, pepper and egg yolks. This mixture should be firm.
- Fill egg whites with mixture and set aside.
- Preheat oven to 350° F.
- Melt butter in a skillet. Sauté onion, bell pepper and mushrooms.
- Add remaining sour cream, heavy cream and pimentos.
- Place deviled eggs in a 9 X 13-inch buttered baking dish. Cover with sauce.
- Sprinkle Cheddar cheese over sauce.
- Bake for 20 to 25 minutes or until bubbly.
- Let stand at least 5 minutes before serving.
- May be held on a hot tray. This is an excellent dish for a buffet.

Egg Soufflé

6	eggs, beaten
1/4	cup butter, melted
1/2	teaspoon baking soda
1	cup cottage cheese
8	ounces Cheddar cheese, grated
	Salt and pepper to taste

Servings: 4
Preparation time: 10 minutes
Baking time: 20 to 25 minutes

- Preheat oven to 400° F.
- Combine all ingredients.
- Pour into a buttered 8 X 8-inch pan.
- Bake for 20 to 25 minutes or until knife inserted in center comes out clean.
- Add diced cooked meat or vegetables for variety.

Golden Egg Casserole

1/2	cup butter
1-1/2	cups all-purpose flour
1	quart warm milk
1-1/2	teaspoons salt
1/4	teaspoon white pepper
3	teaspoons Worcestershire sauce
1	teaspoon curry powder
1/2	cup sour cream
4	ounces cream cheese, sliced
1	pound fresh mushrooms, sliced
1	medium onion, chopped
1/4	cup butter
16 to 18	hard-boiled eggs, sliced
	Lawry's seasoned salt to taste
	Curry powder to taste
3	tablespoons butter
3	slices white bread

Servings: 18 to 20
Preparation time: 1 hour
Baking time: 30 minutes

- Melt 1/2 cup butter in a large saucepan.
- Add flour, then milk, stirring constantly.
- Continue to stir until smooth and thick, at least 10 minutes.
- Add seasonings, sour cream and cream cheese. Stir until smooth.
- Sauté mushrooms and onion in 1/4 cup butter until tender.
- Add to sauce.
- Preheat oven to 350° F.
- Layer a third of the sliced eggs in the bottom of a 3-quart casserole.
- Sprinkle eggs lightly with Lawry's salt and curry powder.
- Cover with a third of the sauce.
- Continue for 2 more layers, ending with sauce.
- Melt 3 tablespoons butter.
- Place bread in a blender, one slice at a time.
- Add crumbs to butter and coat.
- Smooth crumbs evenly over top of casserole.
- Bake for 30 minutes until bubbly.

Spinach-Feta Cheese Quiche

2	tablespoons butter
2	tablespoons finely minced shallots
1-1/2	cups chopped fresh spinach
	Salt and pepper to taste
	Nutmeg to taste
3	eggs
1-1/2	cups heavy cream
6	ounces Feta cheese
1	9-inch deep-dish pie shell
1	tablespoon butter

Servings: 6
Preparation time: 15 minutes
Baking time: 25 to 30 minutes

- Preheat oven to 375° F.
- In a heavy skillet, sauté shallots in butter for 1 minute.
- Add spinach and stir over moderate heat until all water evaporates.
- Stir in salt, pepper and nutmeg.
- Beat eggs and blend with cream.
- Stir spinach into egg mixture.
- Squeeze Feta cheese to get out as much liquid as possible.
- Crumble cheese into spinach mixture and stir.
- Pour into pie shell and dot with butter.
- Bake for 25 to 30 minutes.

Crab Shrimp Quiche

1	9-inch deep-dish pastry shell
1/2	cup mayonnaise
2	tablespoons all-purpose flour
2	eggs, beaten
1/2	cup white wine (sauterne)
1/3	cup sliced celery
1/3	cup sliced green onions with tops
1	cup sliced fresh mushrooms
2	tablespoons butter
1/2	pound crabmeat
1	cup shrimp, cooked and cleaned (cut if large)
8	ounces Swiss cheese, grated

Servings: 6 to 8
Preparation time: 40 minutes
Baking time: 40 minutes

- Bake pastry shell for 5 minutes at 400° F.
- Combine mayonnaise, flour, eggs and wine. Mix until well blended.
- Sauté celery, onions and mushrooms in butter until just tender.
- Stir in crabmeat, shrimp and cheese.
- Combine with mayonnaise mixture.
- Pour into pastry shell.
- Bake at 350° F. for 40 minutes.

Country Vegetable Quiche

1	10-inch pie crust
3	cups sliced fresh mushrooms
2	tablespoons butter
1	cup shredded zucchini
1	cup shredded carrot
1	large onion, diced
1	clove garlic, minced
4	large eggs, beaten
1-1/2	cups shredded Swiss cheese
1	cup Half and Half
1/2	cup sour cream
1	teaspoon dried thyme
1/8	teaspoon ground nutmeg
	Paprika for garnish

Servings: 8
Preparation time: 30 minutes
Cooking time: 40 minutes

- Preheat oven to 350° F.
- Sauté mushrooms in butter. Reserve a small amount for garnish. Spoon remainder into crust.
- Sauté zucchini, carrots, onion and garlic.
- Spoon over mushrooms.
- Combine eggs, 1 cup cheese, Half and Half, sour cream, thyme and nutmeg. Pour over vegetables.
- Top with remaining 1/2 cup cheese.
- Sprinkle with paprika.
- Bake for 40 to 45 minutes.
- Cool 10 minutes before slicing.
- Garnish with reserved mushrooms.
- Excellent with crisp salad and dry white wine.

Crustless Quiche

1/2	pound lean ham, cubed or 12 slices of bacon, fried and crumbled
1	cup (4 ounces) grated Swiss cheese
1/4	cup chopped chives
2	cups milk
1/2	cup Bisquick or Jiffy baking mix
4	medium eggs
1/4	teaspoon salt
1/8	teaspoon pepper

Servings: 6
Preparation time: 30 minutes
Baking time: 50 minutes

- Preheat oven to 350° F. for a metal 9 to 10-inch pie pan or 325° F. for a ceramic quiche dish.
- Lightly grease dish or pan.
- Sprinkle ham, cheese and chives evenly over bottom of dish.
- Put milk, baking mix, eggs, salt and pepper in a blender.
- Mix for 1 minute on high speed.
- Pour milk mixture over meat, chives and cheese.
- Bake for 50 minutes or until a knife comes out clean when inserted in center.
- Let stand for 5 minutes before slicing and serving.
- Serve with spinach salad or tomato aspic.

Italian Lemon Rice

1-1/2 cups raw rice
3 eggs, beaten
2 tablespoons lemon juice
3/4 cup grated Parmesan cheese
 Salt and pepper to taste
2 tablespoons minced parsley
 Parsley for garnish

Servings: 6
Preparation time: 5 minutes
Cooking time: 30 minutes

- Cook rice according to package instructions.
- In a small bowl, combine eggs, lemon juice, cheese, salt, pepper and parsley.
- Add mixture to hot rice 5 minutes before serving.
- Keep warm.
- Garnish with parsley.

Hot Rice Casserole

1 cup raw rice
2 3-ounce cans green chiles, diced
3 cups sour cream
 Salt and pepper to taste
3/4 pound Monterey Jack cheese, cut in strips
1-1/2 cups grated Cheddar cheese

Servings: 8
Preparation time: 35 minutes
Baking time: 30 minutes

- Preheat oven to 350° F.
- Cook rice according to package directions. Measure out 3 cups.
- Combine chiles, sour cream, salt and pepper.
- Layer rice, sour cream mixture, then Monterey Jack cheese in a 9 X 13-inch buttered casserole.
- Top with Cheddar cheese.
- Bake, covered, for 30 minutes.
- Uncover for last few minutes of cooking.
- May be prepared ahead.
- May be frozen.

Amelia Island Rice

2	cups cooked rice
4	ounces vegetable oil
1	6-ounce jar pitted black olives, chopped
1/2	cup mayonnaise
2	red pimentos, chopped
2	teaspoons salt
1	teaspoon pepper

Servings: 4 to 6
Preparation time: 15 minutes
Chilling time: 4 hours
* Combine all ingredients.
* Chill for at least 4 hours.

Rice With Asparagus

2	pounds fresh asparagus, cleaned and trimmed
1	cup raw rice
1/2	cup dry white wine
1-1/2	cups water
	Salt and pepper to taste
1/2	cup grated Parmesan cheese
1/2	cup grated Swiss or Gruyère cheese
6	teaspoons butter
2	tablespoons snipped parsley

Servings: 6 to 8
Preparation time: 10 minutes
Cooking time: 30 minutes
* Cook asparagus in a small amount of lightly salted water for 5 minutes.
* Drain and set aside.
* Cook rice in wine and water.
* Layer rice with asparagus in a shallow 1-1/2-quart baking dish. Lightly salt and pepper each layer.
* Sprinkle cheeses on top.
* Dot with butter and sprinkle parsley on top.
* Place on rack 6 inches from broiler and broil until cheese has melted and dish is heated.

The King's Parsley Rice

3	cups cooked white rice
1	cup finely chopped parsley
1	cup chopped onion
1-1/2	cups grated mild Cheddar cheese
1	3-ounce package cream cheese, diced
3	large eggs, slightly beaten
1-1/2	cups milk
1/2	cup butter, melted
	Salt and pepper to taste

Servings: 6 to 8
Preparation time: 30 minutes
Cooking time: 45 minutes

- Preheat oven to 350° F.
- In a large bowl, toss rice, parsley, onion and 1 cup Cheddar cheese.
- Add cream cheese.
- Combine eggs, milk and butter.
- Add to rice mixture and stir well.
- Season with salt and pepper.
- Pour rice mixture in a greased 2-quart casserole. Top with remaining Cheddar cheese.
- Bake for 45 minutes.

Wild Rice with Fresh Mushrooms

12	ounces raw wild rice
1	cup butter or margarine
1	bunch green onions, minced
1	pound fresh mushrooms, cleaned and sliced
2	10-ounce cans consommé
1	tablespoon vermouth

Servings: 10
Preparation time: 20 minutes
Soaking time: 3 hours
Baking time: 2 hours

- Preheat oven to 275° F.
- Wash wild rice and soak for 3 hours. Drain well.
- In a large skillet, melt butter. Sauté onions and mushrooms until tender.
- Place rice, consommé, mushrooms and onions in a large casserole or roaster.
- Sprinkle vermouth over rice.
- Bake, covered, for 2 hours.
- Remove cover for last few minutes of cooking.

Green Rice

1	10-ounce package frozen chopped spinach
4	tablespoons butter or margarine
1/2	cup finely chopped onion
1	clove garlic, crushed and minced
3	cups cooked rice (1 to 1-1/2 cups raw)
1/4	cup freshly grated Parmesan cheese
1/4	cup grated Cheddar cheese
1/3	cup chopped fresh parsley
2	eggs, beaten
1	cup heavy cream or milk
1	teaspoon salt
1/2	teaspoon pepper
1	tablespoon Worcestershire sauce

Servings: 8
Preparation time: 15 minutes
Baking time: 45 minutes

- Preheat oven to 325° F.
- Cook spinach according to package directions. Squeeze out all water.
- Melt butter in a small skillet.
- Sauté onion and garlic until soft.
- Combine spinach, onion mixture and remaining ingredients.
- Pour into a buttered 2-quart casserole.
- Cover and bake for 45 minutes.
- Remove cover for last 15 minutes of baking.

Herbed Rice

1	onion, finely chopped
3	tablespoons butter
1	cup raw rice
2-1/2	cups chicken stock
2	teaspoons Fines Herbes seasoning
2	cups finely chopped fresh parsley

Servings: 4 to 6
Preparation time: 10 minutes
Cooking time: 30 minutes

- Sauté onion in butter until transparent.
- Add rice, stirring constantly. Cook for 3 minutes.
- Add chicken stock, seasoning and 1-1/2 cups parsley.
- Cover and simmer for 30 minutes.
- Sprinkle with remaining 1/2 cup parsley and serve hot.

Italian Rice and Vegetables

4	tablespoons butter
1/3	cup chopped onion
2	cups raw rice
1/4	cup dry white wine
4-1/2	cups chicken stock
1	tomato, peeled, seeded and chopped
2-1/4	cups cooked zucchini, yellow squash, mushrooms, broccoli, small asparagus or peas in any combination
1/2	cup freshly grated Parmesan cheese

Servings: 10
Preparation time: 30 minutes
Cooking time: 30 minutes

- Melt butter in a large skillet. Sauté onion briefly.
- Add rice and stir to blend.
- Add wine. Simmer, uncovered, for 5 minutes.
- Add chicken stock. Simmer, covered, for 30 minutes.
- Add tomato and cooked vegetables 7 minutes before end of cooking time.
- Toss with Parmesan cheese.

Orange Rice

1/4	cup butter
1/2	cup chopped celery
1/2	cup chopped onion
1	10-1/2-ounce can chicken broth
1	cup orange juice
1/4	cup lemon juice
2	tablespoons grated orange rind
1	teaspoon salt
2	teaspoons sugar
1	cup raw rice

Servings: 6
Preparation time: 10 minutes
Cooking time: 25 minutes

- Melt butter in a saucepan.
- Sauté celery and onion until transparent.
- Add chicken broth, orange juice, lemon juice, orange rind, salt and sugar. Bring to a boil.
- Add rice and reduce heat. Simmer, covered, for 25 minutes.

Fettuccine Alfredo

1	pound fettuccine
1/2	cup sweet butter
1	cup whipping cream
1	cup sour cream
1	cup freshly grated Parmesan cheese
1/2	cup chopped fresh parsley
	Salt and pepper to taste

Servings: 6
Preparation time: 15 minutes
Cooking time: 8 to 10 minutes

- Cook fettuccine according to package directions. Drain.
- Meanwhile, melt butter in a large heavy saucepan.
- Add cream. Stir until cream is warmed through.
- Add sour cream and stir to mix.
- Add fettuccine, Parmesan cheese and parsley. Add salt and pepper.
- Toss gently and serve immediately.

Fettuccine Gorgonzola

3	tablespoons butter
1/4	pound prosciutto ham, cut in thin 1-inch strips
1-1/2	cups heavy cream
1/4	pound grated Gorgonzola cheese
	Nutmeg to taste
	Pepper to taste
1	pound fettuccine

Servings: 4 to 6
Preparation time: 10 minutes
Cooking time: 15 minutes

- Sauté ham in butter over medium heat until lightly browned and crisp.
- Stir in cream, scraping up browned bits from bottom of pan.
- Stir over low heat until slightly thickened.
- Add cheese and seasonings, stirring just until cheese melts.
- Cook fettuccine according to package directions.
- Pour sauce over noodles and toss.

Fettuccine with Zucchini, Mushrooms and Ham

1/2	pound fresh mushrooms, sliced
1/4	cup butter
1	pound zucchini, cut in julienne strips
1/2	pound cooked ham, cut in julienne strips
1	cup heavy cream
1/2	cup butter, cut in bits
	Salt and pepper to taste
1	pound fettuccine, boiled in lightly salted water until tender
3/4	cup freshly grated Parmesan cheese
1/2	cup chopped fresh parsley
	Grated Parmesan cheese
	Parsley for garnish

Servings: 6 to 8
Preparation time: 30 minutes
Cooking time: 10 minutes

- Sauté mushrooms in 1/4 cup butter over moderate heat for 2 minutes.
- Add zucchini, ham, cream, 1/2 cup butter, salt and pepper.
- Simmer for 3 minutes.
- Add fettuccine, 3/4 cup Parmesan cheese and 1/2 cup parsley.
- Mix well.
- Serve on a heated platter.
- Top with Parmesan cheese and parsley.

Spaghetti Florentine

4	tablespoons butter
3	cloves garlic, minced
2	tablespoons Marsala
1/2	pound fresh mushrooms, sliced
	Juice of 1 lemon
1	cup heavy cream
4	cups shredded fresh spinach
	Salt and pepper to taste
1/2	pound spaghetti
	Freshly grated Parmesan cheese

Servings: 4
Preparation time: 15 minutes
Cooking time: 15 minutes

- Sauté garlic in butter.
- Add Marsala and simmer for 5 minutes.
- Squeeze lemon juice over mushrooms.
- Add mushrooms to wine mixture and cook for 5 minutes.
- Add cream, spinach, salt and pepper. Cook for 5 minutes.
- Cook spaghetti according to package directions.
- Pour sauce over spaghetti and toss.
- Top with Parmesan cheese.

Pasta Verde

1	pound pasta
1	head cauliflower
1	small bunch broccoli
1/2	pound asparagus
10	tablespoons butter
1/8	teaspoon ground nutmeg
	Salt and pepper to taste
1/2	teaspoon dried basil or 2 leaves fresh basil
1	tablespoon chopped fresh parsley
3/4	cup freshly grated Parmesan cheese
3/4	cup heavy cream
	Fresh cracked black pepper for garnish
	Grated Parmesan cheese for garnish

Servings: 10
Preparation time: 30 minutes
Cooking time: 10 to 15 minutes

- Cook pasta until tender and drain.
- Divide cauliflower and broccoli into flowerets, leaving 2-inch stems. Cut asparagus into 2-inch pieces.
- Blanch vegetables for 3 to 4 minutes.
- Plunge into cold water to stop cooking.
- Melt 8 tablespoons butter in a large skillet.
- Add herbs and spices to butter and cook for 2 minutes.
- Add vegetables to butter and cook for 5 minutes.
- Coat pasta with remaining 2 tablespoons butter. Add vegetables, cheese and cream.
- Serve with cracked pepper and Parmesan cheese.

Spaghetti Carbonara

8	slices bacon, cut into pieces
1	large onion, chopped
1/4	cup dry white wine
3	eggs, beaten
2/3	cup grated Parmesan cheese
2	tablespoons chopped parsley
	Salt and pepper to taste
1	pound linguine or spaghetti

Servings: 6
Preparation time: 20 minutes
Cooking time: 10 minutes

- Fry bacon. When almost brown, add onion and cook until transparent. Drain bacon and onion on paper towels.
- Pour off all but 1/3 cup bacon grease.
- Add wine and simmer for 8 minutes.
- In a separate bowl, combine eggs, Parmesan cheese, parsley, salt and pepper.
- Cook noodles according to package directions.
- To serve, toss hot noodles with egg mixture, wine mixture, bacon and onion. (Noodles must be hot in order that eggs can be cooked.)

Linguine with Red Clam Sauce

8	ounces Ronzoni linguine
4	tablespoons olive oil
4	tablespoons butter
1	small onion, chopped
1	cup sliced fresh mushrooms
2	cloves garlic, minced
1	cup clam juice (drained from clams)
1	16-ounce can tomato sauce
1/4	teaspoon orégano
2	6-1/2-ounce cans clams, drained
2	tablespoons chopped fresh parsley

Servings: 4
Preparation time: 10 minutes
Cooking time: 20 minutes

- Cook linguine according to package directions.
- In a large heavy skillet, heat oil and butter.
- Sauté onion and mushrooms until just tender.
- Add garlic, clam juice, tomato sauce and orégano.
- Simmer for 10 minutes.
- Add clams and parsley just before serving.
- Spoon sauce over linguine.

Cannelloni

Tomato Sauce

1/4	cup olive oil
1/2	cup chopped onion
2	35-ounce cans tomatoes
2	23-ounce cans tomato purée
1/4	pound pepperoni, boiled to remove fat
	Dried orégano to taste
	Chopped parsley to taste

Servings: 8
Preparation time: 1 hour
Cooking time: 2 hours
Baking time: 30 minutes

- Sauté onion in oil until soft.
- Add remaining ingredients.
- Simmer for 2 hours.
- Remove pepperoni.

Crêpes

6	eggs
1/4	teaspoon salt
1-1/2	cups water
1-1/2	cups all-purpose flour

- Combine all ingredients and beat until smooth.
- Pour 1/4 cup batter into a 6-inch skillet or crêpe maker. Brown both sides quickly. Remove and set aside.

continued...

Cannelloni continued...

Filling

2	tablespoons olive oil	
1/4	cup chopped onion	
3	cloves garlic, minced	
1	10-ounce package frozen chopped spinach, defrosted and squeezed dry	
2	tablespoons butter	
1	pound ground round	
5	tablespoons Parmesan cheese	
2	tablespoons heavy cream	
2	eggs, lightly beaten	
1/2	teaspoon dried orégano, crumbled	

- Heat olive oil in a skillet.
- Sauté onion and garlic.
- Stir in spinach and cook, stirring constantly, for 3 minutes.
- Transfer spinach mixture to a large bowl.
- Brown beef in butter.
- Add to spinach mixture.
- Mix in remaining ingredients and combine.

Besciamella

4	tablespoons butter	
4	tablespoons all-purpose flour	
1	cup milk	
1	cup heavy cream	
1	teaspoon salt	
1/8	teaspoon white pepper	

- Melt butter.
- Stir in flour and cook over low heat for 5 minutes.
- Add milk and cream. Cook, stirring constantly, until sauce thickens.
- Season with salt and pepper.
- Preheat oven to 350° F.
- To assemble, place a small amount of filling in the middle of each crêpe and roll into a tube shape.
- Place crêpes, side by side, in a greased 3-quart oblong ovenproof dish.
- Cover with besciamella and top with tomato sauce.
- Bake for 20 minutes.
- Leftover tomato sauce and sliced pepperoni are wonderful as spaghetti sauce when combined.

Sausage and Spinach Lasagne

1	28-ounce can Italian tomatoes
1	pound bulk pork sausage
1	cup chopped onion
2	cloves garlic, minced
2	6-ounce cans tomato paste
1-1/2	cups water
1/2	pound fresh mushrooms, sliced
1/4	cup chopped fresh parsley
1	teaspoon dried orégano
1	teaspoon dried basil
1/4	teaspoon pepper
	Tabasco sauce to taste
1	bay leaf
2	10-ounce packages chopped spinach, thawed and drained
1	15-ounce carton ricotta cheese
8	ounces mozzarella cheese, shredded
6	tablespoons grated Romano cheese
2	eggs, slightly beaten
	Salt and pepper to taste
1/4	teaspoon ground nutmeg
12	lasagne noodles, cooked and drained

Servings: 8
Preparation time: 45 minutes
Cooking time: 45 minutes
Baking time: 30 minutes

- Purée tomatoes.
- Cook sausage, onion and garlic over medium heat.
- Stir in puréed tomatoes, tomato paste, water, mushrooms, 2 tablespoons parsley, orégano, basil, pepper, Tabasco and bay leaf.
- Simmer for 45 minutes. Remove bay leaf.
- Preheat oven to 350° F.
- Mix spinach, remaining parsley, ricotta cheese, mozzarella cheese, 4 tablespoons Romano cheese, eggs, salt, pepper and nutmeg.
- Pour 1/2 cup of tomato sauce in a 9 X 13 X 2-inch baking dish.
- Put 1/3 cup spinach mixture on each noodle and roll up.
- Place stuffed noodles, seam side down, on sauce in baking dish.
- Pour remaining tomato sauce over stuffed noodles.
- Sprinkle remaining 2 tablespoons Romano cheese on top.
- Bake for 30 minutes.
- May be made ahead and frozen.

Lasagne

Lasagne

1	16-ounce box lasagne noodles
2	cups ricotta cheese
1/4	cup finely chopped green bell pepper
3	tablespoons chopped onion
3	eggs
1	teaspoon salt
1/4	teaspoon black pepper
2	teaspoons dry mustard
1/8	teaspoon ground nutmeg
2	cups milk
1	pound mozzarella cheese, thinly sliced

Servings: 12
Preparation time: 1 hour
Baking time: 1-1/4 hours
Cooking time for sauce: 40 minutes

- Boil pasta for 8 minutes. Drain.
- Preheat oven to 325° F.
- In a small bowl, combine ricotta cheese, green pepper and onion.
- In a separate bowl, beat together eggs, salt, pepper, mustard and nutmeg. Stir in milk.
- In a small buttered 12-inch baking dish, arrange half the noodles. Cover with a third of the mozzarella and half of the ricotta mixture.
- Place half of the remaining mozzarella and all the remaining noodles over this.
- Cover with remaining mozzarella and ricotta.
- Pour milk mixture over all.
- Place dish in a large pan of hot water and bake for 1-1/4 hours.
- Allow to stand 15 minutes before serving.

Lasagne Sauce

1/2	cup butter
1	cup finely chopped green onion
3	cloves garlic, minced
1/2	cup finely chopped green bell pepper
6	tablespoons all-purpose flour
2	14-ounce cans Italian plum tomatoes, drained
6	tablespoons tomato paste
2	teaspoons salt
	Freshly ground black pepper to taste
1	teaspoon dried orégano
1/2	teaspoon dried basil

- In a large saucepan, melt butter. Sauté onion, garlic and green pepper until tender.
- Stir in flour and cook for 2 minutes.
- Add tomatoes, tomato paste, salt, pepper, orégano and basil. Stir constantly until sauce is thickened.
- Simmer for 30 minutes.
- Serve over lasagne.

White Party Pasta

Filling

2	medium onions
4	stalks celery
2	medium carrots
1/4	cup butter
2	teaspoons salt
1	teaspoon pepper
1	teaspoon orégano
1	pound lean chuck
1	pound pork loin, no fat
6	tablespoons tomato sauce
1/2	cup white wine

12   lasagne noodles

Cream Sauce

1/2	cup butter
1/2	cup all-purpose flour
1	teaspoon salt
1	teaspoon pepper
1	quart hot milk
1	cup light cream
3/4	cup finely grated Parmesan cheese
1/2	cup finely grated Romano cheese

Servings: 8 to 10
Preparation time: 30 minutes
Baking time: 30 minutes

- In a food processor, grind onions, celery, carrots and butter for 5 minutes. Set aside in a saucepan.
- Grind together salt, pepper, orégano, chuck and pork. Combine with vegetable mixture.
- Add tomato sauce and wine. Cook over low heat for 15 minutes.
- Drain, reserving liquid to add to boiling water for lasagne. This will add flavor to the lasagne.
- Cook noodles according to package directions. Use reserved liquid from filling in water.
- Preheat oven to 350° F.
- Melt butter in a saucepan.
- Stir in flour.
- Add salt and pepper.
- Add milk. Stir until sauce is smooth and slightly thick. Cover and cook for 5 minutes.
- Remove from heat and stir in cream.
- Combine and mix cheeses.
- Butter a 9 X 13-inch baking or lasagne dish.

continued...

White Party Pasta continued...

- Arrange 4 noodles on bottom.
- Spread a third of the meat filling over noodles.
- Cover with a third of the cream sauce.
- Sprinkle 3 tablespoons cheese mixture over sauce.
- Repeat layers twice, ending with extra cheese on top.
- Bake for 30 minutes or until bubbly.
- Remove from oven when done. Let stand for 10 minutes before cutting and serving.

Vegetarian Lasagne

1/4	cup olive oil
1	cup chopped onion
1	cup chopped parsley
1	pound fresh mushrooms, sliced
3	cloves garlic, minced
1	16-ounce can tomatoes, puréed
1	12-ounce can tomato paste
	Juice of 1/2 lemon
1-1/2	teaspoons Italian herb seasoning
1	teaspoon ground allspice
1-1/2	teaspoons salt
1/2	teaspoon pepper
1-1/2	tablespoons sugar
1	16-ounce package frozen chopped spinach, thawed and well drained
8	lasagne noodles
2	cups ricotta cheese
9	slices mozzarella cheese
1/4	cup freshly grated Parmesan cheese

Servings: 6 to 8
Preparation time: 1 hour
Baking time: 45 minutes

- Sauté onion, parsley, mushrooms and garlic in olive oil.
- Add next 9 ingredients. Simmer for 30 minutes.
- Preheat oven to 350° F.
- Cook lasagne noodles until tender. Drain and cut 2 noodles in half lengthwise.
- Grease a 9 X 13-inch baking dish. Spread a small amount of sauce in bottom.
- Lay 2-1/2 noodles over sauce.
- Spread a thin layer of ricotta over noodles.
- Put 3 slices of mozzarella crosswise over ricotta.
- Repeat layers twice, ending with sauce.
- Sprinkle top with Parmesan cheese.
- Bake, covered, for 30 minutes.
- Uncover and bake 15 minutes longer.

Manicotti

Crêpes
1-1/2 cups water
1-1/4 cups all-purpose flour
5   eggs
1/8   teaspoon salt
       Melted butter as needed

Servings: 8 to 10
Preparation time: 1-1/2 hours
Cooking time: 1-1/2 hours

- Heat a crêpe pan over medium heat for 3 to 5 minutes.
- Blend water, flour, eggs and salt in a blender until smooth.
- Brush pan with melted butter.
- Pour in enough batter to just cover bottom of pan.
- Cook crêpe until dry on top but not browned. Turn crêpe and cook other side.
- Remove crêpe from pan and repeat process until all batter is used. Crêpes for this recipe should be white and not browned.
- Stack crêpes on a wire rack as you make them.

Sauce
1   cup finely chopped onion
1   clove garlic, crushed
1/4   cup olive oil
1   35-ounce can Italian tomatoes
1   6-ounce can tomato paste
3   tablespoons chopped parsley
2-1/4   teaspoons sugar
1-1/2   teaspoons orégano
1/2   teaspoon dried basil
        Freshly ground black pepper to taste

- Sauté onion and garlic in olive oil.
- Add remaining ingredients.
- Bring to a boil. Cover, reduce heat and simmer for 1 hour.

Filling
2   pounds ricotta cheese
8   ounces mozzarella cheese, diced
1/3   cup grated Parmesan cheese
2   tablespoons chopped parsley
        Salt and freshly ground black pepper to taste
        Grated Parmesan cheese

- Combine first 5 ingredients and mix well.
- Preheat oven to 350° F.
- To assemble, pour some sauce on the bottom of a large shallow cassserole.
- Place 1 tablespoon of filling in center of each crêpe. Fold crêpe in thirds and place, seam side down, in dish.
- Cover crêpes with remaining sauce, sprinkle Parmesan cheese on top and bake for 30 minutes.

Sauces, Dressings, Pickles & Jellies

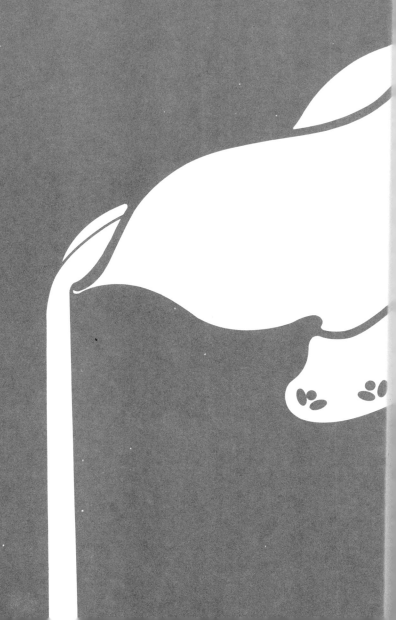

Watercress Mayonnaise

4	egg yolks
2	teaspoons salt
1/8	teaspoon Tabasco sauce
1/2	teaspoon paprika
1/2	teaspoon dry mustard
3	tablespoons cold water
4	cups salad oil
	Juice of 3 lemons
2	cups finely chopped watercress

Servings: 5 cups
Preparation time: 15 minutes

- Beat egg yolks with an electric mixer for 4 minutes until light and lemon colored.
- Add salt, Tabasco, paprika, dry mustard and cold water.
- Add oil slowly, beating constantly at medium speed.
- Add lemon juice.
- Add watercress and continue to beat until well blended.
- Wonderful served over fish or with cold or steamed vegetables.

Low Calorie Curry Sauce

2	cups chicken broth
4	onions, chopped
4	tart apples, peeled, cored and chopped
1	pound yellow squash, chopped
4	tablespoons curry powder
1	teaspoon salt

Servings: 5 cups
Preparation time: 20 minutes
Cooking time: 40 minutes

- Combine first 4 ingredients in a large pot.
- Simmer for 40 minutes.
- Stir in curry powder and salt.
- Allow sauce to cool. Then purée in a blender.
- Add sauce to desired amount of cooked and cubed chicken or shrimp.
- Serve with condiments of chutney, coconut, toasted almonds, crumbled bacon, sliced banana, chopped scallion and chopped egg.

Mustard Sauce

1	cup brown sugar
1/3	cup dry mustard
1	teaspoon all-purpose flour
1/8	teaspoon salt
1/2	cup vinegar
1/2	cup water
2	eggs, beaten

Servings: 2 cups
Preparation time: 5 minutes
Cooking time: 10 minutes

- Mix all dry ingredients in a saucepan.
- Add vinegar and water. Heat over low heat.
- Add eggs.
- Stir slowly until mixture thickens.
- Serve hot or cold over ham.
- May be made ahead.

Vegetable Wine Sauce

1	cup mayonnaise, preferably homemade
1/4	teaspoon curry powder
2	teaspoons lemon juice
1/4	cup dry white wine
1/2	teaspoon salt
1/8	teaspoon white pepper

Servings: 1-1/2 cups
Preparation time: 5 minutes

- Combine all ingredients in a small saucepan or in the top of a double boiler.
- Heat mixture over low heat, stirring constantly.
- Do not boil.
- Wonderful with broccoli or asparagus.

Cumberland Sauce

1	cup red currant jelly
1	small onion, grated
	Grated rind and juice of 1 lemon and 1 orange
1/2	cup red wine (Burgundy or port is best)
1/4	teaspoon Dijon mustard

Servings: 1 cup
Preparation time: 5 minutes
Cooking time: 10 minutes

- Blend all ingredients and bring to a boil in a small saucepan.
- Lower heat and simmer for 10 minutes.
- Strain and serve in a sauceboat with dove, quail or duck.

Barbecue Sauce

1/2	cup butter
1	onion, chopped
1	14-ounce bottle catsup
2-1/2	ounces Worcestershire sauce
1/4	cup vinegar
	Juice of 2 lemons
1	tablespoon brown sugar
1	teaspoon Coleman's dry mustard

Servings: 1 quart
Preparation time: 15 minutes
Cooking time: 10 minutes
- Melt butter in a saucepan.
- Sauté onion.
- Add remaining ingredients.
- Cook over low heat until hot and bubbly.

Dill Sauce

1-1/2	cups sour cream
1/2	cup mayonnaise
1	tablespoon dried dill weed or 1-1/2 tablespoons fresh dill weed
1	teaspoon dried summer savory
1	teaspoon grated onion
1	tablespoon chopped fresh parsley
1/8	teaspoon garlic powder

Servings: 2 cups
Preparation time: 5 minutes
Chilling time: 3 to 4 hours
- Place all ingredients in a mixing bowl. Blend well.
- Refrigerate for 3 or 4 hours or until ready to use.
- Good with cold shrimp or salmon.

Ginger Sauce for Beef

4	tablespoons butter, melted
1/4	cup soy sauce
1/4	cup water
1	tablespoon ground ginger
1-1/2	tablespoons lemon juice
1	tablespoon sugar

Servings: 2/3 cup
Preparation time: 5 minutes
Cooking time: 5 minutes
- Combine all ingredients.
- Simmer for 5 minutes.
- Excellent on tenderloin.
- Use for marinating, basting or as a gravy.

SAUCES, DRESSINGS, PICKLES & JELLIES

Steak Sauce

1/4	cup butter
2	scallions, chopped
2	cloves garlic, minced
2	slices yellow onion
2	carrots, diced
2	sprigs fresh parsley
10	whole black peppercorns
2	whole cloves
2	bay leaves
3	tablespoons all-purpose flour
1	teaspoon beef extract
1	cup beef bouillon
1	cup Burgundy
1/4	teaspoon salt
1/8	teaspoon pepper
2	teaspoons finely chopped fresh parsley

Servings: 3 cups
Preparation time: 15 minutes
Cooking time: 15 minutes

- Melt butter in a large skillet.
- Add vegetables and spices. Cook until soft, about 4 minutes.
- Remove from heat and add flour. Return to heat and cook for 2 minutes.
- Remove from heat and add meat extract, bouillon and 3/4 cup Burgundy. Bring to a boil over medium heat, stirring constantly.
- Simmer for 10 minutes over low heat, stirring frequently.
- Strain.
- Add salt, pepper, parsley and remaining 1/4 cup Burgundy.
- Reheat when ready to serve.
- This makes a good marinade for red meats.

Teriyaki Marinade

1/2	cup soy sauce
1/2	cup vegetable oil
1/4	cup pineapple juice or 1/8 cup lemon juice with 1/8 cup water
2	cloves garlic, minced
1	tablespoon brown sugar
2	tablespoons grated fresh ginger root _or_ 1 teaspoon ground ginger _or_ 2 tablespoons finely chopped candied ginger
1	tablespoon finely grated orange rind _or_ lemon rind

Servings: marinade for 2 pounds of meat
Preparation time: 10 minutes

- Combine all ingredients.
- Pour over meat or chicken.
- Cover and marinate for 5 hours.

Hot Mustard Sauce

2	2-ounce cans Coleman's mustard
1	cup white vinegar
2	eggs
1	cup sugar

Servings: 3 cups
Preparation time: 15 minutes
Standing time: 8 hours
Cooking time: 30 minutes

- Mix mustard and vinegar, stirring well.
- Cover and let stand for at least 8 hours.
- Beat eggs. While continuing to beat, slowly add sugar.
- Add mustard mixture and beat until smooth.
- Put mixture in the top of a double boiler and cook over low heat for 30 minutes. Stir occasionally until sauce becomes thick.
- Cool mixture.
- Store in a covered jar in the refrigerator.
- May be used to baste a pork roast.
- Keeps up to 4 weeks.

Sweet and Sour Sauce

8	teaspoons cornstarch
2	cups water
1/2	cup brown sugar
2	teaspoons chicken bouillon
6	tablespoons vinegar
6	tablespoons soy sauce

Servings: 2-1/2 cups
Preparation time: 5 minutes
Cooking time: 5 minutes

- Make a smooth paste by combining cornstarch and water.
- Add remaining ingredients.
- Bring to a boil over medium heat, stirring constantly.
- Reduce heat and simmer for 2 minutes.
- May be served immediately or refrigerated and reheated.

Wine Sauce

2	tablespoons butter	
1/2	cup minced onion	
1-1/2	tablespoons all-purpose flour	
1/2	teaspoon salt	
1/8	teaspoon pepper	
1/2	teaspoon paprika	
1/2	cup fish stock or milk (use fish stock with fish and milk with vegetables)	
1/4	cup sauterne	
3	tablespoons Half and Half	
1	teaspoon chopped parsley	

Servings: 4
Preparation time: 20 minutes
Cooking time: 10 minutes
• Sauté onion in butter until tender.
• Add flour, salt, pepper and paprika, stirring constantly.
• Gradually stir in fish stock.
• Add sauterne. Bring to a boil, stirring constantly.
• Stir in Half and Half and parsley.
• Serve with fish or vegetables.

Arnold's Hollandaise Sauce

4	egg yolks
	Juice of 1 lemon
1/8	teaspoon salt
1/8	teaspoon white pepper
1/8	teaspoon Worcestershire sauce
6	drops Tabasco sauce
1/4	cup water
	Grated rind of 1 lemon
1/2	cup butter, divided into thirds

Servings: 6
Preparation time: 10 minutes
• Combine first 8 ingredients in the top of a double boiler.
• Add butter, a third at a time, melting each before adding the next.
• Stir until sauce thickens. Then remove from heat. Avoid stirring again or sauce will curdle.
• Serve over broccoli, fish or Eggs Benedict.

Horseradish Sauce

1	cup sour cream
1/2	cup mayonnaise
1	teaspoon lemon juice
4	teaspoons drained horseradish
	Minced garlic to taste
	Salt to taste
	White pepper to taste

Servings: 1-1/2 cups
Preparation time: 5 minutes
Chilling time: 3 to 4 hours
• Blend all ingredients and chill for 3 to 4 hours.

Cinnamon-Sherry Sauce

1/2	cup cream sherry
1	cup water
3/4	cup brown sugar, firmly packed
1 to 2	tablespoons lemon juice
1/2	teaspoon ground cinnamon
	Few grains salt
1	tablespoon cornstarch
1	tablespoon butter

Servings: 8
Preparation time: 10 minutes
Cooking time: 5 minutes

- Combine first 7 ingredients in a small saucepan.
- Bring to a boil, lower heat and simmer for 5 to 10 minutes, stirring occasionally.
- When mixture is clear and thickened, add butter and melt.
- Serve warm over apple pie, cherry pie, cake, gingerbread, etc.

Champagne Chocolate Sauce

6	tablespoons brut champagne
3	ounces (1/2 cup) semisweet chocolate chips
3	tablespoons superfine sugar
2	tablespoons unsalted butter

Servings: 6
Preparation time: 5 minutes
Cooking time: 5 minutes

- Combine champagne, chocolate chips and sugar in a saucepan.
- Stir over low heat until chocolate is melted.
- Whisk in butter, 1 tablespoon at a time.
- Serve at once, while warm.
- May be served over mint ice cream or champagne sherbet.

Praline Sauce

1-1/2	cups brown sugar
2/3	cup light Karo syrup
4	tablespoons butter
1	5.33-ounce can evaporated milk
3/4	cup chopped pecans
1/8	teaspoon salt

Servings: 2 cups
Preparation time: 15 minutes
Cooking time: 10 minutes

- Mix brown sugar, syrup and butter in a saucepan. Bring to boil, stirring constantly.
- After reaching a boil, remove from stove and cool to the lukewarm stage.
- Add milk, pecans and salt. Mix well.
- Remove from saucepan and store in airtight jars.
- May be stored for several months in refrigerator and reheated as needed.
- Especially good with pound cake or ice cream.

Cointreau Strawberry Sauce

3	tablespoons butter
3	tablespoons grated orange rind
1/4	cup orange juice concentrate
2	tablespoons lemon juice
1/2	cup sugar
3	pint baskets strawberries, puréed
3	tablespoons Cointreau
2	tablespoons cognac

Servings: 2 cups
Preparation time: 15 minutes

- In a 3-quart saucepan, combine first 6 ingredients.
- Bring to a boil, stirring constantly.
- Add Cointreau and cognac. Simmer for 5 minutes, stirring occasionally.
- Especially good served with cheesecake.

Hot Fudge Sauce

1/2	cup cocoa
1	cup sugar
1	cup light Karo syrup
1/2	cup light cream
1/4	teaspoon salt
3	tablespoons butter
1	teaspoon salt
1	teaspoon vanilla extract

Servings: 2-1/2 cups
Preparation time: 5 minutes
Cooking time: 8 to 10 minutes

- Combine first 7 ingredients in a saucepan.
- Cook over medium heat, stirring constantly, until mixture comes to a full rolling boil.
- Boil briskly for 3 minutes, stirring occasionally.
- Remove from heat and stir in vanilla.

Honey Dressing

1/4	cup sugar
1	teaspoon dry mustard
1	teaspoon paprika
1	teaspoon celery salt
2	tablespoons minced onion
1	tablespoon lemon juice
5	tablespoons red wine vinegar
1	cup salad oil
1/4	cup honey

Servings: 2 cups
Preparation time: 10 minutes

- Combine all ingredients in a jar. Cover and shake well.
- Refrigerate.

Sour Cream Dressing

1	8-ounce carton sour cream
2	tablespoons lemon juice
2	tablespoons brown sugar
1	tablespoon ground ginger

Servings: 1-1/3 cups
Preparation time: 5 minutes
Chilling time: 1 hour

- Combine all ingredients.
- Cover and refrigerate until chilled.
- Delicious over fresh fruit.

Roquefort Dressing

1/2	teaspoon paprika
1	teaspoon salt
1/4	teaspoon sugar
1/2	cup vegetable oil
1/4	cup wine vinegar
2	tablespoons butter
2	tablespoons Roquefort cheese
1	clove garlic, minced
1	teaspoon Worcestershire sauce

Servings: 1 cup
Preparation time: 8 minutes

- Mix first 5 ingredients in a jar and refrigerate.
- Soften butter and cheese.
- Mix butter, cheese, garlic and Worcestershire sauce. Add to oil and vinegar mixture.
- Shake well.

Golden Dressing

2	egg yolks
1/2	cup heavy cream
2	tablespoons Gulden's mustard
1/2	teaspoon salt
1/8	teaspoon pepper
1/8	cup tarragon vinegar
	Olive oil

Servings: 4 to 6
Preparation time: 10 minutes
- Beat egg yolks.
- Add cream, mustard, salt, pepper and vinegar.
- Place in a jar and shake well.
- Refrigerate until ready to use.
- Lightly coat lettuce with olive oil.
- Pour dressing over lettuce.
- Toss and serve immediately.
- Good on salads, vegetables or cold seafood.

Best Salad Dressing

1	egg
1	egg yolk
1	tablespoon vinegar
1	tablespoon plus 1 teaspoon yellow mustard
1	cup salad oil
2	teaspoons dried orégano
3	teaspoons freshly snipped parsley
2	cloves garlic, minced
3/4	teaspoon salt
1/2	teaspoon pepper

Yield: 2 cups
Preparation time: 10 minutes
- Combine all ingredients in a blender.
- Blend for 1 minute.
- Store in the refrigerator in an airtight jar.
- Before using, shake well to recombine.

Russian Dressing

1	cup vegetable oil
1/2	cup red wine vinegar
1/2	cup catsup
1	teaspoon Worcestershire sauce
1/4	cup sugar
1	teaspoon salt
1	clove garlic, crushed and minced
1	medium onion, finely chopped

Servings: 2-1/2 cups
Preparation time: 10 minutes
- Mix all ingredients until well blended.
- Pour in a covered jar and refrigerate.
- Excellent on citrus and avocado salad.

Roquefort-Mayonnaise Dressing

1	8-ounce carton sour cream
1	small onion, grated
3/4	cup mayonnaise
1/4	cup lemon juice
4	ounces crumbled bleu or Roquefort cheese

Servings: 2 cups
Preparation time: 5 minutes
Chilling time: 1 day
- Mix all ingredients together.
- Put in an airtight container and refrigerate.
- Allow to stand for 1 day so flavors will blend.
- Will keep for at least 2 weeks in refrigerator.

Roquefort-Olive Dressing

1/3	cup chopped ripe olives
1/2	cup mayonnaise
1	tablespoon lemon juice
1	teaspoon grated onion
1/2	teaspoon Worcestershire sauce
2	tablespoons crumbled Roquefort cheese

Servings: 3/4 cup
Preparation time: 10 minutes
- Chop olives in a food processor or by hand.
- Combine olives, mayonnaise, lemon juice, onion and Worcestershire.
- Add Roquefort cheese and blend to combine.

Celery Seed Dressing

1/2	cup sugar
1	teaspoon salt
1	teaspoon dry mustard
1	teaspoon celery seed
1/4	cup grated onion
1	cup salad oil
1/3	cup vinegar

Servings: 10 to 12
Preparation time: 10 minutes
- Combine all ingredients in a blender. Blend for 10 seconds.
- Store in refrigerator.

Calamondin Marmalade

3	quarts calamondins
	Sugar as needed

Servings: 24 1/2-pints
Preparation time: 1 hour
Cooking time: 2 hours
- Wash calamondins.
- Cut calamondins in half. Remove seeds and save.
- Cover seeds with water and let stand overnight.
- Grind fruit and measure.
- Add 2-1/2 measures of water to each measure of fruit.
- Let stand overnight.
- Add water from seeds, pouring through a strainer.
- Put fruit and liquid in a large pot.
- Boil for 20 minutes.
- To each cup of boiled juice, add 1 cup sugar. It's best to make up 4 cups of juice at a time.
- Cook to jellying point, 220° F. to 222° F. on thermometer.
- Pour into sterilized jelly glasses and seal.

Indian Tomato Chutney

5	large, firm, ripe tomatoes
2	cloves garlic, chopped
1	inch fresh ginger root, chopped
1/2	onion, diced
2	tablespoons vinegar
3/4	cup sugar
2	teaspoons raisins
8	whole cardamom seeds or 1/4 teaspoon cardamom powder
1/2	teaspoon cumin seeds
1	inch cinnamon stick
1/2	teaspoon salt
1/4	teaspoon chili powder
2	bay leaves

Servings: 8 to 12 ounces chutney
Preparation time: 1 hour
Cooking time: 30 to 45 minutes
Standing time: 1 day

- Drop tomatoes in boiling water, cover and let stand for 2 minutes.
- Drain tomatoes. Peel. Cut into quarters or chop fine.
- In a saucepan, combine tomatoes, garlic, ginger and onion. Cook over low heat, stirring occasionally until tomatoes are tender and water evaporates.
- Add remaining ingredients.
- Stir over low heat until chutney thickens.
- Remove from heat and cool.
- Remove bay leaves.
- Store in jars.
- Leave out for 1 day.

Hot Pepper Jelly

3	large green or red bell peppers, cut and seeded
8	hot peppers, do not seed
1/2	cup water
3	cups cider vinegar
5	pounds sugar
2	6-ounce bottles Certo
	Green or red food coloring
12	8-ounce canning jars with lids

Servings: 12 8-ounce jars
Preparation time: 45 minutes
Cooking time: 10 minutes

- Finely chop peppers with water in a food processor or mince by hand and combine with water.
- Put in a Dutch oven.
- Add vinegar and sugar.
- Bring to a boil. Boil for 5 minutes.
- Remove from heat and skim.
- Add Certo and food coloring.
- Pour into sterile glass jars.
- Seal and process for 10 minutes.

SAUCES, DRESSINGS, PICKLES & JELLIES

Cranberry Kumquat Relish

2	cups fresh whole cranberries
4	large kumquats or 1 medium orange, peeled
4	ounces (2/3 can) orange juice concentrate
1/2	cup sugar

Servings: 3 cups
Preparation time: 15 minutes
Standing time: 1 to 2 days

- Rinse cranberries and leave in colander to drain.
- Cut kumquats into quarters, removing largest seeds. If using orange, cut into eighths.
- Place concentrate and sugar in a blender jar. Blend well.
- Add kumquats or orange. Blend until peel is coarsely chopped, about 10 to 12 seconds depending on blender.
- Add cranberries with machine running. Blend until whole cranberry is crushed.
- Scrape into a bowl, cover and refrigerate.
- This should be prepared 1 to 2 days prior to serving, as it thickens and deepens in color.
- Serve chilled.
- Will keep refrigerated for several days.

Sweet Pickles

7	cups unpeeled cucumber, thinly sliced
1	cup sliced onion
1	green bell pepper, sliced
2	tablespoons celery seed
1	tablespoon salt
2	cups sugar
1	cup vinegar

Servings: 9 cups
Preparation time: 20 minutes
Refrigeration time: 2 days

- Combine all ingredients and store in refrigerator for 2 days.
- May be frozen in plastic containers.
- Will keep for 2 to 3 weeks in refrigerator.

Minnesota Sandwich Pickles

8 to 10	medium cucumbers
1	large onion, sliced
1/8	cup fresh dill weed
2	cups sugar
3	cups white vinegar
1	cup water
1/2	cup salt

Servings: 5 to 6 pints
Preparation time: 1 hour

- Slice cucumbers lengthwise 1/8-inch thick.
- Dispose of first and last slices from each cucumber.
- Soak sliced cucumbers in ice water for at least 1/2 hour.
- Drain.
- Pack into jars with a slice of onion and some dill in the bottom and on top.
- Bring sugar, vinegar, water and salt to a boil. Boil for 1 minute.
- Pour syrup over cucumbers and seal jars.
- Allow to stand for 24 hours, then chill.
- Best when served cold.

Watermelon Rind Pickles

10	pounds watermelon rind
2	tablespoons lime
8	pounds granulated sugar
2	tablespoons whole cloves
2	tablespoons whole allspice
5	sticks cinnamon
3	ginger roots
1	lemon, sliced
2	cups water
5	cups white vinegar

Servings: approximately 10 pints
Preparation time: 2 hours
Cooking time: 3 hours

- Soak watermelon overnight in one gallon water to which two tablespoons lime have been added.
- Pour off water next morning. Rinse and boil for 20 minutes in strong salt water. Then pour off water.
- Boil 20 minutes in clear water. Drain.
- Bring sugar, spices and vinegar to a rapid boil. Boil for 10 minutes.
- Drop in rind and boil slowly for 1-1/2 to 2 hours.
- DO NOT overcook.
- Green food coloring may be added for color if needed.

Brandied Peaches

Sugar
Water
Peaches
Quart jars, sterilized
Brandy

Preparation time: 1 hour
Standing time: 3 months

- Make a thick syrup of equal parts of sugar and water using 1 cup of sugar and 1 cup of water for every pound of fruit.
- Peel peaches and slice in half lengthwise, removing pit.
- Pack peach halves in jars.
- Add 3 tablespoons brandy to each jar. Then pour in syrup to completely cover fruit and fill jar.
- Seal and process jars in a boiling water bath for 15 minutes.
- Store 3 months before using.
- Chill before serving.

Corn Relish

18	ears of corn
4	cups chopped cabbage
1	cup chopped sweet red pepper
1	cup chopped green bell pepper
1	cup chopped onion
1	tablespoon celery seed
1	tablespoon salt
1	tablespoon turmeric
3	tablespoons mustard seed
1	cup water
4	cups vinegar
2	cups sugar

Servings: 6 pints
Preparation time: 2 hours
Cooking time: 30 minutes

- Cook corn in boiling water for 5 minutes. Cut from cob to measure 8 cups.
- Combine corn with remaining ingredients.
- In a large pot, bring mixture to a boil. Then simmer for 15 minutes.
- Pack relish in hot sterilized jars.
- Seal.
- Process in hot water bath for 15 minutes.

Soups, Sandwiches & Beverages

Gumbo

Roux

4	tablespoons vegetable oil
6 to 7	tablespoons all-purpose flour

Servings: 10
Preparation time: 1 hour
Cooking time: 2-1/2 hours

- Heat oil in a small heavy saucepan. Stir in flour and cook over medium low heat.
- Stir constantly until roux is the color of dark mahogany, about 15 minutes. Do not undercook.
- Set aside.

Gumbo Base

4	tablespoons butter
4	stalks celery, sliced
2	large onions, chopped
4	cups seeded and chopped ripe tomatoes
2	pounds fresh okra, sliced in 1-inch pieces
3	cups strong chicken broth
1	teaspoon cracked red pepper
4	teaspoons salt
2	bay leaves
2	teaspoons Worcestershire sauce
1	teaspoon ground allspice
1/4	teaspoon dried thyme
1/2	teaspoon ground pepper

- Melt butter. Sauté celery and onions until soft.
- Add tomatoes and okra. Cook for 30 minutes.
- Add remaining ingredients and mix well.
- Stir in roux.
- Cover and simmer for 1-1/2 hours.
- May be done ahead to this point and refrigerated.

Seafood

2	tablespoons butter
2	pounds fresh shrimp, butterflied
2	cloves garlic, crushed
1	pound fresh crabmeat
2	cups cooked chicken, cut in bite-size pieces

- Melt butter. Sauté shrimp and garlic for 5 minutes or until shrimp are pink.
- Add shrimp mixture, crabmeat and chicken to gumbo base. Bring to a boil.
- Simmer gently until ingredients are blended, about 30 minutes.
- Serve with white rice.

Filé Seafood Gumbo

2/3	cup vegetable oil
2	cups chopped onion
1/2	cup chopped green onion
2	cups chopped celery
4	cloves garlic, minced
2/3	cup all-purpose flour
1-1/2	quarts water
1	tablespoon salt
1	teaspoon cayenne pepper
1	pound okra, chopped (optional)
2	pounds raw shrimp, peeled and deveined
1	pound crabmeat
1	pint oysters with liquid
1	teaspoon filé powder (available at seafood markets)

Servings: 12
Preparation time: 30 minutes
Cooking time: 1-1/2 hours

- Heat oil in a large heavy sauce pot.
- Sauté onion, celery and garlic until just tender.
- Add flour. Cook and stir constantly until roux is rich and brown, about 15 to 20 minutes.
- Add water, salt, pepper and okra. Simmer for 1 hour.
- Add seafoods and continue to simmer for 30 minutes.
- Do not add filé powder until ready to serve. Then add only to what is being served.
- Serve over rice.

Blue Crab Soup

3	tablespoons butter
3	tablespoons all-purpose flour
4	cups milk, heated
2	cups heavy cream, heated
1	pound white crabmeat, picked and cleaned
1/2	cup finely diced celery
2	ounces sherry
	Salt and pepper to taste
3	hard-boiled eggs, sliced
2	lemons, thinly sliced

Servings: 6
Preparation time: 15 minutes
Chilling time: 2 to 3 hours

- Melt butter in a heavy saucepan. Add flour and stir until smooth.
- Slowly add milk and cream. Simmer, stirring constantly, until thickened.
- Stir in crabmeat, celery and sherry. Season with salt and pepper.
- Serve warm or chilled in mugs. Garnish with slices of egg and lemon.

Cioppino

2	tablespoons olive oil
2	tablespoons butter
2	onions, finely chopped
2	cloves garlic, finely minced
20	fresh mushrooms
1	28-ounce can Italian tomatoes
1	6-ounce can tomato paste
1/2	cup chopped green bell pepper
1	teaspoon dried basil
1/2	teaspoon dried orégano
1/2	cup fresh lemon juice
2	cups dry red wine
1-1/2	pounds red snapper, flounder or bass
24	raw shrimp, shelled
1/2	pound scallops
12	clams

Servings: 6
Preparation time: 30 minutes
Cooking time: 1-1/2 hours

- In a Dutch oven, heat oil and butter.
- Add onions and garlic. Sauté over medium heat until transparent.
- Add mushrooms and sauté an additional 5 minutes.
- Add tomatoes, tomato paste, green pepper, basil, orégano, lemon juice and wine. Stir well to blend.
- Bring to a boil, reduce heat and simmer for 1 hour.
- Add snapper and cook 15 minutes more.
- Add shrimp, scallops and clams. Cook 10 minutes more.
- Serve with crusty garlic bread and a dry red wine.

Oyster and Spinach Soup

1/2	cup chopped onion
2	cloves garlic, minced
1/2	cup butter
12	ounces oysters, drained
1/2	cup all-purpose flour
1-1/2	quarts Half and Half
2	cups chicken broth
2	10-ounce packages frozen chopped spinach, thawed and puréed
1	teaspoon salt
	Pepper to taste

Servings: 8
Preparation time: 15 minutes
Cooking time: 15 minutes

- In a saucepan, sauté onion and garlic in butter until tender.
- Add oysters and cook until edges curl.
- Gradually blend in flour. Cook over low heat until bubbly.
- Gradually add Half and Half, stirring constantly until thickened.
- Stir in broth and spinach. Bring to a low boil.
- Season with salt and pepper.

Fish or Conch Chowder

6	slices bacon
2	medium yellow onions, diced
2	stalks celery, diced
2	cloves garlic, minced
1	cup tomato sauce
2	cups Half and Half
2	pounds white fish or conch, cut into 1-inch pieces
1/2	pound fresh mushrooms
5	medium potatoes, cooked and diced
1/2	cup white wine
	Beau Monde to taste
	Tabasco sauce to taste
	Crazy Jane salt to taste
	Salt and pepper to taste
1/2	cup chopped parsley for garnish

Servings: 6
Preparation time: 20 minutes
Cooking time: 45 minutes

- Fry bacon until crisp. Drain on a paper towel and crumble.
- Pour off all but 3 tablespoons bacon drippings. Sauté onion, celery and garlic until tender.
- Add tomato sauce and Half and Half. Bring just to boiling.
- Add fish, mushrooms and potatoes. Reduce heat and cook chowder over low heat until fish is tender.
- Add wine and crumbled bacon. Simmer for 15 minutes.
- Season to taste.
- Sprinkle parsley on individual servings.

Spinach Shellfish Soup

3	tablespoons butter
1/3	cup finely chopped shallots
1	cup dry white wine
3	tablespoons all-purpose flour
1-1/2	cups clam juice
1	teaspoon garlic salt
1/4	teaspoon white pepper
1	teaspoon Crazy Jane salt
1-1/2	cups light cream
1/2	cup cooked and puréed spinach
1	cup lump crabmeat, cleaned (optional)
1/2	cup sour cream

Servings: 6 to 8
Preparation time: 40 minutes
Cooking time: 30 minutes

- Sauté shallots in butter.
- Add wine. Cook over low heat until reduced by half.
- Dissolve flour in clam juice and add to mixture.
- After mixture thickens, add seasonings, cream and spinach. Heat thoroughly, but do not allow to boil.
- Stir in crabmeat.
- Serve in bowls, topped with a heaping teaspoon of sour cream.

Spinach Soup

1/4	cup finely chopped onion
1/4	cup butter
1/4	cup all-purpose flour
4	cups milk
1	teaspoon salt
2	10-ounce packages frozen chopped spinach, defrosted and drained
	Accent to taste
	Provolone cheese, grated

Servings: 6
Preparation time: 10 minutes
Cooking time: 10 minutes
Standing time: 15 minutes

- Brown onion in butter.
- Stir in flour and cook until bubbly.
- Slowly add milk. Stir with a wire wisk until thickened.
- Add salt, spinach and Accent.
- Let stand for 15 minutes.
- Top with provolone cheese and serve.

Zesty Spinach Soup

2	tablespoons vegetable oil
1/2	medium onion, chopped
1	clove garlic, minced
3/4	pound fresh spinach, finely chopped
1-1/2	cups milk
2	tablespoons grated Parmesan cheese
	Nutmeg to taste
	Salt and pepper to taste
3	teaspoons lemon juice
4	cups chicken stock
2	tablespoons butter
2	tablespoons chopped parsley

Servings: 4
Preparation time: 10 minutes
Cooking time: 10 minutes

- Sauté onion and garlic in oil until soft.
- Add spinach and 1/2 cup milk. Cook for 3 minutes.
- Blend in cheese, nutmeg, salt, pepper and lemon juice. Stir until smooth.
- Add remaining 1 cup milk and stock. Heat through.
- Stir in butter and parsley.
- May be reheated but do not boil.

Broccoli Soup

1	pound fresh broccoli, trimmed
1	quart chicken broth
1	small onion, chopped
2	stalks celery with leaves, chopped
4 to 5	sprigs fresh parsley, chopped
1	large carrot, diced
1	teaspoon salt
1/4	teaspoon cayenne pepper
2	tablespoons cornstarch
1	cup sour cream (use less if desired)
1	tablespoon chopped chives

Servings: 6 to 8
Preparation time: 30 minutes
Cooking time: 20 minutes

- Wash broccoli. Cut off heads and peel and slice stalks. Place all in a large pot with next 7 ingredients.
- Bring to a boil, reduce heat and simmer for 20 minutes.
- Mix cornstarch with a little cold water and add to soup.
- Simmer and stir until thick.
- Purée in a blender until smooth.
- May be frozen at this point.
- Soup may be served either hot or cold.
- If serving cold, refrigerate at this point. When ready to serve, add sour cream and garnish with chives.
- If serving hot, gently heat before adding sour cream.

Broccoli Bisque

1	large bunch fresh broccoli
1/4	cup chopped onion
2	cups chicken broth
2	tablespoons butter
1	tablespoon all-purpose flour
2	tablespoons salt
1/4	teaspoon pepper
2	cups Half and Half

Servings: 6
Preparation time: 15 minutes
Cooking time: 10 to 14 minutes

- Steam broccoli until tender. Chop.
- In a saucepan, combine broccoli, onion and chicken broth. Bring to a boil. Reduce heat and simmer for 10 minutes.
- Purée mixture in a blender until smooth.
- Melt butter in a saucepan. Add flour, salt and pepper. Stir until smooth.
- Stir in Half and Half.
- Combine sauce and broccoli purée.
- Cook over medium heat, stirring until soup bubbles.
- Serve hot or cold.

Cold Zucchini Soup

2	medium zucchini, sliced	
1	green bell pepper, sliced	
1	medium onion, sliced	
3	cups chicken stock	
1	cup sour cream	
1	teaspoon dried dill weed	
1	tablespoon chopped parsley	

Servings: 6 to 8
Preparation time: 10 minutes
Cooking time: 20 minutes
Chilling time: 1-1/2 hours

- Simmer zucchini, bell pepper and onion in chicken stock for 20 minutes.
- Remove vegetables and purée in a food processor or blender.
- Return puréed vegetables to stock and cool.
- Add sour cream, dill and parsley.
- Chill thoroughly, at least 1-1/2 hours.

Zucchini Bisque

1/2	cup butter
1	medium onion, finely chopped
1-1/2	pounds zucchini, grated
2-1/2	cups chicken stock
1/2	teaspoon ground nutmeg
1	teaspoon fresh basil
1	teaspoon salt
	White pepper to taste
1	cup heavy cream

Servings: 8
Preparation time: 15 minutes
Cooking time: 15 minutes
Chilling time: 2 to 3 hours

- Melt butter in a large heavy saucepan. Add onion and sauté until soft.
- Add zucchini and stock to onion and simmer for 15 minutes.
- In a food processor or blender, purée zucchini mixture in two batches, adding half of the seasonings to each batch.
- Combine batches, add cream and stir until mixed.
- Correct seasonings.
- Serve warm or chill for 2 to 3 hours.

Mushroom Bisque

1	pound fresh mushrooms, chopped
1	medium onion, chopped
4	cups chicken broth or enough broth to cover vegetables
7	tablespoons butter
6	tablespoons all-purpose flour
3	cups milk
1	cup heavy cream
3	teaspoons dry sherry
	Parsley for garnish

Servings: 8
Preparation time: 15 minutes
Cooking time: 1 hour

- Simmer mushrooms, onion and chicken broth in a large pot for 45 minutes.
- Purée vegetables and broth. Return to pot.
- In a separate pot, melt butter. Blend in flour, stirring constantly, for 3 minutes.
- Gradually add milk and simmer until thick.
- Combine sauce and mushroom broth mixture. Add cream and sherry, stirring to combine.
- Garnish with parsley and serve.
- For a thicker soup, reduce amount of chicken broth.

Mushroom Broth

1	pound fresh mushrooms, cleaned and chopped
2	tablespoons butter
1	quart rich chicken broth
1/2	teaspoon grated lemon peel
1	1/2-inch slice of large onion
1/4	cup chopped parsley
1/2	cup dry white wine
	Mushroom slices for garnish
	Lemon slices for garnish

Servings: 6 to 8
Preparation time: 15 minutes
Cooking time: 1 hour

- Sauté mushrooms in butter over low heat until tender.
- Put mushrooms in a pot with broth, lemon peel, onion and parsley.
- Cover. Simmer over low heat for 1 hour.
- Filter soup through fine cheesecloth. Set aside.
- Before serving, reheat and add wine.
- Season to taste.
- Garnish with mushroom slices or lemon slices.
- May be made ahead.
- Freezes well.

Cold Cucumber-Dill Soup

2	tablespoons butter
3	cucumbers, peeled and chopped
1	large leek, white part only, chopped
1	bay leaf
1	tablespoon all-purpose flour
3	cups chicken stock
1	teaspoon salt
1/4	teaspoon pepper
1	cup heavy cream
	Juice of 1/2 lemon
1	teaspoon finely chopped fresh dill weed
	Sour cream

Servings: 6
Preparation time: 15 minutes
Cooking time: 30 minutes
Chilling time: 3 hours

- Melt butter in a large heavy pot.
- Sauté cucumbers, leek and bay leaf until vegetables are soft.
- Stir in flour, chicken stock, salt and pepper.
- Simmer for 30 minutes. Remove bay leaf.
- Purée mixture in a blender.
- Stir in cream, lemon juice and dill.
- Correct seasonings. Chill for several hours.
- Float a spoonful of sour cream on each portion when serving.

Yogurt Cucumber Soup

2	medium onions
2	large cucumbers
2	pints plain yogurt
2	pints sour cream
1	cup chicken stock
1/2	teaspoon white pepper
1/2	teaspoon garlic salt
1	teaspoon Worcestershire sauce

Servings: 6
Preparation time: 20 minutes
Chilling time: 1 to 2 hours

- Chop onions and cucumbers to a fine consistency in a blender or food processor.
- Mix yogurt, sour cream and chicken stock in a large bowl.
- Add onions and cucumbers to yogurt mixture.
- Add all seasonings to mixture and chill.
- If soup is too thick, thin with heavy cream.
- Soup may be stored in refrigerator for 3 to 4 days.

Potage Cressonaire

2	leeks, chopped
2	tablespoons butter
3	medium potatoes, sliced
2	10-3/4-ounce cans chicken broth
2	cans water
1	bunch watercress
	Salt and pepper to taste
1	cup heavy cream
	Watercress for garnish

Servings: 6 to 8
Preparation time: 30 minutes
Cooking time: 35 minutes

- Sauté leeks in butter until soft.
- Add potatoes, broth and water.
- Bring to a boil. Reduce heat and simmer for 30 minutes.
- Add watercress, salt and pepper. Simmer another 5 minutes.
- Cool.
- Purée in a blender until smooth and creamy.
- Add cream. Reheat gently before serving or refrigerate and serve cold.
- Garnish with watercress.

Vichyssoise

6	tablespoons butter
4	medium onions, diced
4	medium potatoes, peeled and diced
2	cups chicken stock
1	cup heavy cream
1	cup Half and Half
1	cup milk
1	teaspoon salt
1/8	teaspoon white pepper
2	tablespoons chopped chives

Servings: 8
Preparation time: 20 minutes
Cooking time: 45 minutes
Chilling time: 3 hours

- In a large heavy pot, melt butter. Sauté onions until soft.
- Add potatoes and chicken stock.
- Cover and simmer for 45 minutes.
- Cool.
- Purée mixture in a blender or processor.
- Stir in creams, milk and seasonings.
- Chill well.
- Stir before serving.
- Garnish with chives.

Jellied Borscht

1-1/2	envelopes unflavored gelatin
1/3	cup sherry
1	tablespoon lemon juice
1	cup beet juice
4	cups consommé
2	2-ounce jars caviar
	Sour cream
	Parsley for garnish
	Nutmeg

Servings: 6 to 8
Preparation time: 10 minutes
Refrigeration time: 3 to 4 hours

- Dissolve gelatin in sherry and lemon juice.
- Heat beet juice and consommé.
- Add gelatin mixture to heated liquids. Stir until gelatin is dissolved.
- Put 1 teaspoon caviar in the bottom of each bouillon cup. Pour consommé gently into cup.
- Chill until firm.
- Scoop a tablespoon of consommé from the center of each cup. Fill hole with sour cream.
- Top with small sprig of fresh parsley and sprinkle with nutmeg.

Hearty Gazpacho

1	cup finely chopped and peeled tomatoes
1/2	cup finely chopped celery
1/2	cup finely chopped green bell pepper
1/2	cup finely chopped cucumber
1/4	cup finely chopped onion
2	teaspoons snipped parsley
1	teaspoon snipped chives
1	small clove garlic, minced
2 to 3	tablespoons tarragon wine vinegar
2	tablespoons olive oil
1	teaspoon salt
1/4	teaspoon black pepper
1/2	teaspoon Worcestershire sauce
2	cups tomato juice
	Chives for garnish
	Croutons for garnish

Servings: 4 to 5
Preparation time: 20 minutes
Chilling time: 4 hours

- Combine first 14 ingredients.
- Cover and chill for at least 4 hours.
- <u>Hint</u>: If using the food processor to chop vegetables, <u>do not over chop</u>. This is best if vegetables have some texture and crunch.
- Garnish with chives or croutons.

SOUPS, SANDWICHES & BEVERAGES

Song of India Soup

1	medium onion, chopped
4	tablespoons butter
1	cup peeled and shredded apples
2	teaspoons curry powder
1-1/2	cups yellow squash, cooked and mashed
2	cups chicken broth
1	cup Half and Half
1	tablespoon lemon juice
	Lemon juice for apples
	Mint leaves for garnish
	Apple slices for garnish

Servings: 6
Preparation time: 30 minutes
Cooking time: 25 minutes

- Sauté onion in butter in a large saucepan.
- Add apples and curry powder. Stir until well blended.
- Cook for 5 minutes.
- Add squash and broth.
- Bring to a boil, stirring frequently.
- Reduce heat, cover and simmer for 10 minutes, stirring occasionally.
- Purée in a blender.
- Stir in Half and Half and lemon juice.
- Sprinkle lemon juice on apple slices.
- Garnish with mint leaves and apple slices.
- May be served hot or cold.

Greek Lemon Egg Soup

8	cups chicken broth
3/4	cup raw rice
	Salt to taste
4	eggs
	Juice of 2 lemons
	Lemon slices for garnish

Servings: 6
Preparation time: 30 minutes
Cooking time: 20 minutes

- Bring chicken broth to a boil. Add rice and salt. Cover and simmer for 20 minutes.
- When done, remove from heat.
- Beat eggs until light and frothy.
- Slowly add lemon juice, beating continuously.
- Dilute mixture with 2 cups of hot soup, beating constantly until well mixed.
- Add diluted egg mixture to rest of soup, beating constantly.
- Bring almost to the boiling point, but do not boil or soup will curdle.
- Serve at once with thin lemon slices for garnish.

"The Sisters" Cheese Soup

1/4	cup margarine or butter
1	cup diced potato
1/2	cup diced carrot
1/2	cup diced celery
1/2	cup diced green bell pepper
1/2	10-ounce package frozen green peas
1-1/2	quarts chicken broth
1	cup grated sharp Cheddar cheese
1	cup diced Velveeta cheese
1/4	cup chopped parsley
1/4	cup cornstarch
1	cup milk
	Salt and pepper to taste

Servings: 8
Preparation time: 15 minutes
Cooking time: 40 minutes

- Melt butter in a large soup pot. Sauté vegetables until just tender.
- Add broth. Simmer over low heat for 30 minutes.
- Add cheeses and parsley. Continue to cook over low heat until cheese has melted.
- Add cornstarch to milk. Stir until well blended.
- Add milk to soup and stir until thickened.
- Add salt and pepper.
- Serve immediately.

Pumpkin Soup

1-1/2	quarts chicken broth
1/4	cup chopped onions
1/4	teaspoon ground nutmeg
1/2	teaspoon paprika
1/4	teaspoon garlic powder
1	cup mashed pumpkin
1/4	cup cornstarch
1-1/2	cups milk
1	egg yolk
1/8	cup dry sherry

Servings: 8
Preparation time: 10 minutes
Cooking time: 35 minutes

- Pour chicken broth in a large soup pot.
- Add onion, nutmeg, paprika, garlic powder and pumpkin. Simmer over low heat for 30 minutes.
- Mix cornstarch with milk. Add to soup and stir until thick.
- Add egg yolk to 1 cup of soup mixture. Beat well and return to soup.
- Add sherry. Stir until well blended.
- Serve immediately.

Winter Green Soup

2	quarts boiling water
1/2	pound white bacon, chopped
2	ham hocks
4	chorizos or pepperoni, sliced thin
1	large Spanish onion, chopped
1 to 2	cloves garlic, minced (optional)
2	15-ounce cans collard greens, drained
2	16-ounce cans great northern beans, do not drain
	Salt and pepper to taste
6	large potatoes, cubed

Servings: 10
Preparation time: 20 minutes
Cooking time: 2 hours

- In 2 quarts boiling water, combine bacon, ham hocks, chorizos, onion and garlic. Cook, covered, for 1/2 hour.
- Add collard greens and beans. Cook over low heat for 1/2 hour.
- Add salt, pepper and potatoes. Continue cooking, covered, for 1 hour.
- Serve with cornbread.

Lentil Soup

1	pound dried lentils
2	quarts boiling water
1	cup chopped onion
1	cup chopped celery
1	clove garlic, minced
1/2	green bell pepper, chopped
1/4	cup bacon grease
2	beef bouillon cubes
1	tablespoon sugar
1	tablespoon salt
1	teaspoon pepper
1/4	cup catsup
1/2	teaspoon dried thyme
2	bay leaves
2	tablespoons sherry
1-1/2	cups diced potatoes
1-1/2	cups diced carrots

Servings: 12
Soaking time: overnight
Preparation time: 30 minutes
Cooking time: 1-1/2 hours

- Soak lentils in cold water overnight.
- Drain lentils and simmer in boiling water for 45 minutes.
- In a large skillet, sauté onion, celery, garlic and pepper in bacon grease until soft.
- Add sautéed vegetables to lentils.
- Stir in next 8 ingredients.
- Bring to a boil. Add potatoes and carrots.
- Reduce heat and simmer for 30 minutes.
- Correct seasonings and cook another 30 minutes.
- Serve with crusty bread and salad.

Country Chicken Soup

Chicken Broth

1	fryer, hen or equivalent chicken parts
	Water to cover
2	onions, halved
2	carrots, diced
2	stalks celery with leaves, diced
2	chicken bouillon cubes
	Salt and pepper to taste

Soup

3	carrots, chopped
3	stalks celery, chopped
2	large fresh mushrooms, sliced
1	zucchini, sliced
3	tomatoes, skinned and chopped
1/2	cup frozen tiny peas
1	cup canned corn
1/4	cup raw rice
1/2	cup barley
1/2	cup vermicelli, broken into 3-inch pieces
	Chicken broth (from above recipe)
	Chicken meat (from fryer used to make broth), diced
3	tablespoons chopped fresh parsley

Servings: 8
Preparation time: 35 minutes
Cooking time: 3-1/2 hours

- Make a strong broth by simmering chicken, vegetables, and seasonings in a large pot for 2 to 3 hours or until meat falls from bones.
- Remove from heat, skim broth, strain and reserve.
- Add first 10 ingredients to chicken broth and cook over low heat until all are tender.
- Add diced chicken and parsley.
- Serve with corn bread or seasoned Arabic bread.
- May be prepared ahead.

Vegetable Chicken Soup

4	cups chicken broth
4	medium onions, chopped
1	16-ounce can tomato wedges
2	tablespoons sugar
1	12-ounce package frozen soup vegetables
1/4	cup barley
1/4	cup macaroni
	Salt and pepper to taste
	Worcestershire sauce to taste
1	teaspoon Fines Herbes seasoning
2	cups cooked diced chicken

Servings: 8 to 10
Preparation time: 20 minutes
Cooking time: 1 hour

- Combine first 10 ingredients in a Dutch oven.
- Simmer over low heat for 1 hour.
- Add chicken shortly before serving.
- May be prepared ahead.

Peanut Soup

1	medium onion, finely chopped
1	cup diced celery
1/2	cup butter
2	tablespoons all-purpose flour
2	quarts chicken broth
1	cup creamy peanut butter
1	cup Half and Half
1/4	cup chopped parsley
1/4	cup chopped salted peanuts

Servings: 8
Preparation time: 15 minutes
Cooking time: 10 minutes

- Sauté onion and celery in butter until tender.
- Stir in flour, blending well.
- Stir in chicken broth. Bring mixture to a low boil.
- Reduce heat and simmer.
- Stir in peanut butter and Half and **Half**.
- Simmer for 10 minutes.
- Garnish with parsley and peanuts.

Ram's Steak Sandwich

2/3	cup beer
1/3	cup vegetable oil
1-1/4	teaspoons salt
1/2	teaspoon pepper
2	cloves garlic, minced
2	pounds flank steak
4	tablespoons butter
1/2	teaspoon paprika
3	cups sliced onions
6	tablespoons butter, softened
1/4	teaspoon parsley
1/4	teaspoon dried tarragon
1/4	teaspoon dried orégano
1/4	teaspoon dried thyme
6	sourdough rolls, cut in half
1-1/2	cups sour cream
2	tablespoons horseradish
	Paprika for garnish

Servings: 6
Preparation time: 30 minutes
Baking time: 20 minutes
Marinating time: 4 hours

- Combine beer, oil, salt, pepper and garlic in a jar. Shake well.
- Score steak and place in a shallow dish. Pour marinade over meat and let stand for 4 hours.
- Preheat oven to 350° F.
- Melt 4 tablespoons butter with paprika. Sauté onions until tender.
- Mix 6 tablespoons butter with herbs. Spread on each half of a roll.
- Wrap rolls in foil and bake for 20 minutes.
- Remove steak from marinade and broil for 5 minutes on each side.
- Thinly slice meat on the diagonal.
- Heat sour cream and horseradish.
- Place 2 roll halves open face on each plate.
- Place slices of meat on roll, cover with onion mixture and top with sour cream mixture. Sprinkle with paprika.

Artichoke Puffs

3	English muffins, halved	
	Mayonnaise	
3/4	cup mayonnaise	
1/2	medium onion, chopped	
3/4	cup sharp Cheddar cheese spread	
	Salt and pepper to taste	
6	tomato slices	
12	artichoke hearts, halved	
	Paprika for garnish	

Servings: 6
Preparation time: 15 minutes
Baking time: 15 minutes
- Preheat oven to 350° F.
- Spread muffin halves with mayonnaise.
- Combine 3/4 cup mayonnaise, onion, cheese, salt and pepper.
- Put a slice of tomato on each muffin.
- Top with 4 artichoke heart halves.
- Spoon cheese mixture on top.
- Sprinkle with paprika.
- Bake for 15 minutes.

Guten Tog

2	tablespoons butter
1	pound fresh mushrooms, sliced
6	slices rye bread
1/2	cup mayonnaise
1/2	cup mustard
6	slices lean smoked ham
3/4	cup sour cream
6	slices Swiss cheese

Servings: 6
Preparation time: 15 minutes
Baking time: 10 minutes
- Preheat oven to 400° F.
- Sauté mushrooms in butter.
- Toast rye bread and place on a cookie sheet.
- Spread each piece of toast with equal parts mayonnaise and mustard.
- Place a slice of ham on each piece of toast.
- Top ham with a heaping spoonful of sour cream.
- Lay slices of Swiss cheese on top.
- Bake until cheese melts, about 10 minutes.
- Spoon sautéed mushrooms over the top.

Hot Brown Sandwich

1/3	cup butter
1	medium onion, minced
1/3	cup all-purpose flour
3	cups hot milk
1	teaspoon salt
	Red pepper to taste
3	tablespoons chopped fresh parsley
	Nutmeg to taste
2	egg yolks, beaten
1/4	cup grated Cheddar cheese
1/2	cup grated Parmesan cheese
6 to 8	slices of bread
	Sliced turkey, chicken or ham (a combination is great!)
	Crisp bacon strips (optional)
	Mushroom caps, sliced and sautéed (optional)

Servings: 3 to 4
Preparation time: 25 minutes
Cooking time: 5 minutes

- Melt butter in the top of a double boiler.
- Add onion and cook until soft.
- Add flour. Blend to make a smooth paste.
- Add milk, salt, red pepper, parsley and nutmeg.
- Cook until sauce is thick and smooth, stirring constantly.
- Add a little hot sauce to yolks to temper them.
- Stir yolks into sauce.
- Set pan over hot water.
- Add cheeses. Blend until melted.
- To assemble sandwiches, trim crust from 2 slices of bread for each serving, toast and lay on an ovenproof dish.
- Spread bread with a thin coating of sauce.
- Cover generously with meat, then with a large portion of sauce, so that all of the toast is covered.
- Run under a preheated broiler until sauce browns and puffs up.
- Garnish with bacon strips and mushrooms, if desired.

Ham Topped Muffins

1	cup cooked ham, cut in 1/4-inch cubes
1/4	cup grated Cheddar cheese
1/3	cup sour cream
1/4	cup finely chopped onion
1-1/3	cups all-purpose flour
2	tablespoons sugar
2-1/2	teaspoons baking powder
3/4	teaspoon salt
1	egg
3/4	cup milk
1/3	cup vegetable oil
	Snipped parsley for garnish

Servings: 12 muffins
Preparation time: 15 minutes
Baking time: 25 minutes

- Preheat oven to 400° F.
- Combine ham, cheese, sour cream and onion. Set aside.
- Stir together flour, sugar, baking powder and salt.
- Make a "well" in center of dry ingredients.
- In a small bowl, slightly beat egg with milk and oil.
- Add all at once to dry ingredients.
- Stir just until moist. Batter will be lumpy.
- Spoon batter into a twelve 2-1/2 to 2-3/4-inch muffin tin, filling 2/3 full.
- Top each with 1 rounded tablespoon of ham mixture.
- Bake for 25 minutes.
- Remove from tin and garnish with parsley.
- May refrigerate leftovers and warm later.
- These freeze beautifully.

Jacksonville Sangria

1	quart Burgundy
3	lemons
3	oranges
1	jigger brandy
1	jigger Cointreau
2	tablespoons white crème de menthe
	Sugar to taste
1/2	quart soda water, chilled

Servings: 8
Preparation time: 15 minutes
Chilling time: 1-1/2 hours

- Combine all spirits and sugar with the juice of the oranges and lemons.
- Chill well.
- Serve in a glass pitcher with the orange and lemon rinds sliced as garnish.
- Add chilled soda just before serving.

Blazing Spice Wine Punch

1/4	cup sugar
2	sticks of cinnamon, broken
8	whole cardamom seeds, crushed
8	whole cloves
4	whole allspice
	Thin peel from 1 orange
1/2	cup water
1/2	gallon dry red wine
2	cups ruby port wine
1	cup seedless raisins
1	cup almonds
1	orange, sliced
20	sugar cubes
1	lemon peel, studded with 2 cloves
1	cup brandy, divided
	Cinnamon sticks for stirring

Servings: 20
Preparation time: 15 minutes
Standing time: 3 to 4 hours

- Combine first 7 ingredients in a saucepan and bring to a boil.
- Cover and simmer over low heat for 5 minutes.
- Let stand for several hours.
- Strain, reserving liquid and discarding spices and orange peel.
- Combine wine, port, raisins and almonds in a large pot.
- Add strained spice liquid and bring just to boiling.
- Pour into a heat-proof punch bowl and float orange slices on top.
- Place sugar cubes and lemon peel in a large punch ladle.
- Add 1/4 cup warm brandy to ladle and pour the rest over surface of punch.
- Hold ladle over punch bowl. Ignite mixture in ladle. Rotate and shake ladle until sugar is almost dissolved. Lower ladle into punch to ignite brandy. Stir slowly a few times. When flames die, serve.
- Serve in a cup with a few almonds, raisins and a cinnamon stick.

Hot Mulled Wine

5	cups water
1-1/2	cups sugar
15	whole cloves
2	cinnamon sticks
1/2	gallon Burgundy

Servings: 3 quarts
Preparation time: 5 minutes
Cooking time: 20 minutes

- Combine water, sugar, cloves and cinnamon sticks. Bring to boil.
- Simmer for 20 minutes, stirring occasionally.
- Add wine.
- Heat until just hot.
- Serve in mugs.

Hot Buttered Rum

1	pound butter, softened
2	pounds light brown sugar
2	eggs
1	teaspoon ground nutmeg
1	teaspoon ground cinnamon
1	teaspoon ground allspice
	Cinnamon sticks
	Rum as needed
	Water as needed
	Butter for garnish

Servings: 50 cups
Preparation time: 1 hour

- Combine first 6 ingredients.
- Beat with an electric mixer at medium speed for 1 hour, scraping sides of bowl every 15 minutes.
- Pour into a 2-quart covered container and refrigerate.
- When ready to serve, place 1 cinnamon stick, 2 tablespoons of butter mixture and 2 ounces of rum in a mug.
- Fill with boiling water and stir.
- Garnish with a pat of butter.
- This will keep in the refrigerator for weeks and may also be frozen.

Coffee Punch

1	gallon milk
1/2	cup instant coffee
1/3	cup sugar
1	6-ounce can Hershey's chocolate syrup
1/2	gallon vanilla ice cream
2	cups heavy cream, whipped for garnish
	Ground cinnamon for garnish
	Ground nutmeg for garnish
	Chocolate curls for garnish

Servings: 20
Preparation time: 15 minutes
Chilling time: 3 hours

- Scald milk.
- Add coffee, sugar and chocolate syrup.
- Refrigerate.
- Soften ice cream and add to chilled mixture in a punch bowl.
- For a decorative touch, put part of milk mixture in a ring mold and freeze to use in punch bowl.
- Garnish with whipped cream or chocolate curls or dust with cinnamon or nutmeg.

Ruth's Coffee

6	heaping teaspoons instant coffee
4	cups hot water
1/2	teaspoon ground cinnamon
3	teaspoons sweet butter
6	ounces Kahlua
	Orange peel studded with cloves
	Whipping cream, whipped

Servings: 8
Preparation time: 10 minutes
Cooking time: 15 minutes

- Mix first 6 ingredients in a saucepan.
- Cover and simmer over low heat for 15 minutes. This will keep longer if cooked over low heat.
- Serve in demitasse cups topped with whipped cream.

Frozen Bourbon Sour

2	tea bags, individual size
1	cup boiling water
1/2	cup sugar
2-1/2	cups water
1	6-ounce can orange juice concentrate
1	6-ounce can limeade concentrate
1	cup bourbon
	Lemon twists for garnish
	Mint sprigs for garnish

Servings: 1-1/2 quarts
Preparation time: 10 minutes

- Steep tea bags in boiling water for 5 minutes. Then discard.
- Add sugar to tea and stir until dissolved.
- Add water, orange juice and limeade concentrates and bourbon. Mix well.
- Pour into containers, cover and freeze.
- To serve, spoon into cocktail glasses. Garnish with lemon twists and mint sprigs.

Boston Club Punch

1/2	cup water
4	tablespoons sugar
	Juice of 2 lemons
4	ounces bourbon
10	ice cubes
1	teaspoon Cointreau
4	teaspoons maraschino cherry juice
2	lemon slices

Servings: 2
Preparation time: 10 minutes

- Combine first 6 ingredients in a cocktail shaker.
- Shake well.
- Put 2 teaspoons cherry juice and 1 lemon slice in each of 2 glasses.
- Pour in mixture and serve.

Champagne Punch

1/2	cup superfine sugar
1	cup Grand Marnier
2	10-ounce packages frozen peaches (in quick thaw pouch)
1	bottle dry white wine, chilled
2	bottles champagne, chilled

Servings: 25
Preparation time: 10 minutes
- Combine sugar and Grand Marnier in a punch bowl. Stir until sugar dissolves.
- Add peaches, wine and champagne.
- Serve chilled.

Holiday Eggnog

1	dozen eggs, separated
1	cup sugar
3/4	cup bourbon
1/4	cup rum
1/4	cup crème de cacao
1	quart heavy cream
	Nutmeg

Servings: 25
Preparation time: 30 minutes
- Beat egg yolks and sugar together until light in color.
- While beating, slowly add bourbon, rum and crème de cacao.
- Beat egg whites until stiff. Fold into yolk mixture.
- Whip cream and fold into egg mixture.
- Refrigerate.
- This is better made a day ahead.
- Sprinkle with nutmeg before serving.

Famous Mint Iced Tea

4-1/2 cups water, divided
6 sprigs of mint
3 tea bags, individual size
3/4 cup sugar
Juice of 3 lemons
2 cups cold water
Lemon slice and mint for garnish

Servings: 6
Preparation time: 25 minutes
- Make 2 separate pots of boiling water, 2-1/4 cups each.
- In one pot, put mint and tea bags. Cover and let sit for 15 minutes.
- In the other pot, put sugar and lemon juice.
- Pour water in pots through a strainer and combine.
- Add 2 cups cold water and refrigerate.
- When ready to serve, pour over ice.
- Garnish with lemon slice and fresh sprig of mint.
- If tea should cloud, add a bit of boiling water to clear.

Desserts

Caramel Soufflé with English Custard Sauce

Soufflé
4	cups sugar
12	egg whites
2-1/2	tablespoons water

English Custard
3/4	cup sugar
3	cups milk
12	egg yolks
2	tablespoons butter
1	teaspoon vanilla extract
1	cup heavy cream

Servings: 8
Preparation time: 1-1/2 hours
Baking time: 1 hour

- Preheat oven to 300° F.
- Put 1-1/2 cups sugar in a skillet and heat over medium heat until it turns light brown and liquid.
- Pour immediately into a greased 3-quart casserole or bundt pan, turning pan to coat sides and bottom.
- Beat egg whites until stiff.
- Add 2 cups sugar gradually, beating constantly.
- Brown remaining 1/2 cup sugar in skillet. Add approximately 2-1/2 tablespoons water and cook until syrup forms a thread.
- Beat egg whites with a mixer at medium speed while adding syrup. Then finish blending at high speed.
- Pour into casserole, place in a shallow pan of water and bake for 1 hour or until firm but light.
- Cool. Invert onto a serving platter and cover with English custard.

- Mix sugar and milk. Cook in the top of a double boiler until hot.
- Beat egg yolks until they are thick and lemon colored.
- Add butter and egg yolks to hot sugar and milk mixture.
- Continue to cook until mixture thickens slightly and coats a spoon.
- Remove from heat and allow to cool.
- Add vanilla and either whipped or unwhipped cream.

Frozen Chocolate Crêpes with Custard Sauce

Crêpes

2	eggs
1/2	cup Bisquick
3/4	cup milk
1	tablespoon Crisco, melted
1	teaspoon vanilla extract
1	tablespoon sugar
2-1/2	tablespoons unsweetened cocoa
	Additional Crisco for greasing pan

Chocolate Filling

1	12-ounce package semisweet chocolate chips
1-1/2	teaspoons vanilla extract
1/8	teaspoon salt
1-1/2	cups whipping cream, scalded
6	egg yolks

Servings: 16
Preparation time: 20 minutes
Cooking time: 5 minutes
Freezing time: 2 hours

- Combine first 7 ingredients. Process in a blender until smooth. Batter will be thin and creamy.
- Let rest in refrigerator for 1/2 hour.
- Heat a 6-1/2-inch crêpe pan or iron skillet over medium high heat. Grease bottom lightly with Crisco.
- Using a 1-ounce measure, pour a scant measure of batter into hot pan. Tilt to cover bottom.
- Cook until crêpe looks almost dry on top, turn and brown other side.
- Turn crêpe onto waxed paper. Grease pan with Crisco again, repeating step between each crêpe.
- Layer crêpes between sheets of waxed paper.

- Combine chocolate, vanilla and salt in blender. Add cream and mix for 30 seconds or until chocolate melts.
- Add yolks. Mix for 5 seconds. Transfer to a bowl and cool.
- Divide filling mixture among crêpes, using a generous tablespoon for each crêpe.
- Roll up and wrap well for freezer. Freeze.

continued...

Frozen Chocolate Crêpes with Custard Sauce continued...

Custard Sauce

4	large egg yolks
1-1/2	tablespoons cornstarch
1/2	cup sugar
1-1/2	cups Half and Half
1/2	teaspoon vanilla extract
	Chocolate curls for garnish

- Combine egg yolks, cornstarch and sugar in a small bowl.
- Scald Half and Half. Add slowly to yolk mixture, whisking rapidly.
- Pour into the top of a double boiler. Cook over simmering water until thickened.
- When thickened, cool quickly by putting pan into cold water and stirring with whisk.
- Add vanilla. Strain into bowl to remove lumps.
- To serve, remove crêpes from freezer 20 minutes before serving. Custard sauce should be sitting in warm water ready to use. Spoon sauce over each crêpe and garnish with chocolate curls.

Baked Brie in Puff Pastry

4	Pepperidge Farms puff pastry patty shells
2	4-1/2-ounce rounds of Brie cheese
1	large egg
1	tablespoon milk
3	ripe pears
3	crisp apples

Servings: 8
Preparation time: 10 minutes
Cooking time: 25 to 30 minutes

- Thaw patty shells.
- Preheat oven to 425° F.
- Place 2 patty shells next to each other. roll into a large circle, blending shells together.
- Place a round of cheese in center of pastry. Bring edges together as though wrapping a package. Seal edges together by pressing dough.
- Repeat procedure with other 2 patty shells.
- Beat egg and milk together. Brush each round with mixture until well coated.
- Place rounds on a buttered baking sheet.
- Bake for 25 to 30 minutes, until pastry is puffed and brown.
- Serve with slices of fresh fruit.

Crêpes Floridian

Dessert Crêpes

1	cup all-purpose flour
1	cup milk
1/8	teaspoon salt
3	eggs
2	tablespoons butter, melted
1	tablespoon sugar

Servings: 6 to 7
Preparation time: 1-1/2 hours
Cooking time: 15 minutes
Standing time: 1 hour

- Combine all ingredients in a blender. Blend until all lumps are dissolved.
- Let mixture stand at room temperature for 1 hour or chill overnight in refrigerator.
- If necessary, add more milk to make batter the consistency of light cream.
- Lightly brush a 7-inch crêpe pan with oil and heat until a drop of batter sizzles when dropped in pan.
- Pour 2 to 3 tablespoons of batter into pan, turning quickly to coat bottom evenly.
- Cook over medium heat until crêpe browns on bottom.
- Turn crêpe over and brown other side.
- Makes 12 to 14 crêpes.

Filling

1	12-ounce package cream cheese
1/4	cup sugar
1-1/2	tablespoons freshly grated orange rind
3 to 4	tablespoons orange juice
1/4	cup finely chopped pecans

- Combine all ingredients and whip until fluffy.

continued...

Please note the following corrections to Jacksonville & Company:

p. 20   "Bacon and Onion Roll-Ups"
Last instruction should be "Bake for 15 minutes."

p. 21   "Chicken Teriyaki"
Baking time should be "15 minutes".

p. 87   "Chicken Breasts and Artichokes in Champagne Sauce"
First instruction should be "Preheat oven to 375°F."
Fifth instruction of top section add "Reduce oven temperature to 200°F."

p. 110   "Mosquito Lagoon Duck Breasts"
This recipe is particularly for wild duck.

p. 169   "Dill Muffins"
First instruction should be "Spoon into greased miniature muffin tins, filling 2/3 full."

p. 212   "Hot Fudge Sauce"
Delete "1 teaspoon salt" from ingredients.

p. 228   "Broccoli Bisque"
"2 tablespoons salt" should be "2 teaspoons salt."

p. 281   "Mrs. Dearing's Mayonnaise Cake"
"5 cups cocoa" should be "1/2 cup cocoa."

Crêpes Floridian continued...

Sauce

1/2	cup sugar
1-1/2	tablespoons cornstarch
1-1/2	cups orange juice
1/8	teaspoon salt
1/4	cup chopped pecans
1	ounce Curaçao liqueur (optional)
2	tablespoons butter
	Thinly sliced orange for garnish

- Mix sugar and cornstarch with 1/4 cup orange juice.
- Heat remaining 1-1/4 cups orange juice to boiling point. Add sugar mixture and cook, stirring constantly, until clear and thickened.
- Remove from heat, add remaining ingredients and stir until butter melts.
- To assemble, spoon 2 tablespoons of filling in the middle of each crêpe.
- Roll crêpe and place, folded side down, in an electric skillet or baking dish.
- Set aside until time to serve.
- Just before serving, pour sauce over crêpes and heat until sauce bubbles.
- Garnish with orange slices and serve warm.

Spiked Apple Crisp

5	cups peeled and sliced apples
1/2	teaspoon ground cinnamon
1	teaspoon grated lemon rind
1	teaspoon grated orange rind
1	ounce Grand Marnier
1	ounce Amaretto
3/4	cup sugar
1/4	cup light brown sugar
3/4	cup all-purpose flour, sifted
1/4	teaspoon salt
1/2	cup butter

Servings: 8
Preparation time: 30 minutes
Baking time: 1 hour

- Preheat oven to 350° F.
- Arrange apple slices in a greased 2-quart casserole.
- Sprinkle cinnamon, lemon and orange rinds, Grand Marnier and Amaretto on top of apples.
- Combine sugars, flour, salt and butter until crumbly.
- Spread sugar mixture over apples.
- Bake for approximately 1 hour or until apples are tender and top is brown.
- Serve topped with vanilla ice cream or whipped cream.

Apple Dumplings

Sauce

2	cups sugar
2	cups water
1	teaspoon ground cinnamon
1	teaspoon ground nutmeg
4	tablespoons butter

6 to 8   medium apples

Dumplings

2	cups all-purpose flour
1	teaspoon salt
2	teaspoons baking powder
3/4	cup shortening
1/2	cup milk
	Sugar to taste
	Ground cinnamon to taste
1	tablespoon butter, per apple
	Heavy cream, lightly whipped

Servings: 6 to 8
Preparation time: 1 hour
Cooking time: 1 hour

- Preheat oven to 375° F.
- Combine all ingredients in a medium saucepan.
- Cook for 5 minutes. Set aside.
- Core and peel apples.
- Sift all dry ingredients.
- Cut in shortening and add milk.
- Roll dough to a 1/8-inch thickness and cut into squares large enough to cover each apple.
- Place an apple in the center of each pastry square, sprinkle with sugar and cinnamon and dot with butter.
- Fold corners to top and seal.
- Place apples in a 9 X 13-inch baking dish. Pour sauce around apples.
- Bake for 1 hour.
- Serve warm with whipped cream.

Pineapple Sherbet

1	cup unsweetened pineapple juice
1-1/3	cups sugar
	Juice and grated rind of 1 lemon
1	quart milk

Servings: 8
Preparation time: 5 minutes
Freezing time: 6 hours

- Mix pineapple juice and sugar.
- Add lemon juice and rind.
- Add milk and stir.
- Pour into a loaf pan and freeze.

Lemon Snow Pudding with Custard Sauce

DESSERTS

Pudding

1	envelope unflavored gelatin
1/2	cup cold water
3/4	cup boiling water
3/4	cup sugar
1/4	teaspoon salt
1/4	cup fresh lemon juice
1	teaspoon grated lemon rind
2	egg whites, stiffly beaten
	Fruit for garnish

Servings: 6
Preparation time: 30 minutes
Chilling time: 3 hours

- Soften gelatin in cold water.
- Add boiling water, sugar and salt. Stir until all is dissolved.
- Stir in lemon juice and rind.
- Chill until mixture is slightly thick. Then whip with electric mixer until light and fluffy.
- Fold in egg whites.
- Spoon mixture into an oiled 1-quart mold or 6 small molds. Chill until firm.
- Unmold and serve with custard sauce. Garnish with fruit.

Custard Sauce

2	egg yolks
3	tablespoons sugar
1/8	teaspoon salt
1	cup milk
1/2	teaspoon vanilla extract

- Combine first 4 ingredients in top of a double boiler.
- Cook over simmering water until mixture thickens.
- Stir in vanilla.
- Pour into a covered container and chill.

Strawberries au Chocolat

1	pint fresh strawberries, rinsed and hulled
2	tablespoons sugar
1/4	cup cognac
1/2	pint heavy cream
1	tablespoon confectioners' sugar
4	chocolate dessert cups (see Index) or buy prepared cups

Servings: 4
Preparation time: 20 minutes

- Sprinkle with sugar and cognac. Allow to sit for 15 minutes.
- Meanwhile, whip cream with confectioners' sugar until thick.
- Gently remove strawberries with a slotted spoon and place in chocolate cups, reserving 4 small berries.
- Cover with whipped cream and place a berry on top of each dessert.

257

Meringues with Strawberries and Custard

Meringues

1	cup sugar
1/2	teaspoon baking powder
1/8	teaspoon salt
3	egg whites at room temperature (use extra large eggs)
1	teaspoon cold water
1	teaspoon vanilla extract
1	teaspoon vinegar

Custard

3	egg yolks
1/4	cup sugar
1/8	teaspoon salt
1-1/2	cups milk
1	teaspoon vanilla extract
2	pints strawberries
1/4	cup sugar
	Whipped cream for garnish

Servings: 12
Preparation time: 30 minutes
Baking time: 2 hours

- Preheat oven to 275° F.
- Mix sugar, baking powder and salt. Set aside.
- Whip egg whites slowly until stiff. Add cold water and continue beating. Slowly add sugar mixture, 1 tablespoon at a time, beating constantly. Add vanilla and vinegar.
- Dampen a piece of brown paper cut to fit a cookie sheet. Form 12 cups of meringue on paper.
- Bake for 1 hour, turn off oven and leave meringues in oven for 1 more hour.

- Put yolks in the top of a double boiler and beat with whisk. Add half each of the sugar, salt and milk, mixing until smooth. Add rest of sugar, salt and milk. Stir well.
- Cook over hot water, stirring constantly, until mixture coats spoon.
- Remove from heat and set pan in cold water to cool.
- Stir in vanilla.
- Wash strawberries before capping, cap and toss with sugar. Chill.
- To serve, fill meringues with strawberries and spoon custard over berries. Garnish with whipped cream.

Frozen Grand Marnier Soufflé with Hot Strawberry Sauce

Soufflé

2	pints vanilla ice cream
4	macaroons, crumbled
8	teaspoons Grand Marnier
1	cup heavy cream
4	teaspoons slivered almonds, toasted
4	teaspoons confectioners' sugar

Servings: 8
Preparation time: 15 minutes
Freezing time: 6 hours or overnight

- Slightly soften ice cream.
- Stir in macaroons and Grand Marnier.
- Whip cream until thick. Fold into ice cream mixture.
- Spoon into a 6-cup metal mold or individual molds.
- Sprinkle with almonds and confectioners' sugar.
- Cover and freeze for 6 hours or overnight.
- To unmold, wrap in a hot towel and loosen edges with a knife.
- Spoon hot strawberry sauce over the top.

Sauce

1	pound whole frozen strawberries, thawed
	Sugar to taste
8	teaspoons Grand Marnier

- Put berries in a saucepan with sugar and simmer until berries are just soft.
- Remove from heat and stir in Grand Marnier.

Green Grapes in Snow

2	pounds Thompson grapes, stemmed and washed
1/2	cup kirsch
1	pint sour cream
1/2	cup brown sugar
	Mint leaves for garnish

Servings: 6 to 8
Preparation time: 15 minutes
Soaking time: 2 hours

- Soak grapes in kirsch for 2 hours.
- Just before serving, stir in sour cream.
- Serve in champagne glasses. Sprinkle with brown sugar and garnish with mint leaves.
- Strawberries may also be used.

DESSERTS

Charlotte Malakoff

1	envelope Knox unflavored gelatin
2	tablespoons cold water
3	1-ounce squares semisweet chocolate
1/2	cup water
4	egg yolks
1/2	cup sugar
	Salt to taste
1	teaspoon vanilla extract
4	egg whites
1/2	teaspoon cream of tartar
1/4	cup sugar
1/2	cup chopped pecans
1/4	cup heavy cream, whipped
3	dozen single lady fingers or 18 double lady fingers, dipped in crème de cacao
	Whipped cream for garnish
	Chocolate for garnish

Servings: 8 to 10
Preparation time: 1 hour
Cooking time: 15 minutes
Chilling time: 8 hours

- Must be prepared ahead.
- Soften gelatin in cold water.
- In a saucepan, combine chocolate and water.
- Stir constantly over low heat until chocolate melts and is smooth.
- Remove chocolate mixture from heat and add gelatin. Stir.
- Set aside to cool.
- Beat egg yolks with a mixer until thick and lemon colored. Gradually beat in 1/2 cup sugar. Add salt and vanilla.
- Gradually beat in chocolate mixture.
- Beat egg whites and cream of tartar until soft peaks form. Gradually add 1/4 cup sugar.
- Fold egg whites into chocolate mixture. Fold in whipped cream and pecans.
- Set aside 10 single lady fingers.
- Line the bottom of an 8-inch spring-form pan (or a crystal or silver bowl) with lady fingers, cutting to fit. Line sides by standing lady fingers on end.
- Fill with half the chocolate mixture, layer the reserved lady fingers. Then top with the remaining chocolate.
- Chill for 8 hours or overnight.
- Garnish top with whipped cream and shaved chocolate.

Fresh Lemon Charlotte Russe

4	eggs, separated
1/2	cup fresh lemon juice
1/8	teaspoon salt
1	envelope unflavored gelatin
1-1/2	cups sugar, divided
3	tablespoons butter
1-1/2	teaspoons grated lemon rind
1	teaspoon vanilla extract
24	double lady fingers, split in half
1	cup heavy cream, whipped
	Whipped cream for garnish
	Lemon slices for garnish

Servings: 10
Preparation time: 45 minutes
Chilling time: 6 hours

- Combine egg yolks, lemon juice and salt in the top of a double boiler. Mix well.
- Stir in gelatin and 1 cup sugar.
- Cook over simmering water for 15 minutes or until thickened, stirring constantly.
- Add butter, lemon rind and vanilla, stirring until butter melts.
- Chill mixture until partially thickened.
- Arrange lady fingers around bottom and sides of a 9-1/2-inch spring-form pan, cutting to make fit.
- Beat egg whites until soft peaks form. Then gradually add remaining 1/2 cup sugar. Continue beating until stiff peaks form.
- Fold whipped cream and gelatin mixture into egg whites.
- Spoon into prepared pan.
- Cover and chill for 5 hours or overnight.
- Garnish with whipped cream and twisted slice of lemon.

Pears Poached in Wine

3	firm ripe pears
1/2	cup port or Dubonnet
1/2	teaspoon grated lemon rind
4	tablespoons mild honey
2	tablespoons lemon juice
2	tablespoons water
1	cup heavy cream, whipped

Servings: 4
Preparation time: 5 minutes
Cooking time: 15 minutes

- Peel and quarter pears.
- Combine pears, port, lemon rind, honey, lemon juice and water in a saucepan.
- Poach for 15 minutes.
- Chill in sauce.
- Garnish with whipped cream before serving.

Fresh Fruit in Grand Marnier Sauce

Fruit

4	navel oranges, peeled and sliced
2	medium bananas, sliced
2	medium apples, sliced
1-1/2	cups fresh strawberries
1-1/2	cups seedless grapes
2	tablespoons sugar

Grand Marnier Sauce

4	egg yolks
2	teaspoons cornstarch
1/2	cup sugar
1	cup milk, scalded
1/4	cup Grand Marnier
1	teaspoon vanilla extract
1	teaspoon grated orange rind
1/2	cup heavy cream

Servings: 6
Preparation time: 30 minutes
Chilling time: 2 hours

- Combine all the fruit in a large glass bowl. Sprinkle with sugar. Cover and refrigerate.
- Combine egg yolks, cornstarch and sugar in the top of a double boiler.
- Add milk. Mix with a wire whisk.
- Cook over simmering water, stirring constantly with whisk, until custard thickens and will coat a spoon.
- Remove from heat and stir in Grand Marnier, vanilla and orange rind.
- Cool sauce completely. Then chill for at least 2 hours.
- Just before serving, whip cream and fold into sauce.
- Drain any liquid from fruit. Pour sauce over all.

Strawberry Sorbet

3	pints fresh strawberries
2	cups sugar
1-1/2	cups orange juice
1/2	cup lemon juice
1/2	cup Grand Marnier
	Mint leaves and strawberries for garnish

Servings: 8
Preparation time: 20 minutes
Freezing time: 6 hours

- Wash and hull strawberries.
- Combine strawberries, sugar and juices in a blender or food processor. Pulverize to liquid form.
- Add Grand Marnier and stir.
- Pour into a 2-1/2-quart baking dish and freeze to the consistency of sherbet.
- Scoop into balls and serve in a crystal bowl garnished with fresh strawberries and mint leaves.

Chocolate Cups

1	6-ounce package semisweet chocolate chips
8	paper cupcake liners

Servings: 8 cups
Preparation time: 20 minutes
Cooking time: 5 minutes
Chilling time: 1 hour

- Melt chocolate in the top of a double boiler, over hot, not boiling, water.
- When chocolate is almost melted, remove from heat and let stand to complete melting.
- Brush chocolate on inside of cupcake liners, building sides thickly and dividing equally into cups.
- Chill to harden.
- Peel off paper and store in a cool place until ready to use.
- May fill cups with chocolate mousse, champagne mousse or any ice cream topped with sauce.

Honey Ice Cream

1	cup heavy cream
2	cups light cream
2	egg yolks, beaten
1/3	cup honey
1/4	teaspoon salt
1	tablespoon vanilla extract

Servings: 6 to 8
Preparation time: 20 minutes
Cooking time: 20 minutes
Freezing time: 1 hour in freezer
　　　　　　　4 hours in trays

- Whip heavy cream. Cover and refrigerate.
- In the top of a double boiler, combine light cream, yolks, honey and salt.
- Cook over simmering water, stirring constantly, until mixture thickens and coats a spoon.
- Remove from heat and stir in vanilla.
- Cool thoroughly. Then fold in whipped cream.
- Freeze according to ice cream freezer instructions, or in ice trays, stirring once during freezing time.

Fresh Coconut Torte

1	pint heavy cream
3	eggs, separated
	Juice of 1 orange
	Grated rind of 1 orange
	Juice of 1-1/2 lemons
	Grated rind of 1 lemon
1/2	cup butter, softened
1-1/4	cups confectioners' sugar
1	cup grated fresh coconut
30	ladyfingers
3	tablespoons confectioners' sugar
1	cup grated fresh coconut
1	dozen or more perfect strawberries

Servings: 12
Preparation time: 30 minutes
Chilling time: 8 hours

- Whip cream. Set aside.
- Whip egg whites until stiff. Set aside.
- Beat egg yolks, citrus juices and rinds together with a fork. Set aside.
- Cream butter and sugar in a large mixing bowl.
- Gradually beat yolk mixture into sugar and butter.
- Fold half the whipped cream into mixture. Cover and refrigerate remaining whipped cream.
- Fold egg whites into mixture.
- Fold in 1 cup coconut.
- Line a large mold, bowl or springform pan with waxed paper.
- Split ladyfingers. Line bottom and sides of bowl.
- Pour half the mixture over ladyfingers.
- Place a layer of ladyfingers on mixture and top with remaining mixture.
- Cover and chill for at least 8 hours.
- Turn out on a silver platter or plate. Ice with remaining whipped cream.
- Sprinkle with confectioners' sugar and 1 cup coconut.
- Garnish with strawberries.

Watermelon Ice

2/3	cup sugar
3/4	cup water
3-1/2	cups chopped, seeded watermelon
1/2	cup lemon juice

Servings: 8 to 10
Preparation time: 15 minutes
Freezing time: 4 to 6 hours

- Combine sugar and water in a saucepan. Bring to a boil over high heat.
- Boil mixture gently for 4 minutes. Remove from heat and cool.
- Purée watermelon in a blender or food processor. Add sugar mixture and lemon juice while continuing to process.
- If using processor, freeze mixture in processor bowl. If not using processor, freeze in a metal bowl.
- Freeze until a solid rim of ice is around the edge of bowl and the center is mushy, about 3 to 4 hours.
- Process or blend again for approximately 2 to 3 minutes, until light.
- Return to freezer and freeze until firm.

The Girdlebuster

1/2	gallon coffee ice cream
1/2	gallon chocolate ice cream
2	dozen coconut macaroons
6	Heath bars, cracked
	Hot Fudge Sauce (see Index)

Servings: 16
Preparation time: 30 minutes
Freezing time: 3 hours

- Soften coffee and chocolate ice cream.
- In the bottom of a 9-inch spring-form pan, crumble 3 macaroons to form a thin layer.
- Add a fourth of the coffee ice cream.
- Crumble 3 more macaroons and press into layer.
- Add a fourth of the chocolate ice cream.
- Sprinkle on a fourth of the Heath bars.
- Repeat all steps to form three more layers, ending with Heath bars.
- Freeze for 3 hours.

Coconut Mousse

3	envelopes unflavored gelatin
1/3	cup boiling water
1	pint Half and Half
2	cups freshly grated coconut (grated by hand)
1	cup sugar
1	teaspoon almond extract
1-1/2	pints heavy cream

Servings: 10
Preparation time: 30 minutes
Chilling time: 6 hours

- Dissolve gelatin in boiling water.
- In a saucepan, bring Half and Half to boiling. Then cool.
- Add coconut.
- Add gelatin mixture and sugar. Stir to dissolve.
- Add almond extract to heavy cream. Beat until stiff.
- Fold whipped cream into coconut mixture and pour into an 8-cup mold.
- Chill for 6 hours.
- Decorate with fresh flowers.

Kahlua Mousse

5	cups milk
9	egg yolks
3/4	cup sugar
1/8	teaspoon salt
1/4	cup sherry
2	teaspoons vanilla extract
1	cup heavy cream
2	dozen ladyfingers
	Kahlua

Servings: 16
Preparation time: 30 minutes

- Heat milk in the top of a double boiler until bubbles form around edge of pan.
- Beat egg yolks with sugar and salt until well blended.
- Gradually pour hot milk into egg mixture, beating constantly. Return to double boiler. Cook, stirring constantly, until custard is "batter" thick.
- Remove from heat. Add sherry and vanilla. Cover and refrigerate until cool.
- Whip heavy cream until stiff. Fold into custard.
- Line a clear glass bowl with ladyfingers sprinkled heavily with Kahlua.
- Fill bowl a third full with custard. Place a layer of ladyfingers on top. Repeat layers until bowl is full.
- Top may be decorated with more saturated ladyfingers and whipped cream.

Champagne Mousse

3/4 cup brut champagne
1/2 cup sugar
5 egg yolks
1-1/2 cups heavy cream
Chocolate Cups (see Index)
Champagne Chocolate Sauce (see Index)

Servings: 8
Preparation time: 30 minutes
Cooking time: 15 minutes
Freezing time: overnight

- Combine 1/2 cup champagne with sugar and bring to a boil in a saucepan.
- Slowly boil, *without stirring*, until syrup registers 236° F. on a candy thermometer or is at the soft ball stage.
- In a large bowl beat egg yolks until light and lemon colored.
- Add syrup in a thin stream, beating constantly.
- Continue beating until mixture is thick and creamy, about 10 minutes.
- Gradually blend in remaining 1/4 cup champagne.
- Whip cream until stiff. Fold into champagne mixture.
- Cover and freeze overnight.
- Serve in Chocolate Cups with Champagne Chocolate Sauce (see Index).

Chocolate Mint Ice Cream

2 eggs
3 cups whipping cream
1 cup milk
1/2 cup sugar
1/4 cup light Karo syrup
1 teaspoon vanilla extract
1/4 teaspoon salt
1/3 cup green crème de menthe
4 to 6 drops green food coloring
2 1-ounce squares semisweet chocolate, shaved

Servings: 8
Preparation time: 20 minutes
Freezing time: 4 hours

- Beat eggs for 4 minutes on high speed.
- Add cream, milk, sugar, Karo syrup, vanilla and salt.
- Beat until sugar is dissolved.
- Add crème de menthe and food coloring. Pour into a 4-quart ice cream freezer.
- Freeze according to manufacturer's directions.
- Stir in chocolate and cover.
- Pack with additional salt and ice using 1 part salt to 4 parts ice.
- Freeze for 4 hours.

Cheese Blintzes

Blintzes

2	eggs
1/2	teaspoon salt
1	cup all-purpose flour, sifted
1	cup water

Servings: 12
Preparation time: 40 minutes
Cooking time: 15 minutes

- Combine eggs and salt. Beat until lemon colored.
- Alternately add flour and water, beating until smooth. Should be the consistency of cream. Add more water if mixture is too thick.
- Grease a 6-inch skillet and heat on medium heat.
- Pour enough batter into skillet to make a very thin pancake, tilting skillet from side to side to cover bottom.
- Cook on one side only.
- Cool on paper towel, bottom side up.
- Regrease skillet after each pancake is made.

Filling

1	3-ounce package cream cheese
1	pound farmers cheese
1	egg, beaten
	Sugar to taste
1/4	teaspoon salt
	Sour cream
	Sugar

- Combine cheeses.
- Add egg and stir until smooth.
- Add sugar and salt.
- Place rounded tablespoon of filling on each pancake and fold over from all sides into an envelope shape.
- Serve hot with sour cream and sugar on top.
- May be made ahead and frozen.

Exceptional Chocolate Mousse

DESSERTS

8	ounces semisweet chocolate
1/2	pound butter
8	egg yolks
1/2	teaspoon vanilla extract
2	tablespoons chocolate mint, coffee or almond liqueur
8	egg whites
1	cup sugar
1/2	cup toasted almonds or shaved chocolate for garnish

Servings: 8 to 10
Preparation time: 40 minutes
Freezing time: 4 hours

- Melt chocolate and butter in the top of a double boiler or microwave oven.
- Stir to blend. Then remove from heat.
- Stir in egg yolks, vanilla and liqueur. Set aside to cool.
- Beat egg whites until fluffy.
- Add sugar gradually while beating.
- Fold in melted chocolate mixture.
- Pour into a 2-quart dish or individual parfaits.
- Cover with plastic wrap and freeze.
- Before serving, sprinkle with almonds or shaved chocolate.

Orange Ice

1	envelope unflavored gelatin
1/4	cup cold water
1	cup sugar
1	cup water, boiling
3	cups fresh orange juice
4	tablespoons fresh lemon juice
1/2	pint whipping cream
4	tablespoons plus 1 teaspoon sugar
1	cup chopped pecans, toasted

Servings: 6
Preparation time: 20 minutes
Freezing time: 4 hours

- Dissolve gelatin in 1/4 cup water.
- Add 1 cup sugar to 1 cup water. Stir until dissolved.
- Add orange juice, lemon juice and gelatin. Mix well.
- Pour into a deep ice tray and freeze. Stir occasionally.
- When ready to serve, scoop orange ice into sherbet or parfait glasses. Whip cream with 4 tablespoons plus 1 teaspoon sugar.
- Spoon on ice.
- Sprinkle pecans on top and serve at once.

Cold Lemon Soufflé

1	envelope unflavored gelatin
1/4	cup cold water
5	egg yolks
3/4	cup lemon juice
2	teaspoons grated lemon rind
3/4	cup sugar
5	egg whites
3/4	cup sugar
1	cup heavy cream
1	10-ounce package frozen raspberries

Servings: 6
Preparation time: 45 minutes
Chilling time: 4 hours

- Sprinkle gelatin over water. Set aside.
- Combine egg yolks, lemon juice, lemon rind and 3/4 cup sugar in the top of a double boiler.
- Cook mixture over simmering water for 20 minutes.
- Remove custard from heat and stir in gelatin.
- Put custard in refrigerator or freezer to cool, about 15 minutes.
- When custard is cool, beat egg whites until they hold their peaks. Then gradually add 3/4 cup sugar.
- Whip cream until stiff.
- Fold together whipped cream, egg whites and lemon mixture.
- Pour into a 2-quart dish. Cover and chill.
- Purée raspberries in a blender and spoon over soufflé when serving.

Caramelized Pears

1	29-ounce can pear halves
4	tablespoons unsalted butter
1/2	teaspoon ground cinnamon
1/4 to 1/2	cup sliced almonds, toasted
1/2	cup heavy cream

Servings: 8
Preparation time: 20 minutes
Baking time: 20 to 30 minutes

- Preheat oven to 350° F.
- Drain pears and reserve syrup.
- Boil syrup until only a few tablespoons remain or until caramelized.
- Add butter and cinnamon. Mix well.
- Arrange pears in a large, round, shallow dish with narrow end of pears toward center.
- Pour sauce over pears and sprinkle with almonds.
- Bake for 20 to 30 minutes.
- Pour cream over center of pears and serve.

Cakes & Pies

"The Sisters" Bourbon Pound Cake

Cake

1	cup margarine
2-1/2	cups sugar
6	eggs
3	cups all-purpose flour
2	teaspoons baking powder
1	teaspoon salt
1/2	teaspoon ground nutmeg
1	cup sour cream
1/2	cup bourbon
1	cup finely chopped pecans

Bourbon Glaze

3/4	cup water
1	cup sugar
1/4	cup bourbon

Servings: 16
Preparation time: 30 minutes
Baking time: 1-1/4 hours

- Preheat oven to 325° F.
- Spray a 10-inch tube pan with Pam.
- Cream margarine and sugar with an electric mixer until light and fluffy.
- Add eggs, one at a time.
- Sift together flour, baking powder, salt and nutmeg.
- To batter, add flour mixture alternately with sour cream and bourbon, beginning and ending with flour.
- Stir in pecans.
- Turn batter into prepared pan.
- Bake on lower rack in oven for 1-1/4 hours or until done.
- After removing cake from oven, pour bourbon glaze over cake while it is still in pan.

- Combine water and sugar in a small saucepan.
- Bring to a low boil. Boil for 5 minutes.
- Remove glaze from heat and stir in bourbon.

Coconut Pound Cake

1	cup evaporated milk
6	eggs
1/2	cup butter
1	cup Crisco
3	cups sugar
3	cups all-purpose flour
1	teaspoon baking powder
1/2	teaspoon salt
1	teaspoon vanilla extract
1	teaspoon lemon extract
1	7-ounce package Angel Flake coconut

Servings: 12
Preparation time: 20 minutes
Baking time: 1-1/4 hours

- Have milk, eggs and butter at room temperature.
- Preheat oven to 350° F.
- Cream butter, Crisco and sugar in a large bowl.
- Add eggs, one at a time, beating after each addition.
- Sift dry ingredients. Add alternately with milk to butter mixture.
- Add vanilla and lemon extracts.
- Stir in coconut.
- Bake in a greased tube pan for 1-1/4 hours.

Fresh Apple Pound Cake

1-1/2	cups vegetable oil
2	cups sugar
3	eggs
3	cups all-purpose flour
1	teaspoon salt
1	teaspoon baking soda
2	teaspoons vanilla extract
3	large apples, peeled and diced
1	cup chopped pecans

Servings: 12
Preparation time: 30 minutes
Baking time: 1 hour, 20 minutes

- Preheat oven to 325° F.
- Combine oil, sugar and eggs. Beat for 3 minutes.
- Add flour, salt and soda. Blend well.
- Add vanilla.
- Fold in apples and pecans.
- Pour batter into a greased and lightly floured bundt or tube pan.
- Bake for 1 hour and 20 minutes.
- Cool for 20 minutes before covering with sauce.

Sauce

1/2	cup butter
1/2	cup brown sugar, lightly packed
2	tablespoons milk

- Combine butter, brown sugar and milk in a saucepan.
- Bring to boil over medium heat, stirring constantly. Continue to cook for 10 minutes.
- While sauce is still hot, drizzle over cooled cake.

Bloomingdale's Pound Cake

Cake

1	cup butter, softened
2	cups sugar
4	eggs
2	teaspoons vanilla extract
1	cup milk
3	tablespoons baking powder
3	cups all-purpose flour
1-1/2	ounces sweet chocolate, melted
1/8	teaspoon salt
1/8	teaspoon baking soda
2	tablespoons milk
	Powdered sugar

Servings: 12
Preparation time: 30 to 45 minutes
Baking time: 45 minutes

- Preheat oven to 350° F.
- Grease, flour and sugar a 10-inch tube pan. Chill while preparing batter.
- Cream butter and sugar. Add eggs, one at a time.
- Add vanilla, 1 cup milk, baking powder and flour in order listed.
- Pour half the batter into prepared pan.
- Mix chocolate, salt, baking soda, 2 tablespoons milk and 2 tablespoons of the reserved batter.
- Pour this mixture over the first layer of batter and swirl with 2 knives to marbleize.
- Pour remaining batter on top and place pan on a baking sheet in middle of oven.
- Bake for 45 minutes. Do not overcook.
- Sprinkle with powdered sugar.
- Serve with rum sauce while cake is warm.
- May be made a day ahead, wrapped in foil and warmed in a 200° F. oven.
- May be frozen several months if wrapped well.

Rum Sauce

6	egg yolks
1	cup sugar
2/3	cup light or dark rum
1	cup heavy cream, slightly whipped

- Beat egg yolks and sugar.
- Add rum and stir gently until thickened.
- Add whipped cream.
- Warm in the top of a double boiler and serve over warm pound cake.

Lafayette Grill Cake

Cake

4	squares unsweetened chocolate
1/2	cup butter
1	cup water
2	cups sugar
1/2	cup sour cream
1-1/2	teaspoons baking soda
2	cups all-purpose flour
2	eggs

Custard

1/2	cup all-purpose flour
4/5	cup sugar (1 cup less 5 teaspoons)
1-1/2	cups milk
1-1/2	squares unsweetened chocolate
2	egg yolks
1	teaspoon vanilla extract

Icing

2	egg whites
1-1/2	cups sugar
5	tablespoons water
1/4	teaspoon cream of tartar
6	marshmallows
1	teaspoon vanilla extract

Servings: 16
Preparation time: 30 minutes
Cooking time: 55 minutes

- Preheat oven to 350° F.
- In a small saucepan, melt chocolate and butter. When melted, pour into a large bowl.
- Bring water to a boil in the pan chocolate was in.
- Add water to chocolate mixture. Mix only by hand.
- Blend sugar, sour cream and baking soda. Add to batter and mix by hand.
- Blend in flour and eggs, one at a time.
- Pour into two 9-inch layer pans lined with waxed paper.
- Bake for 25 minutes.
- While cakes bake, prepare custard.

- Combine flour and sugar.
- Melt chocolate and milk together.
- Add flour mixture. Stir on top of stove until thick and lumpy.
- Add some custard to egg yolks. Then blend egg yolks back into remaining chocolate.
- Cook 1 minute longer. Remove from heat.
- Fold in vanilla. Cover with plastic wrap and cool.

- In the top of a double boiler, place first 5 ingredients and put over boiling water. Beat for 7 minutes with an electric mixer on high speed while ingredients are cooking.
- Remove from heat and continue beating until thick enough to spread. Add vanilla.
- Place custard between completely cooled cake layers. Frost with icing.
- If made ahead, do not refrigerate.

No Mix Chocolate Cake

Cake

1	cup butter
4	tablespoons cocoa
7/8	cup water
2	cups all-purpose flour
2	cups sugar
1	teaspoon salt
1/2	cup buttermilk
2	eggs, slightly beaten
1	teaspoon baking soda
1	teaspoon vanilla extract

Servings: 12
Preparation time: 15 minutes
Baking time: 25 minutes

- Preheat oven to 400° F.
- Bring butter, cocoa and water to a boil in a saucepan.
- Combine flour, sugar and salt in a large bowl.
- Pour butter mixture into flour mixture. Stir to combine.
- Add remaining ingredients. Blend well.
- Pour into a greased and floured 9 X 14-inch baking pan.
- Bake for 25 minutes.
- Prepare chocolate icing 5 minutes before cake is done.

Chocolate Icing

1/2	cup butter
1/8	teaspoon salt
4	tablespoons cocoa
6	tablespoons milk
1	16-ounce box confectioners' sugar
1	teaspoon vanilla extract
1	cup broken pecan pieces or top with Peppermint Icing

- In a saucepan, bring butter, salt, cocoa and milk to a boil.
- Remove from heat and stir in sugar and vanilla.
- Add pecans to icing if not using Peppermint Icing.
- Spread on cake while cake is still hot.

Peppermint Icing

3	cups confectioners' sugar
5	tablespoons butter, softened
6	tablespoons milk or light cream
1	teaspoon peppermint extract Red or green food coloring to tint (optional)

- If icing with Peppermint Icing, be sure cake is completely cooled.
- Combine all ingredients in a large bowl.
- Stir by hand with a wooden spoon to combine.
- Spread on cake.

Sunshine Cake

Cake

8	egg whites
1/2	teaspoon cream of tartar
1-1/4	cups sugar
8	egg yolks
1	cup cake flour

Servings: 10 to 12
Preparation time: 2 hours
Baking time: 45 minutes
Chilling time: 12 to 24 hours

- Must be prepared 12 to 24 hours ahead.
- Preheat oven to 350° F.
- Beat egg whites until stiff. Add cream of tartar and sugar.
- Beat egg yolks until light and lemon colored. Fold into egg whites.
- Sift flour 3 times and carefully fold into egg mixture.
- Pour into an ungreased tube pan. Bake for 45 minutes.
- Remove from pan and cool.

Bavarian Cream Frosting

2-1/2	cups milk
1	cup sugar
1	tablespoon all-purpose flour
4	egg yolks, beaten
1	envelope Knox unflavored gelatin
3	tablespoons cold milk
1	teaspoon vanilla extract
1	cup heavy cream, whipped

- Combine milk, sugar and flour in the top of a double boiler.
- Cook over medium heat, stirring constantly, until thickened.
- Slowly add egg yolks and stir until thickened.
- Dissolve gelatin in cold milk and add to custard. Chill until firm but not set.
- Fold in vanilla and whipped cream.
- Chill until firm.
- Slice cake horizontally into three equal layers.
- Top each layer with Bavarian frosting.
- Once assembled, cover entire cake with frosting.
- Refrigerate until ready to serve.
- Use your favorite garnish for added color. Fresh sliced strawberries would enhance the appearance and taste.

Blueberry Cake

1/2	cup butter
1	cup sugar
3	eggs
1	cup sour cream
2	cups all-purpose flour, sifted
1	teaspoon baking powder
1/2	teaspoon salt
1	teaspoon vanilla extract
2-1/2	cups fresh blueberries, rinsed, drained and floured
3/4	cup brown sugar, firmly packed
3/4	cup chopped nuts
1	teaspoon ground cinnamon
	Whipped cream or confectioners' sugar

Servings: 12
Preparation time: 25 minutes
Baking time: 40 to 45 minutes

- Preheat oven to 350° F.
- Butter a 9 X 13 X 2-inch baking pan.
- Cream butter and sugar until fluffy.
- Add eggs, one at a time.
- Stir in sour cream.
- Add flour, baking powder, salt and vanilla. Beat until just blended.
- Gently fold in blueberries.
- Spread half the batter in baking pan.
- Mix brown sugar, nuts and cinnamon.
- Sprinkle mixture evenly over batter.
- Spread remaining batter in pan. Bake for 40 to 45 minutes.
- Cool in pan and cut into squares.
- Serve warm or cool, with confectioners' sugar or whipped cream.

Black Russian Cake

Cake

1	box Duncan Hines chocolate cake mix
1/2	cup salad oil
1	4-1/8-ounce box instant chocolate pudding
4	eggs
3/4	cup strong coffee
6	tablespoons Kahlua
6	tablespoons crème de cacao

Servings: 15 to 20
Preparation time: 20 minutes
Baking time: 45 minutes

- Preheat oven to 350° F.
- Combine all ingredients.
- Mix well.
- Pour in a greased and floured bundt pan.
- Bake for 40 to 45 minutes.
- Cool and remove from pan.

Icing

1	cup powdered sugar
2	tablespoons strong coffee
4	tablespoons crème de cacao

- Combine powdered sugar, coffee and crème de cacao.
- Punch holes in top of cake and drizzle icing over top.

Caramel Cake with Caramel Icing

Cake
1	cup butter
2	cups sugar
4	large eggs
3	cups sifted all-purpose flour
1	cup milk
1	tablespoon baking powder
1	teaspoon vanilla extract

Caramel Icing
2	pounds light brown sugar
4	tablespoons all-purpose flour
1/2	teaspoon salt
1-1/2	cups evaporated milk
3	tablespoons butter
2	tablespoons vanilla extract

Servings: 16
Preparation time: 20 minutes
Baking time: 25 minutes
Cooking time: 15 minutes

- Have butter, eggs and milk at room temperature.
- Preheat oven to 350° F.
- Cream butter and sugar in a large mixing bowl at high speed until sugar is dissolved.
- Separate eggs. Beat yolks until thick.
- Add yolks to creamed butter and sugar.
- Mix well.
- Set mixer on low speed. Add flour and milk alternately, beginning and ending with flour. Put baking powder in last addition of flour.
- Beat egg whites until stiff but not dry. Fold into batter.
- Add vanilla.
- Pour batter into 3 greased and lined 9-inch cake pans.
- Bake for 25 minutes.
- When cake is cool, frost with caramel icing.

- Mix sugar, flour and salt in a large heavy saucepan. Add milk.
- Let mixture come to a boil slowly. Continue cooking until it forms a firm ball when dropped in cold water, about 15 minutes or 225° F. on a candy thermometer.
- Remove from heat. Add butter and cool.
- Add vanilla and beat with mixer until thick and creamy.
- Add a few drops of evaporated milk as needed if icing becomes too thick to spread.

Mrs. Dearing's Mayonnaise Cake

Cake

1	cup sugar
2	cups all-purpose flour
2	teaspoons baking soda
5	cups cocoa
1	cup Hellmann's mayonnaise
1	cup cold water
1/8	teaspoon salt
1	teaspoon vanilla extract or 1 tablespoon dark rum

Sallie's White Icing

1	cup sugar
1	egg white (large egg)
1/4	teaspoon cream of tartar
1/2	cup boiling water
1	teaspoon vanilla extract or peppermint extract

Servings: 10 to 12
Preparation time: 30 minutes
Baking time: 25 minutes

- Preheat oven to 350° F.
- Sift sugar into a mixing bowl.
- Combine flour, soda and cocoa. Sift into sugar.
- Add mayonnaise, water, salt and vanilla. Beat with an electric mixer at medium speed until a few bubbles appear.
- Divide batter between 2 lightly greased and floured 9-inch cake pans.
- Bake for 25 minutes.
- Cool pans on wire racks. Turn out layers by inverting pans on brown paper.

- Warm the large bowl of mixer with hot water. Dry thoroughly.
- Blend sugar and egg white at low speed.
- Add cream of tartar, then boiling water. Turn mixer slowly to high speed.
- Beat until white holds a peak firmly, but not until stiff.
- Add extract.
- Ice cake.
- May decorate with shaved chocolate curls or melted chocolate drizzled over cake.
- This is best served on a plate with a fork. It is too moist for buffet serving with napkin only.

Aunt Em's Strawberry Shortcake

2	cups all-purpose flour
3	teaspoons baking powder
1/2	teaspoon salt
1/2	cup Crisco
2/3	cup milk
4	tablespoons butter
1/4	cup sugar
2	pints fresh strawberries, sliced
1/2	cup sugar
1	pint heavy cream, whipped
6	perfect strawberries for garnish

Servings: 8
Preparation time: 25 minutes
Baking time: 20 minutes

- Preheat oven to 450° F.
- Butter a 9-inch cake pan.
- Sift flour, baking powder and salt.
- Cut in shortening with a knife and fork until mixture resembles coarse meal.
- Add enough milk to make a soft dough.
- Turn onto a lightly floured surface and knead a few times.
- Divide dough in half.
- Pat half of dough into a 9-inch circle. Place in pan and brush with 2 tablespoons butter.
- Pat other half of dough into a 9-inch circle and place on top. Brush with 2 tablespoons butter.
- Bake for 20 minutes.
- After removing cake from oven, sprinkle top with 1/4 cup sugar.
- Toss strawberry slices with sugar.
- Pull apart layers of shortcake. Spoon strawberries between layers and on top.
- Top with whipped cream and garnish with whole strawberries.
- Shortcake is best when just out of oven.

Miniature Cream Cheese Tarts with Cherry Sauce

CAKES & PIES

Pastry
2	3-ounce packages cream cheese, softened
1	cup butter, softened
2	cups all-purpose flour

Filling
1	pint sour cream
5	tablespoons sugar
2	teaspoons vanilla extract

Cherry Sauce
1-1/2	tablespoons cornstarch
1/8	teaspoon ground cinnamon
1	16-ounce can pitted dark sweet cherries
2	tablespoons brandy
1/2	teaspoon lemon juice

Servings: 4 dozen tarts
Preparation time: 1 hour
Baking time: 15 to 20 minutes
Chilling time: 1 hour

- Mix cream cheese, butter and flour by hand. Form into a ball.
- Cover and chill for 1 hour.
- Form dough into 1-inch balls and press to fit in ungreased miniature muffin tins.
- Preheat oven to 350° F.
- Blend all ingredients.
- Fill each muffin cup with a heaping teaspoon of filling.
- Bake for 15 to 20 minutes, or until pastry is light brown and filling bubbles.
- Cool slightly in tins. Then remove to cooling racks.
- Combine cornstarch and cinnamon in a small saucepan.
- Drain cherries, reserving liquid.
- Gradually add cherry liquid to cornstarch mixture.
- Cook over medium heat, stirring constantly, until mixture thickens.
- Remove from heat and stir in brandy, lemon juice and cherries. Cool.
- Spoon a little sauce into each tart.

Kentucky Butter Cake

Cake

3	cups all-purpose flour
1	teaspoon baking powder
1	teaspoon salt
1/2	teaspoon baking soda
1	cup butter, softened
2	cups sugar
4	eggs
1	cup buttermilk
2	teaspoons vanilla extract

Sauce

1-1/2	cups sugar
1/3	cup water
3/4	cup butter
1-1/2	teaspoons vanilla extract

Servings: 12
Preparation time: 20 minutes
Baking time: 1-1/4 hours

- Preheat oven to 325° F.
- Sift all dry ingredients together. Set aside.
- Cream butter and sugar until well blended.
- Add eggs, one at a time, mixing well after each addition.
- Add buttermilk and vanilla. Mix well.
- Gradually add dry ingredients.
- Grease and flour only the bottom of a tube pan.
- Pour batter into pan. Bake for 1-1/4 hours.
- When cake as baked for 1 hour, combine all ingredients in a small saucepan. Heat until sugar dissolves, stirring frequently.
- After baking cake for final 15 minutes, remove from oven. Prick top of cake with a toothpick.
- Pour hot sauce over top of cake while still in pan.
- Allow cake to cool completely before removing from pan.

Lemon Garden Cake

1	envelope unflavored gelatin
1/4	cup cold water
6	eggs, separated
3/4	cup sugar
1/2	cup lemon juice
	Grated rind of 1 lemon
1/2	cup sugar
1/8	teaspoon salt
	Large angel food cake
1/2	pint heavy cream, whipped

Servings: 12
Preparation time: 1 hour
Chilling time: 6 to 8 hours

- Soften gelatin in water.
- Beat egg yolks until lemon colored. Add 3/4 cup sugar and beat well. Add lemon juice and lemon rind.
- Cook in the top of a double boiler over simmering water until mixture is thickened and will mound. Stir constantly while cooking.
- Add gelatin. Then set aside to cool.
- Beat egg whites until stiff. Gradually add 1/2 cup sugar and salt.
- Fold cooled custard into egg whites.
- Tear angel food cake into bite-size pieces.
- Stir cake pieces and custard together in a large bowl until cake pieces are well coated.
- Pour into either a greased tube pan or a 9 X 13-inch baking dish.
- Chill overnight or at least 6 to 8 hours.
- When ready to serve, unmold cake from pan and frost with whipped cream.
- May garnish with thinly sliced lemon wedges.

Chocolate Ricotta Cheesecake

Crust
1-1/2 cups graham cracker crumbs
1/3 cup light brown sugar
1/2 teaspoon ground cinnamon
1/3 cup butter, melted

Servings: 10
Preparation time: 30 minutes
Baking time: 35 minutes
Chilling time: 4 hours
* Preheat oven to 350° F.
* Combine all ingredients.
* Press lightly into an 8-inch spring-form pan.

Filling
1   8-ounce package cream cheese, softened
1-1/2 cups ricotta cheese
1   cup semisweet chocolate bits, melted
2   eggs, beaten
1/2 cup sugar
1/2 teaspoon vanilla extract
1   cup sour cream

* Mix first 6 ingredients in a food processor or mixer until smooth.
* Pour mixture into crust and bake for 35 minutes or until set.
* Spread cheesecake with sour cream while still hot. Then cool thoroughly.
* Chill for several hours or overnight.

Most Requested Cheesecake

Crust
1-3/4 cups graham cracker crumbs
1/4 cup chopped walnuts
1-1/2 teaspoons ground cinnamon
2   tablespoons sugar
1/2 cup butter, melted

Servings: 8 to 10
Preparation time: 30 minutes
Baking time: 45 minutes
Chilling time: 2 hours
* Preheat oven to 375° F.
* Mix all ingredients together and press in bottom and up sides of a spring-form pan.

Filling
1-1/2 pounds cream cheese, softened to room temperature
1   cup sugar
3   eggs, beaten
1/2 teaspoon vanilla extract

* Beat cream cheese thoroughly with an electric mixer. Add sugar gradually. Add eggs, one at a time, then vanilla.
* Pour into crust and bake for 40 minutes.

continued...

Most Requested Cheesecake continued...

Topping
1	pint sour cream
2	tablespoons sugar
1/2	teaspoon vanilla extract
2	cups fresh fruit or berries

- Whip sour cream. Add sugar and vanilla. Pour over pie and bake for 5 minutes at 500° F.
- Chill. Best if you can chill overnight.
- Just before serving, top with fresh fruit or berries.

Buttermilk Orange Cupcakes with Fresh Orange Sauce

Cupcakes
1/2	cup butter, softened
1	cup sugar
2	eggs
1	teaspoon baking soda
2	cups all-purpose flour
1/4	teaspoon salt
2/3	cup buttermilk

Servings: 60 miniature cakes
Preparation time: 20 minutes
Baking time: 12 minutes

- Preheat oven to 375° F.
- Cream butter and sugar.
- Add eggs, one at a time.
- Sift dry ingredients. Add to mixture, alternating with buttermilk.
- Spoon mixture into greased miniature muffin tins until tins are half full.
- Bake for 10 to 12 minutes. Do not overcook.

Orange Sauce
	Juice of 2 oranges
	Grated rind of 1 orange
1	cup sugar

- Simmer all ingredients over low heat until
- sugar dissolves.
- Spoon 1 teaspoon of sauce over each
- cupcake while cakes are warm and still in the pan.
- Allow cakes to cool in tins. Then remove and store in covered container.

Lighter Than Air Date Torte

1	8-ounce package pitted dates
3	tablespoons butter
1	cup boiling water
1	teaspoon baking soda
1	cup sugar
1	cup all-purpose flour
1	egg
1	cup chopped pecans
1/2	pint whipping cream
3	tablespoons sugar
1	ounce brandy

Servings: 10 to 12
Preparation time: 20 minutes
Standing time: 20 minutes
Baking time: 20 minutes

- Preheat oven to 350° F.
- Put dates, butter, boiling water and baking soda in a large mixing bowl. Mix well. Let stand for 20 minutes.
- Combine sugar and flour.
- Add to date mixture.
- Add egg and pecans. Mix until well blended.
- Pour into a greased 9 X 13-inch baking dish.
- Bake for 20 minutes.
- Cut into squares while warm.
- Whip cream. Add sugar and brandy.
- Serve each square with a dollop of whipped cream mixture on top.

Chocolate Chip Pie

1	9-inch pie shell
1	6-ounce package chocolate chips
2	eggs, beaten
1/2	cup butter, melted
1	cup sugar
1	teaspoon vanilla extract
1/2	cup all-purpose flour

Servings: 6
Preparation time: 10 minutes
Baking time: 50 to 60 minutes

- Preheat oven to 350° F.
- Bake crust for 8 minutes.
- Put chocolate chips in crust.
- Combine eggs, butter, sugar, vanilla and flour.
- Pour over chocolate chips.
- Bake for 50 to 60 minutes.

Frozen Chocolate Pie with English Custard Sauce

Filling
2	cups semisweet chocolate chips
1-1/2	teaspoons vanilla extract
1/8	teaspoon salt
1-1/2	cups whipping cream, scalded
6	egg yolks

Crust
3/4	cup graham cracker crumbs
3	tablespoons margarine, not butter, melted
1/4	teaspoon ground cinnamon
2	tablespoons brown sugar, firmly packed

Sauce
6	egg yolks
2	tablespoons cornstarch
3/4	cup sugar
2-3/4	cups Half and Half
1	teaspoon vanilla extract
	Crushed toasted almonds for garnish

Servings: 10
Preparation time: 1 hour
Freezing time: 2 hours

- Put chocolate chips, vanilla and salt in a blender.
- Add cream and blend at medium speed for 30 seconds.
- Add egg yolks and blend for 5 seconds.
- Transfer mixture to a bowl and allow to cool while making crust.
- Combine all ingredients. Pat on the bottom of a 9-inch pie pan.
- Pour cooled chocolate filling into pie crust and freeze.
- Combine yolks, cornstarch and sugar in a bowl.
- Scald Half and Half. Gradually add to egg mixture, whisking rapidly.
- Pour mixture in the top of a double boiler and cook over barely simmering water until thickened. Do not overcook.
- Cool sauce rapidly to stop cooking by putting pan into cold water and stirring.
- Add vanilla. Strain sauce into bowl to remove any lumps.
- Remove pie from freezer 20 minutes before serving time if pie has been in freezer for more than 3 hours, otherwise, take it out when ready to serve.
- Pour custard sauce over pie and sprinkle with almonds.

Goodstuff's Bourbon Pie

Crust

2	ounces unsweetened chocolate
1/2	cup butter
2	eggs
1	cup sugar
1/2	teaspoon vanilla extract
1/2	cup all-purpose flour
1/4	teaspoon salt

Filling

5	egg yolks
3/4	cup sugar
1	envelope unflavored gelatin
1/4	cup cold water
6	tablespoons bourbon, divided
1	cup heavy cream

Topping

1	cup heavy cream
4	tablespoons confectioners' sugar
1	egg white, beaten until stiff

Servings: 8 to 10
Preparation time: 25 minutes
Baking time: 20 minutes

- Grease a 10-inch pie pan.
- Preheat oven to 350° F.
- Melt chocolate and butter in the top of a double boiler over hot water. Stir until smooth. Remove from heat and cool.
- In a medium mixing bowl, beat eggs and sugar until thick and light in color, about 5 minutes.
- Stir in vanilla, flour, salt and cooled chocolate mixture. Blend thoroughly.
- Turn batter into prepared pie pan.
- Bake for 20 minutes. Do not overbake. Remove from oven and cool completely.
- In a large mixing bowl, lightly beat egg yolks. Gradually add sugar and continue to beat until mixture is very thick, about 10 minutes.
- In a small heatproof bowl, sprinkle gelatin over water. Stir to dissolve.
- Blend in 3 tablespoons bourbon. Let stand until thickened.
- Place bowl in a small pan of hot water over moderate heat. Stir mixture until gelatin is completely dissolved.
- With a wire whisk, blend gelatin mixture into yolks.
- Blend in remaining 3 tablespoons bourbon. Set aside.
- In a small mixing bowl, beat cream until thickened. Fold into bourbon mixture.
- Pour filling over cooled brownie crust and refrigerate until firm before covering with topping.
- In a small bowl, combine cream and sugar. Beat until thickened. Fold in egg white.
- Fill a pastry bag, fitted with a large open-star tube, with whipped cream. Pipe a lattice design on top of pie.
- Chill until time to serve.

French Silk Pie

3	egg whites
1/8	teaspoon salt
1/4	teaspoon cream of tartar
3/4	cup sugar
1/2	cup chopped pecans
1/2	teaspoon vanilla extract
4	ounces sweet baking chocolate
3	tablespoons water
1	tablespoon brandy
2	cups whipping cream
	Shaved chocolate for garnish

Servings: 6 to 8
Preparation time: 45 minutes
Baking time: 50 minutes
Chilling time: 5 hours

- Preheat oven to 300° F.
- Beat egg whites with salt and cream of tartar until soft peaks form.
- Gradually add sugar and beat until stiff.
- Fold in nuts and vanilla.
- Pour into a greased 9-inch pie pan building up sides to form a rim.
- Bake for 50 minutes. When done, remove from oven and cool.
- In the top of a double boiler, melt chocolate with water. Add brandy.
- Whip 1 cup cream and fold into chocolate mixture.
- Allow chocolate mixture to cool. Then pile into meringue shell.
- Chill for 5 hours.
- When ready to serve, whip remaining 1 cup cream and spread over top of pie, or put a dollop on each slice.
- Garnish with shaved chocolate.

Louisville Pie

1/2	cup butter
1	cup sugar
4	eggs
1	cup light Karo syrup
1/4	cup all-purpose flour
1	cup finely chopped walnuts
1/2	scant cup chocolate chips
1	teaspoon vanilla extract
1	unbaked 9-inch deep-dish pie shell

Servings: 8
Preparation time: 15 minutes
Baking time: 45 minutes

- Preheat oven to 350° F.
- Melt butter and cool.
- Beat sugar, eggs, syrup and flour until light and creamy.
- Add butter and beat again.
- Add nuts, chocolate chips and vanilla.
- Pour into pie shell.
- Bake for 45 minutes.
- Best when served warm with a dollop of fresh whipped cream.

Brandy Alexander Pie

1	envelope unflavored gelatin
1/2	cup cold water
2/3	cup sugar
1/8	teaspoon salt
3	eggs, separated
1/4	cup cognac
1/4	cup crème de cacao
2	cups heavy cream, whipped
1	9-inch deep-dish graham cracker crust
	Chocolate curls for garnish

Servings: 8
Preparation time: 1 hour
Chilling time: 4 hours

- Sprinkle gelatin over cold water in a saucepan.
- Add 1/3 cup sugar, salt and egg yolks, blending well.
- Cook over low heat, stirring constantly, until gelatin dissolves and mixture thickens. Do not boil.
- Remove from heat. Stir in cognac and crème de cacao. Chill until mixture starts to mound.
- Beat egg whites until stiff. Gradually add remaining 1/3 cup sugar. Fold whites into thickened custard.
- Fold half the whipped cream into mixture. Then turn into crust.
- Chill pie for 4 to 5 hours or until set.
- When ready to serve, spread remaining whipped cream over top of pie and garnish with chocolate curls.

Nantucket Cranberry Pie

2	cups fresh cranberries, picked over
1/2	cup chopped walnuts
1/2	cup sugar
1	cup all-purpose flour
3/4	cup butter or margarine, melted
1	tablespoon almond extract
1	cup sugar
2	eggs, slightly beaten

Servings: 8
Preparation time: 15 minutes
Baking time: 40 minutes

- Preheat oven to 325° F.
- Place cranberries, walnuts and 1/2 cup sugar in the bottom of a 10-inch pie pan.
- Mix flour, butter, almond extract, 1 cup sugar and eggs.
- Pour mixture over berries. Bake for 35 to 40 minutes.

Best Pumpkin Pie

2	cups cooked or canned pumpkin, strained
1-1/2	cups sugar
1	teaspoon ground cinnamon
1/4	teaspoon ground cloves
1/4	teaspoon ground allspice
1	teaspoon powdered ginger
2	tablespoons brandy
1/2	teaspoon salt
2	eggs, beaten
2	tablespoons butter, melted
1	tablespoon molasses
1	unbaked 9 or 10-inch pie shell, baked 8 minutes in a hot oven
1	cup heavy cream, whipped
2	tablespoons brandy

Servings: 6
Preparation time: 25 minutes
Baking time: 1 hour, 10 minutes

- Preheat oven to 425° F.
- Mix first 11 ingredients in order given. Pour into pie shell.
- Bake in oven for 10 minutes. Then reduce temperature to 300° F. and bake for 1 hour.
- Serve with brandy flavored whipped cream.

Pecan Tart

20	Ritz crackers, crushed
1	cup sugar
3/4	cup chopped pecans
3	egg whites
1/2	pint heavy cream, whipped
6 to 8	pecan halves

Servings: 6 to 8
Preparation time: 20 minutes
Baking time: 50 minutes

- Preheat oven to 300° F.
- Combine crackers, 1/2 cup sugar and nuts.
- Beat egg whites until stiff, gradually adding remaining 1/2 cup sugar.
- Fold cracker mixture into egg whites.
- Spoon mixture into a buttered pie dish and bake for 50 minutes.
- Top individual slices with whipped cream and pecan halves before serving.

Spectacular Peach Pie

3-1/2	cups peeled and sliced fresh peaches
2	cups sugar
2	tablespoons all-purpose flour
1	teaspoon ground nutmeg
3/4	cup butter
1	teaspoon salt
2	cups all-purpose flour
2/3	cup Crisco
1/2	cup cold water

Servings: 12
Preparation time: 30 minutes
Baking time: 45 minutes

- Preheat oven to 350° F.
- Place peaches in the bottom of a buttered 9 X 13-inch baking dish.
- Pour sugar evenly over peaches.
- Dust with 2 tablespoons flour. Sprinkle nutmeg over all.
- Cut butter into pats and place evenly over all.
- Sift salt and 2 cups flour. Cut in Crisco. Sprinkle cold water on top and blend with fingers until a ball can be formed.
- Roll out on a floured surface and cut into strips. Lay on top of peaches crosswise and lengthwise to form a lattice top.
- Bake for 45 minutes.

Angel Pie

Meringue Shell

4	egg whites
1/2	teaspoon baking powder
1/4	teaspoon cream of tartar
1/8	teaspoon salt
1	teaspoon vanilla extract
1	teaspoon white vinegar
1	teaspoon water
1	cup sugar

Servings: 6 to 8
Preparation time: 45 minutes
Baking time: 1 hour
Setting time: 1 hour

- Preheat oven to 275° F.
- Beat egg whites with baking powder, cream of tartar and salt until stiff.
- Put vanilla, vinegar and water in a cup.
- Add sugar and liquid alternately to egg whites.
- Place in a 9-inch greased pie pan.
- Bake for 1 hour.
- Turn off oven. Open door to broil position. Leave meringue in oven for 1 hour.

continued...

Angel Pie continued...

Filling

4	egg yolks, beaten
1/2	cup sugar
4	tablespoons lemon juice
	Juice and rind of 1 lemon
1	tablespoon all-purpose flour
1/2	cup water
1/2	pint whipping cream
1/2	teaspoon vanilla extract
	Shaved chocolate for garnish

- Mix first 6 ingredients. Cook in the top of a double boiler until thickened.
- Cover and allow to cool.
- Whip cream with vanilla.
- Spread whipped cream over meringue.
- Pour cooled filling on top of cream.
- Garnish with shaved chocolate.

"The Sisters" Famous Peanut Butter Pie

3/4	cup sifted confectioners' sugar
1/3	cup crunchy peanut butter
1	9-inch deep-dish pie shell
2/3	cup sugar
1/4	cup cornstarch
1	tablespoon all-purpose flour
1/2	teaspoon salt
3	cups milk
3	egg yolks, beaten
1-1/2	teaspoons vanilla extract
2	tablespoons butter, melted
3	egg whites

Servings: 8
Preparation time: 1 hour

- Preheat oven to 450° F.
- Combine sugar and peanut butter with fingers until crumbs are formed. Set aside.
- Brown pie shell on middle rack in oven for 8 minutes. Cool.
- Fill shell with crumbs, reserving 2 tablespoons for top.
- Combine sugar, cornstarch, flour and salt in the top of a double boiler.
- Add milk. Cook over boiling water until thick enough to mound, beating often with a wire whisk.
- Add a little hot mixture to egg yolks. Then add yolks to mixture.
- Stir in vanilla and butter.
- Cool over ice, beating with whisk to prevent crusting.
- Pour custard into pie shell.
- Beat egg whites until stiff. Spoon on top of custard.
- Sprinkle top with reserved crumb mix.
- Bake at 400° F. for 5 minutes on lower rack in oven.

Chocolate Torte

3/4	of 16-ounce box graham crackers, crushed
1/2	cup sugar
1	cup butter, melted
2	12-ounce packages chocolate chips
4	tablespoons sugar
6	tablespoons milk
8	eggs, separated
2	teaspoons vanilla extract
1/2	pint heavy cream, whipped
5	tablespoons sugar

Servings: 10
Preparation time: 30 minutes
Baking time: 10 minutes
Chilling time: 5 hours

- Preheat oven to 300° F.
- Make torte shell by combining crushed crackers, 1/2 cup sugar and butter. Mix well.
- Press mixture 1/2-inch deep and 4 inches up on sides of a tube or 9-inch spring-form pan.
- Spoon any remaining crumbs over bottom of shell.
- Bake for 10 minutes. Then cool.
- Make filling by blending together chocolate chips, 4 tablespoons sugar and milk in the top of a double boiler over hot water. Set aside.
- When cool, beat in egg yolks, one at a time. Add vanilla.
- Beat egg whites until stiff peaks form.
- Fold in chocolate mixture. Spoon mixture into torte shell.
- Refrigerate for at least 5 hours.
- One hour before serving, frost with whipped cream sweetened with 5 tablespoons sugar.
- Return to refrigerator until ready to serve.

Cookies & Candies

Peppermint Chocolate Meringues

3	egg whites
3/4	cup sugar
1/2	teaspoon cream of tartar
1	6-ounce package semisweet chocolate chips
1/2	cup crushed peppermint candy
1/2	cup chopped pecans
1	teaspoon vanilla extract

Servings: 18 meringues
Preparation time: 12 minutes
Baking time: 4 hours or overnight

- Preheat oven to 400° F.
- Whip egg whites until stiff.
- Fold in remaining ingredients.
- Drop by spoonfuls onto a cookie sheet covered with brown paper, a grocery bag is good.
- Put cookies in oven and turn oven off.
- Leave cookies in oven for at least 4 hours or overnight.
- For best results, do not open oven door.
- Store cookies in a covered tin.
- May be prepared ahead.

Meringues Pistachio

4	egg whites
1	cup sugar
1/2	teaspoon vanilla extract
2	squares unsweetened chocolate, finely grated
1	6-ounce package semisweet chocolate chips
1/4	cup milk
1	2-1/4-ounce package pistachio nuts, chopped

Servings: 48 meringues
Preparation time: 20 minutes
Baking time: 45 minutes

- Preheat oven to 275° F.
- Beat egg whites until stiff.
- Gradually add sugar, beating continuously until whites hold peaks.
- Add vanilla and grated chocolate, folding gently.
- Cover a cookie sheet with brown paper cut from paper bags.
- Drop meringues by teaspoonfuls onto paper.
- Bake for 45 minutes.
- Cool and remove from paper with a spatula.
- Melt chocolate chips and milk in the top of a double boiler.
- Dip tops of meringues first in melted chocolate, then in nuts.
- Allow chocolate to harden before storing.

Cocoa Clouds

3	egg whites
1/8	teaspoon salt
1	cup sugar, sifted
2	teaspoons water
1	teaspoon vanilla extract
3	tablespoons cocoa
1/2 to 1	cup chopped pecans (optional)

Servings: 40 clouds
Preparation time: 15 minutes
Baking time: 30 minutes

- Preheat oven to 250° F.
- Beat egg whites and salt until stiff but not dry.
- Add half the sugar and beat until mixed.
- Combine water and vanilla.
- Alternating with vanilla mixture, add remaining sugar to egg whites.
- Fold in cocoa and nuts by hand.
- Immediately drop batter by teaspoonful, 1 inch apart, onto a greased cookie sheet.
- Bake for 30 minutes.
- These are fragile. Remove carefully from cookie sheet.
- Serve with sorbets.

Guava Dainties

1	3-ounce package cream cheese, softened
1/2	cup butter
1	cup all-purpose flour, sifted
1/2	cup guava jelly or paste
1/3	cup finely chopped pecans
	Confectioners' sugar, sifted

Servings: 36 dainties
Preparation time: 30 minutes
Cooking time: 12 minutes
Chilling time: Overnight

- Combine cream cheese and butter.
- Gradually add flour and mix well.
- Divide dough into two parts and shape into balls.
- Wrap balls in waxed paper and refrigerate overnight.
- Preheat oven to 350° F.
- Roll dough to 1/8-inch thickness. Spread a *very* thin layer of guava jelly over pastry.
- Sprinkle with pecans.
- Roll up and slice 1/2-inch thick.
- Place on a baking sheet and bake for 12 minutes.
- Remove from pan and sift confectioners' sugar on top.

Tea Cakes

8	tablespoons butter
1	cup sugar
2	egg yolks
1	teaspoon vanilla extract
1-1/2	cups cake flour
1	teaspoon baking powder
1/8	teaspoon salt
2	egg whites
1	cup dark brown sugar
1	cup chopped pecans

Servings: 24 squares
Preparation time: 30 minutes
Baking time: 30 minutes

- Preheat oven to 300° F.
- Cream butter and sugar together.
- Add egg yolks and vanilla. Mix well.
- Sift flour, baking powder and salt. Add to butter mixture and mix well.
- Press mixture into a greased 8-inch pan.
- Beat egg whites until fluffy. Gradually add brown sugar.
- Spread meringue evenly over mixture in pan.
- Sprinkle pecans over meringue.
- Bake for 30 minutes.
- Remove from oven and immediately cut into 1-1/2 to 2-inch squares.
- Do not remove from pan until completely cool.
- Store in an airtight container.

Praline Cookies

1/2	cup dark brown sugar
1/2	cup light brown sugar
2	tablespoons all-purpose flour
1/2	teaspoon salt
1	egg white
1	teaspoon vanilla extract
2	cups whole pecans

Servings: 5 dozen cookies
Preparation time: 20 minutes
Baking time: 25 minutes

- Preheat oven to 275° F.
- Sift sugars, flour and salt together.
- Beat egg white until stiff.
- Fold egg white and vanilla into sugar mixture.
- Gently fold in pecans.
- Drop by teaspoonfuls onto a well greased cookie sheet.
- Bake for 25 minutes.

Sugar Cookies

2-1/2 cups all-purpose flour
1/2 teaspoon baking soda
1 teaspoon salt
1 egg, beaten
2 tablespoons vinegar
2 teaspoons grated lemon peel
1 teaspoon vanilla extract
1/2 cup butter
1/2 cup Crisco
1 cup sugar
1/2 cup sugar

Servings: 5 dozen cookies
Preparation time: 20 minutes
Baking time: 10 to 12 minutes
- Preheat oven to 400° F.
- Sift together flour, soda and salt.
- Combine egg, vinegar, lemon peel and vanilla.
- Cream butter and Crisco. Then gradually add 1 cup sugar.
- Add dry ingredients alternately with egg mixture.
- Drop by teaspoonfuls onto an ungreased cookie sheet.
- Flatten with a fork and sprinkle with 1/2 cup sugar.
- Bake for 10 to 12 minutes.

Oatmeal Crisp Cookies

1 cup butter
2 tablespoons water
2 tablespoons maple syrup
1 cup all-purpose flour
1 cup sugar
1/2 teaspoon baking soda
1 teaspoon baking powder
2-1/2 cups quick cooking oatmeal
1/2 cup sugar

Servings: 6 dozen cookies
Preparation time: 15 minutes
Baking time: 12 to 15 minutes
- Preheat oven to 350° F.
- Melt butter in water. Add syrup.
- Sift dry ingredients together. Then blend in oatmeal.
- Combine butter mixture with dry ingredients.
- Cover dough and chill for 1 hour.
- Form dough into 1-inch balls and roll in sugar.
- Place balls on ungreased cookie sheets and flatten slightly.
- Bake for 12 to 15 minutes.
- Remove from cookie sheets immediately and cool on racks.

Bourbon Fruitcake Cookies

1	pound raisins	
1	pound coarsely chopped candied cherries	
1	pound coarsely chopped candied pineapple	
2	cups bourbon	
2	cups brown sugar	
1/2	cup butter	
4	eggs, beaten	
3	cups all-purpose flour	
3	teaspoons baking soda	
1/4	teaspoon salt	
1	teaspoon ground cinnamon	
1	teaspoon ground nutmeg	
1	teaspoon ground cloves	
1	pound chopped pecans	

Servings: 12 to 15 dozen
Preparation time: 30 minutes
Standing time: overnight
Baking time: 15 minutes

- Soak raisins, cherries and pineapple overnight in bourbon.
- Preheat oven to 350° F.
- Cream sugar and butter.
- Add eggs.
- Fold in flour, baking soda, salt, cinnamon, nutmeg and cloves.
- Add soaked fruit and pecans. Mix well.
- Bake in miniature cupcake tins or drop as cookies on a cookie sheet.
- Bake for 15 minutes.
- Cool and store in tightly sealed container.

Mint Surprise Cookies

3	cups all-purpose flour
1	teaspoon baking soda
1/2	teaspoon salt
1	cup butter
1	cup sugar
1/2	cup brown sugar, firmly packed
2	eggs, beaten
1	teaspoon vanilla extract
36	Andes green mints
	Walnuts

Servings: 3 dozen cookies
Preparation time: 30 minutes
Chilling time: 2 hours
Baking time: 9 to 12 minutes

- Sift together flour, soda and salt.
- Cream butter and sugars.
- Add eggs and vanilla.
- Blend in dry ingredients.
- Cover and chill for at least 2 hours.
- Preheat oven to 375° F.
- To shape cookies, enclose each mint in a tablespoon of chilled dough.
- Place on an ungreased baking sheet 2 inches apart.
- Place a walnut on top of each cookie.
- Bake for 9 to 12 minutes.

Exquisite Mint Sticks

Mint Sticks

2	1-ounce squares unsweetened chocolate
1/2	cup butter
2	eggs
1	cup sugar
1-1/2	teaspoons peppermint extract
3/4	cup all-purpose flour
1/4	teaspoon salt
1/2	cup chopped pecans (optional)

Icing

2	tablespoons butter
1-1/4	cups confectioners' sugar
1	tablespoon heavy cream
2	teaspoons peppermint extract
1	1-ounce square unsweetened chocolate
1	tablespoon butter

Servings: 2 to 3 dozen sticks
Preparation time: 20 minutes
Baking time: 25 minutes

- Preheat oven to 350° F.
- Melt chocolate and butter in the top of a double boiler.
- Beat eggs until frothy.
- Add sugar, peppermint extract and chocolate mixture.
- Add flour, salt and pecans. Mix thoroughly.
- Pour into a greased 9-inch square pan.
- Bake for 25 minutes.

- Mix together butter, sugar and cream.
- Add peppermint extract.
- Melt chocolate and butter. Set aside.
- Spread creamed icing over cake and drizzle chocolate mixture on top.
- Cut into squares.
- These may be frozen.

Rich Brownies

6	1-ounce squares unsweetened chocolate
1-1/2	cups butter
2-1/4	cups sifted all-purpose flour
1-1/2	teaspoons baking powder
1-1/2	teaspoons salt
3	cups sugar
6	eggs
2	teaspoons vanilla extract
2	cups chopped pecans or English walnuts

Servings: 2 dozen
Preparation time: 20 minutes
Baking time: 40 minutes

- Preheat oven to 350° F.
- Melt chocolate and butter in the top of a double boiler over medium heat.
- Let cool and add dry ingredients.
- Beat eggs and vanilla. Stir in nuts.
- Fold into chocolate mixture.
- Pour batter in a buttered 9 X 13-inch pan.
- Bake for 35 to 40 minutes.
- Do not overbake. Should be moist.
- Let cool. Cut into squares.

Miniature Individual Cheesecakes

	Butter
3/4	cup graham cracker crumbs
2	8-ounce packages cream cheese, softened
3/4	cup sugar
3	egg yolks
	Juice of 1 lemon
	Grated rind of 1 lemon
3	egg whites
3/4	cup sour cream
2	tablespoons sugar
1/2	teaspoon vanilla extract

Servings: 60 cheesecakes
Preparation time: 20 minutes
Baking time: 10 to 15 minutes

- Preheat oven to 350° F.
- Generously butter miniature muffin tins.
- Crush graham cracker crumbs and put about 1/2 teaspoon in each muffin cup. Shake tin around. The crumbs that stick to the butter will form a crust. Gently shake out excess crumbs.
- Combine cream cheese, sugar, egg yolks, lemon juice and rind.
- Beat egg whites until they hold their peaks. Then fold into cream cheese mixture.
- Fill muffin cups 3/4 full. Bake for 10 to 15 minutes, watching closely. When they puff up, cracks appear on top and are faintly brown, they are done. Turn out on a tea towel. Turn oven up to 400° F.
- Blend sour cream, sugar and vanilla. Put in a small casserole and bake for 5 minutes.
- Each cheesecake will have an indentation on the top. Put a teaspoonful of baked sour cream mixture in it and serve.
- Cheesecakes may be frozen.
- May garnish with fruit and a melted red currant jelly glaze.

COOKIES & CANDIES

Luscious Squares

1	6-ounce package butterscotch chips
1/4	cup butter
3/4	cup self-rising flour
1/3	cup brown sugar
1/2	teaspoon vanilla extract
1	egg
1	cup miniature marshmallows
1	6-ounce package chocolate chips
1/4	cup chopped nuts

Servings: 20 squares
Preparation time: 15 minutes
Baking time: 20 to 25 minutes

- Preheat oven to 350° F.
- Melt butterscotch chips and butter over low heat.
- Add flour, brown sugar, vanilla and egg.
- Fold in marshmallows, chocolate chips and nuts.
- Spread mixture in a 9-inch square pan.
- Bake for 20 to 25 minutes. *Do not overbake.* Squares are soft at end of baking time, but harden.
- Cool before cutting.

Chocolate Toffee Yummies

2	cups all-purpose flour
1/2	cup butter, softened
1	cup light brown sugar
1	cup coarsely broken pecans
2/3	cup butter
1/2	cup light brown sugar
1	cup chocolate chips

Servings: 30 squares
Preparation time: 15 minutes
Baking time: 20 minutes

- Preheat oven to 350° F.
- Combine first 3 ingredients with an electric mixer on medium speed for 3 minutes.
- Firmly pat mixture into the bottom of a 9 X 13 X 2-inch pan.
- Sprinkle pecans on crust.
- Mix butter and sugar. Cook over medium heat until bubbly, stirring constantly.
- Pour butter mixture over crust.
- Bake for 20 minutes.
- Remove from oven and immediately sprinkle chocolate chips on top.
- Swirl chips with a knife to evenly coat cookie.
- Cool and cut into squares.

Chocolate-Caramel Layer Squares

1	14-ounce bag caramels
2/3	cup evaporated milk
1	18-1/2-ounce package German chocolate cake mix
3/4	cup butter, softened
1	cup chopped pecans
1	6-ounce package semisweet chocolate chips

Servings: 5 dozen bars
Preparation time: 40 minutes
Baking time: 25 minutes
Chilling time: 30 minutes

- Preheat oven to 350° F.
- In the top of a double boiler, combine caramels and 1/3 cup evaporated milk. Cook, stirring constantly, until caramels have melted.
- In a mixing bowl, combine cake mix, remaining 1/3 cup evaporated milk and butter. Mix with an electric mixer until dough sticks together.
- Stir in pecans.
- Press half of cake mixture in a greased 9 X 13 X 2-inch pan.
- Bake in oven for 6 minutes.
- Remove from oven and sprinkle chocolate chips over crust.
- Pour caramel mixture over chocolate, spreading evenly.
- Crumble remaining cake mixture over caramel mixture.
- Return pan to oven and bake for 15 to 18 minutes.
- Remove from oven and let cool. Chill in refrigerator for 30 minutes.
- Cut into small bars.

Chocolate Cheesecake Muffins

1	3-ounce package cream cheese, softened
3	tablespoons sugar
1-3/4	cups all-purpose flour
3/4	cup sugar
3	tablespoons unsweetened cocoa
2-1/2	teaspoons baking powder
3/4	teaspoon salt
1	egg, beaten
3/4	cup milk
1/3	cup vegetable oil
1	teaspoon vanilla extract
1/2	cup powdered sugar

Servings: 12 muffins
Preparation time: 30 minutes
Baking time: 20 minutes

- Preheat oven to 400° F.
- In a small mixing bowl, beat cream cheese and 3 tablespoons sugar until light and fluffy. Set aside.
- In a large mixing bowl, stir together flour, 3/4 cup sugar, cocoa, baking powder and salt.
- Make a "well" in center of dry ingredients.
- Combine egg, milk, oil and vanilla. Pour into "well."
- Stir until just moistened. Batter will be lumpy.
- Spoon 2 tablespoons batter into each of 12 buttered muffin cups.
- Drop a teaspoonful of cream cheese mixture into each cup. Top with remaining batter, completely covering cream cheese.
- Bake for 20 minutes.
- Cool slightly. Then roll in powdered sugar.

Pecan Pie Bars

1	18-1/2-ounce package yellow cake mix
1/2	cup butter, melted
1	large egg

Servings: 36 bars
Preparation time: 30 minutes
Cooking time: 45 minutes

- Preheat oven to 350° F.
- Grease bottom and sides of a 9 X 13-inch baking dish.
- Set aside 2/3 cup cake mix.
- In a large mixing bowl, combine remaining cake mix, butter and egg.
- Mix ingredients until crumbly.
- Press into prepared pan and bake for 15 minutes.

continued...

Pecan Pie Bars continued...

Filling

2/3	cup reserved cake mix
1/2	cup brown sugar, firmly packed
1-1/2	cups dark corn syrup
1	teaspoon vanilla extract
3	large eggs
1	cup chopped pecans

- While crust bakes, prepare filling.
- Mix first 5 ingredients with an electric mixer.
- Pour filling into crust. Sprinkle pecans over all.
- Bake at 350° F. for 30 minutes.
- Cool and cut into bars.

Chocolate Perfections

Crust

1/2	cup plus 1 tablespoon light brown sugar
1	cup plus 1 tablespoon all-purpose flour
1/2	cup finely chopped pecans
1/2	cup butter, melted

Servings: 20
Preparation time: 1 hour
Baking time: 10 to 12 minutes
Chilling time: 4 hours

- Preheat oven to 400° F.
- Combine brown sugar, flour, pecans and butter.
- Press evenly in the bottom of a 9 X 13-inch pan.
- Bake for 10 to 12 minutes until it looks like a cookie.
- Crumble crust and again press evenly into bottom of pan.
- Chill.

Filling

1	cup butter, softened
1-1/2	cup sugar
1	teaspoon vanilla extract
1	tablespoon good rum
3	ounces Baker's unsweetened chocolate, melted and cooled
4	eggs, chilled

- In a large mixing bowl, cream butter and sugar until light and fluffy.
- Add vanilla, rum and chocolate. Mix well.
- Add eggs, one at a time, beating 3 to 5 minutes after each addition.
- Pile into cold crust and chill for 3 hours. May be chilled as long as 2 days.
- Cut into squares to serve.
- Sprinkle any loose crumbs on top of squares.
- May also use a ready-made graham cracker or chocolate cookie crust.

Peanut Buttercups

1	15-ounce roll peanut butter cookie dough
36	Reese's miniature peanut butter cups

Servings: 36
Preparation time: 5 minutes
Baking time: 10 minutes
Chilling time: 30 minutes

- Slice cookie dough according to package directions. This makes 36 pieces.
- Using 3 miniature muffin tins, place one piece of dough in each cup.
- Bake according to package directions.
- While cookies are baking, unwrap peanut butter cups.
- When cookies are done, remove from oven and immediately place one peanut butter cup on top of each cookie. Wait 5 minutes. Then swirl top of peanut butter cup so that ridges of cup are covered.
- Refrigerate for 30 minutes or until hard.
- Remove from tin and serve.
- These freeze beautifully.

Incredible Edibles

2	cups graham cracker crumbs
2	cups confectioners' sugar
3/4	cup margarine, melted
1	12-ounce jar crunchy peanut butter
1	12-ounce package chocolate chips

Servings: 24 cookies
Preparation time: 20 minutes

- Mix cracker crumbs, sugar, margarine and peanut butter with hands.
- Pat in a greased 11 X 13-inch baking dish.
- Melt chocolate chips in the top of a double boiler.
- Spread over cookie mix.
- Let cool. Cut into squares.
- Store in refrigerator in an airtight container.

Russian Rocks

1	cup butter
2	cups brown sugar
3	eggs, beaten
3	cups all-purpose flour
2	teaspoons ground cinnamon
1	teaspoon baking soda
2	cups raisins
1-1/2	cups chopped pecans

Servings: 6 dozen cookies
Preparation time: 15 minutes
Baking time: 10 to 12 minutes

- Preheat oven to 325° F.
- In a mixing bowl, cream butter and sugar.
- Add eggs, one at a time. Blend to mix well.
- Sift together flour, cinnamon and soda.
- Add dry ingredients to sugar mixture, blending on low setting until just mixed.
- Stir in raisins and pecans by hand.
- Drop by teaspoonfuls onto greased cookie sheets.
- Bake cookies for 10 to 12 minutes.

Peanut Butter Balls

1	cup butter
1	12-ounce jar creamy peanut butter
1	16-ounce box confectioners' sugar
1	12-ounce package semisweet chocolate bits
1	2-inch strip of paraffin
	Toothpicks

Servings: 4 dozen peanut butter balls
Preparation time: 20 minutes
Chilling time: 1-1/2 hours

- Cream butter and peanut butter with a mixer or food processor.
- Blend in sugar, a little at a time.
- Form mixture into a ball. Cover and chill for 1 hour.
- Form dough into small balls.
- Place on cookie sheets lined with waxed paper. Chill for 1/2 hour.
- Melt chocolate and paraffin in the top of a double boiler.
- Dip each ball into chocolate using toothpicks.
- Return to cookie sheets lined with waxed paper and chill.
- Will keep in refrigerator for several weeks if stored in an airtight container.

English Toffee

3/4	cup finely chopped pecans
2	cups sugar
2	cups butter
1	12-ounce package chocolate chips

Servings: 2 cookie sheets of toffee
Preparation time: 45 minutes
Cooking time: 30 minutes
Chilling time: 1 hour

- Line 2 cookie sheets with waxed paper.
- Sprinkle half the pecans on each sheet of waxed paper.
- Mix sugar and butter over medium high heat, stirring often.
- Bring sugar mixture to the hard crack stage on a candy thermometer, 300° F.
- Pour at once over pecans on waxed paper.
- Pour chocolate chips onto both sheets, dividing evenly.
- Let stand 2 to 3 minutes.
- Spread melted chips over surface with a knife.
- Sprinkle the remaining half of the pecans on top.
- Refrigerate for 1 hour.
- Break into pieces.

Pralines

1/2	cup butter
1-1/2	cups light brown sugar
1-1/2	cups granulated sugar
1	cup Pet milk
1/2	teaspoon vanilla extract
2	cups pecan halves

Servings: 18
Preparation time: 5 minutes
Cooking time: 30 minutes

- Combine first 5 ingredients in a heavy 3-quart saucepan.
- Simmer until syrup forms a soft ball when dropped in ice water.
- Stir in pecans.
- Drop by spoonfuls onto waxed paper. Put newspaper under waxed paper to protect table surface or countertops.

Foolproof Fudge

2-1/4	cups sugar
3/4	cup Pet evaporated milk
12	large marshmallows
1/4	cup butter
1/4	teaspoon salt
1	6-ounce package semisweet chocolate chips
1	teaspoon vanilla extract
1	cup broken pecans

Servings: 30 pieces
Preparation time: 15 minutes
Cooking time: 5 minutes

- In a heavy 2-quart saucepan, combine first 5 ingredients.
- Bring to a boil over medium heat, stirring constantly.
- Cook and stir for 5 minutes.
- Remove from heat. Stir in chocolate chips, then vanilla and nuts.
- Spread into a greased 8-inch square pan.
- Cool. Cut into 30 pieces.

Peanut Butter Fudge

3	cups sugar
3/4	cup butter
2/3	cup evaporated milk
1	12-ounce jar crunchy peanut butter
1	teaspoon vanilla extract
1	7-ounce jar marshmallow cream
2	cups dry roasted peanuts

Servings: 40 small squares
Preparation time: 15 minutes
Cooking time: 5 minutes

- Combine sugar, butter and milk in a heavy pot.
- Bring to a boil and boil for 5 minutes.
- Add peanut butter, vanilla and marshmallow cream.
- Stir and put in a buttered 9 X 13-inch pan.
- Sprinkle peanuts on top.
- When cool, cut into bite-size squares.

Bourbon Balls

1	cup chopped pecans
6	tablespoons bourbon
1/2	cup butter
1	16-ounce box plus 3 tablespoons confectioners' sugar
5	ounces semisweet chocolate
1	1-inch strip of paraffin
	Toothpicks

Servings: 3 to 4 dozen candies
Soaking time: overnight
Preparation time: 30 minutes
Chilling time: 1-1/2 hours

- Soak pecans in bourbon overnight.
- Mix butter and sugar by hand. Add pecans and bourbon.
- Wrap in plastic wrap and refrigerate for 1 hour.
- Form into small balls.
- Place on a cookie sheet lined with waxed paper. Chill for 30 minutes.
- In the top of a double boiler, melt chocolate and paraffin.
- Dip balls in chocolate using toothpicks.
- Return to cookie sheet lined with waxed paper and refrigerate.
- Will keep for several weeks if covered tightly.

Mint Balls

1/4	cup butter
1	16-ounce box confectioners' sugar
1/3	cup crème de menthe
1	cup chopped pecans
3-1/2	squares unsweetened chocolate
1/6	cup shaved paraffin

Servings: 100 mint balls
Preparation time: 1 hour
Chilling time: 3 hours

- Melt butter and combine with powdered sugar.
- Add crème de menthe and pecans.
- Roll into 3/4-inch balls and place on a cookie sheet lined with waxed paper.
- Refrigerate for several hours.
- Using a slotted spoon, dip balls into chocolate that has been melted with paraffin in the top of a double boiler.
- Place balls on waxed papered cookie sheet and refrigerate.
- Will keep in refrigerator in airtight tins for several weeks.
- Serve in silver bowls with sprigs of holly.

Cooking with Herbs

Herbs
The Magic Ingredient

Cooking with fresh herbs has become increasingly popular in contemporary American households for many good reasons.

A veritable renaissance of interest in good, natural food and seasonings has focused unprecedented attention on the virtues and pleasures of culinary herbs.

Preservatives, artificial flavorings and colorings, bulk processing and like dangers to good health present in foods, have resulted in their loss of nutritional value, natural flavor and the scrupulous cook's confidence.

More than ever before, salt and refined sugar are looked on with suspicion and disapproval for all ages. Low-fat diet restrictions, as well as salt and sugar-free meals, have brought to the fore many palatable and nourishing possibilities that herbs offer as replacements.

Younger generations, carefully nurturing family fitness and sound nutrition, are responding with imaginative ways to use fresh products and herb seasonings, as enjoyable and beneficial substitutes for processed foods. Educating young palates to savor the superior quality of fresh, natural ingredients, enhanced with the stimulating zest of herbs, predictably leads to a greater respect for healthful practices.

For those new to herb seasoning, start simply with those you can have the most fun using and growing, such as one of the container-grown "collections" which range from the simplest bouquet-garni bachelor pots to the more sophisticated finesherbes strawberry jars or a summer salad planter.

For sheer joy, convenience and possibly least demanding gardening adventure, culinary herbs are peerless. In addition, most kitchen herbs are equipped with a built-in disease and insect resistance. Container-grown herbs require evenly moist soil, neutral to alkaline in makeup. They have one compelling demand to grow vigorously, a well-drained location with partial shade in hot climates. Magic is their name!

The very best way to get acquainted with herbs is to grow them and learn firsthand their distinguishing characteristics, as well as their compatible qualities. Their very scents offer helpful guidance to the beginning herbalist. Some herbs and foods have a special affinity for one another. Some time-honored combinations are:

Basil Good used in tomato and egg dishes, soups, chowders, fish dishes, beans, eggplant, squash, onions, liver, lamb and chicken. Basil enthusiasts steam it as a vegetable served with herbed butter, freshly ground pepper and topped with a garnish of lightly salted, chopped tomatoes.

Chervil Add to sauces, especially béarnaise, egg dishes, soups, salads, spinach and beets.

Chives Use with any dish where a subtle onion flavor is desired.

Dill Add to any fish sauce. Sprinkle generously on potatoes, cucumbers, green salads, slaw and beans. The green dill weed is lighter in flavor and more versatile than the seed.

Marjoram Enhances many vegetables, especially mushrooms, and most egg dishes, lamb, beef, poultry, onion soup and mixed green salads.

Orégano Flavors all tomato dishes, spaghetti, chili, meat loaf, cream sauces, roasted meats, stews and poultry.

Parsley Packed with vitamins A and C, thiamin, riboflavin (B_2), niacin, calcium, iron, magnesium and phosphorous, it is a great loss when quantities of the valuable herb are so casually tossed out with the leftovers. Try substituting finely chopped parsley for spinach in spinach quiche, similar to the early English practice of using the entire plant, stemmed, for a parsley pie. Parsley is very useful to slimmers as it helps remove excess fluid from body tissue.

Rosemary Rub into beef, pork, veal and lamb roasts. Especially good used with chicken, capon, duck, rabbit and fruit compotes.

Sage Add to lima beans, tomatoes, pork stews, turkey, rabbit, stuffings, sausage, meat loaf, eggplant and sharp cheese.

Savory Also called the bean herb. Use with potatoes, soup, roasted meats, especially pork and veal, chicken stuffing, halibut, salmon, potato salad and stewed pears.

Tarragon This herb speaks French. Use with vinegar dressings, mushrooms, veal, sweetbreads, béarnaise sauce, tartare, mustard sauce, tomato soup and juice, egg dishes, fish, poultry and asparagus.

Thyme Use in tomato and creole dishes, gumbo and chowders, carrots, onions, aspics, cottage cheese, dips, meat loaf, veal, liver, scallops, crab, sole and flounder.

Fines-herbes Specific herbs used may vary, but usually include marjoram, summer savory and parsley. For "fines-herbes," the accomplished French cook would finely snip the above mentioned combination to either stir in a dish while cooking or if just using parsley, to sprinkle on top for color or flavor.

Bouquet-garni herbs In classical French cooking, a "bouquet-garni" is a combination of parsley, marjoram, thyme and a bay leaf (½ of a bay leaf is often ample for most recipes). The herbs should be tied in cheesecloth and dropped into simmering food that cooks long enough for the flavor to go out of the herbs and into the pot. Then the herbs should be discarded. The Americanized "bouquet-garni" or "broth posy" may contain a variety of combinations according to the foods being used.

Summer Salad Planter Box Includes basil, chervil, chives, tarragon, thyme, orégano, parsley, marjoram and dill.

If fresh herbs are unavailable, good quality commercially dried herbs may be substituted if given proper attention.

Most dried herbs lose flavor and color within a year, and the purchase date should be noted on the label. Since an expiration date does not appear on spice and herb packaging, it is important to be familiar with the following ways to maintain and use purchased dried or home preserved herbs:

Store dried herbs in airtight containers in a cool, dark place, preferably the refrigerator.

To test the strength or freshness of dried herbs, finely crush a small amount. A freshlike aroma should result.

Before adding dried herbs to a recipe, help release the full flavor by either gently crushing the palm of one hand against the heel of the other, with a mortar and pestle or between waxed paper with a rolling pin.

Delicately flavored and ground herbs should be added toward the end of the cooking time to prevent the loss of flavor from steam. Bay leaves require longer, slower cooking to bring out their best flavor.

Add slightly stronger crushed dried herbs along with salt and freshly ground pepper. Avoid long cooking of herbs in foods such as stews. It is best to add during last half hour to prevent overcooking or bitterness.

Generally speaking, fresh and dried herbs may be used interchangeably by transposing. The favored formula is: 1 part dried herbs closely approximates 3 parts fresh herbs.

A good way to revitalize dried herbs is to soak them for about 10 minutes in 1 teaspoon lemon juice.

After dried herbs have been added, allow time for flavor to develop before testing.

Dried herbs added to juices, sauces and butters should be allowed ample time to blend, preferably overnight.

Basil and Garlic Butter

1/2	cup butter or margarine, softened
2	cloves garlic, pressed
2	tablespoons finely snipped fresh basil

Servings: 3/4 cup
Preparation time: 5 minutes
Standing time: 2 to 3 hours

- Combine all ingredients. Mix thoroughly and place in a container. Allow flavors to blend at room temperature for 2 to 3 hours before refrigerating.
- May be made in a food processor.
- Delicious served with lamb chops, steaks, broiled tomatoes, broiled flounder or other white fish.

Yogurt Herb Spread

1	cup plain yogurt
2	tablespoons good mayonnaise
2	teaspoons lemon juice
2	tablespoons each: finely snipped fresh basil, chives, orégano, parsley, tarragon

Servings: 1-1/4 cups
Preparation time: 10 minutes
Standing time: 2 hours

- Combine all ingredients and blend thoroughly.
- Let stand for 2 hours for flavors to blend.
- Chill before serving.

Boursin

1	8-ounce carton whipped butter
2	8-ounce packages cream cheese, softened
1	teaspoon dill seed
1/2	teaspoon each: dried basil, chives, marjoram, thyme
2	teaspoons lemon juice
2	cloves garlic, pressed

Servings: 2 cups
Preparation time: 15 minutes

- Cream butter and cream cheese in a processor or blender.
- Soften herbs in lemon juice for 5 minutes. Add garlic.
- Add herb mixture to processor. Blend.
- Store Boursin in two 8-ounce cartons with tight lids to refrigerate or freeze.

Mixed Herb Butter

1 pound butter or margarine
1 cup mixed herbs: snipped fresh tarragon, chervil, thyme, chives, summer savory, orégano
1 tablespoon lemon juice

Servings: 2 cups
Preparation time: 5 minutes
Standing time: 2 to 3 hours

- Use kitchen shears to finely snip the stipel leaves and tender tips of the herbs. This bruises and releases the essential oils which flavor the butter.
- Warm 1/2 cup butter in a small saucepan.
- Add herbs. Mix well and bruise herbs to further increase flavor while lightly sautéing, about 3 minutes.
- Add lemon juice.
- Add remaining 1-1/2 cups butter and mix thoroughly. Transfer to a plastic container and refrigerate.
- Herb butter may be made in a food processor with good results if butter is firm. Herbs may be coarsely chopped. After mixing, allow to stand at room temperature for 2 to 3 hours before chilling so flavors will blend.
- Serve herb butter with any food usually accompanied with butter such as: pasta, breads, rice, broiled steak, fish fillets, baked potato and toast.
- Unsalted, steamed and drained vegetables of any kind become exquisite taste treats with the addition of 1 tablespoon or more herb butter per 4 servings.
- Large quantities of butter should be made because of its many uses and time saving readiness on hurried occasions.

Parsley Sauce

1	cup water	
1	cup finely snipped parsley leaves	
2	tablespoons butter or margarine	
1/2	teaspoon lemon juice (optional)	

Servings: 3/4 cup
Preparation time: 10 minutes
Cooking time: 5 to 10 minutes
- Bring water to a boil in a heavy saucepan.
- Add parsley to blanch for 1 minute. Drain.
- Heat butter and lemon juice in saucepan.
- Add parsley and sauté for 2 minutes.
- Pour all over steamed and drained vegetables or potatoes.

Quick Herb Sauce

1	cup good mayonnaise
1	teaspoon Dijon mustard
1	tablespoon lemon juice
1/4	cup mixed herbs: finely snipped fresh chervil, dill, chives, tarragon, watercress, thyme

Servings: 1-1/4 cups
Preparation time: 10 minutes
Standing time: 2 to 3 hours
- Mix mayonnaise, mustard and lemon juice until smooth.
- Stir in herbs.
- Allow flavors to blend for several hours before using.
- Serve as a sandwich spread or with salads, crudités, deviled eggs or stuffed eggs.

Herb Dip

1	cup sour cream
1	8-ounce package cream cheese
2	teaspoons grated onion
1/2	teaspoon Worcestershire sauce Tabasco sauce to taste
1	tablespoon each: snipped fresh chives, parsley, tarragon, dill Milk

Servings: 2 cups
Preparation time: 20 minutes
- In a processor or blender, whirl first 5 ingredients until smooth.
- Add herbs and mix.
- Add milk by tablespoonful to get desired consistency.
- Use as a dip for raw vegetables or as dressing for a tomato salad.

Vinaigrette with Mixed Herbs

	Freshly ground black pepper to taste
1	teaspoon Dijon mustard
1/4	cup wine vinegar
1	cup vegetable oil
1	tablespoon lemon juice
1/2	cup mixed herbs: finely snipped fresh tarragon, chervil, chives, dill, thyme, basil, marjoram (others may be used)
1	clove garlic

Servings: 2 cups
Preparation time: 10 minutes

- Combine pepper and mustard in a mixing bowl.
- Add vinegar and stir until dissolved.
- Add oil slowly, beating well to make an emulsion.
- Stir in lemon juice.
- Add mixed herbs.
- Peel and halve garlic clove. Put in dressing.
- Serve with tossed salads of all kinds and asparagus.
- May substitute 3 tablespoons finely chopped fresh basil for mixed herbs and serve with tomato or mixed lettuce salads.

Sesame Salt

1	cup sesame seeds
1/4	cup salt

Servings: 1-1/4 cups
Preparation time: 20 minutes
Baking time: 10 to 15 minutes

- Preheat oven to 325° F.
- Place sesame seeds in a shallow baking pan.
- Toast until slightly brown, stirring occasionally. Watch carefully so as not to burn.
- Combine seeds with salt and whirl in a processor or blender.
- Store in an airtight container.
- If salt is not dry enough to shake, place in a 200° F. oven for 5 minutes to remove moisture.

Yogurt Salad Dressing

1/4	cup cider or wine vinegar
2	tablespoons water
1	envelope Italian salad dressing mix
1	tablespoon each: finely snipped fresh chives, marjoram, tarragon, summer savory, thyme
2/3	cup plain yogurt

Servings: 1 cup
Preparation time: 10 minutes

- Place vinegar and water in a cruet or wide-mouth bottle with a tight lid.
- Add dressing mix and shake well.
- Add herbs and yogurt. Shake thoroughly and chill before using.

Tomato Soup with Basil

4	tablespoons butter or margarine
1	large mild onion, chopped
1-1/2	pounds firm ripe tomatoes, peeled and chopped
2-1/2	cups hot chicken stock
	Freshly ground black pepper to taste
3	tablespoons finely cut fresh basil

Servings: 4
Preparation time: 30 minutes
Cooking time: 20 minutes

- Melt butter in a large heavy saucepan.
- Gently sauté onion until tender.
- Add tomatoes and cook for 5 minutes.
- Pour in stock. Bring to a boil, lower heat and simmer for 20 minutes. Add pepper.
- Blend in processor until smooth.
- Return to saucepan to reheat. Stir in basil.
- May be served chilled with a dollop of sour cream and fresh chives.

Slimmer's Herbed Gazpacho

1	medium carrot, coarsely grated
1	stalk celery, finely chopped
1	spring onion, finely chopped
1	tender cucumber, finely chopped
1	cup V-8 juice
1	cup yogurt
1/2	teaspoon sesame or plain salt
2	tablespoons lemon juice
1/2	cup snipped parsley leaves
1	tablespoon each: finely snipped fresh chives, basil, tarragon

Servings: 3 to 5
Preparation time: 20 minutes
• Combine all ingredients and blend thoroughly.
• Chill until ready to serve.
• For variation, add one 8-ounce can crushed pineapple with juice.

Chervil Soup

4	tablespoons herbed butter or margarine
2	medium onions, thinly sliced
3	medium carrots, thinly sliced
2	medium potatoes, thinly sliced
3-1/2	cups hot chicken stock
1	cup chopped fresh chervil
	Freshly ground black pepper to taste
1/2	cup light cream

Servings: 4
Preparation time: 15 minutes
Cooking time: 35 minutes
• Melt butter in a large saucepan.
• Sauté vegetables for 10 minutes.
• Add stock, chervil and pepper. Bring to a boil.
• Reduce heat and simmer, covered, for 35 minutes.
• Cool slightly. Then blend in processor until smooth.
• Return to saucepan to reheat. Stir in cream.

Tomatoes Stuffed with Herbed Orzo

6	medium to large firm ripe tomatoes
	Salt and freshly ground black pepper to taste
	Herbed or vegetable oil
1/3	cup uncooked orzo (rice shaped pasta)
1/3	cup each: finely snipped fresh basil, parsley, chives
1/2	cup freshly grated Parmesan cheese or crumbled Feta cheese
2	tablespoons aromatic or vegetable oil
	Salt and freshly ground black pepper to taste

Servings: 6
Preparation time: 30 minutes
Baking time: 35 minutes

- Preheat oven to 325° F.
- Core and cut a 1/2-inch slice from stem end of tomatoes. Reserve slices. Remove and reserve seeds, pulp and liquid from tomatoes and leave a 1/2-inch shell.
- Sprinkle insides of tomatoes lightly with salt and pepper. Brush with herbed oil.
- Arrange tomatoes, hollow side up, in a lightly oiled shallow baking dish.
- Bake for 15 minutes. Remove tomatoes and invert on a rack to drain.
- In a saucepan of lightly salted boiling water, cook orzo until tender. Drain.
- Chop reserved tomato slices and pulp. Put in a bowl.
- Add orzo and herbs.
- Add Parmesan cheese, oil, salt and pepper. Mix thoroughly.
- Fill tomatoes with mixture, mound and return to baking dish. Bake at 325° F. for 20 minutes.

Summer Squash and Chervil

2	tablespoons butter or margarine
6	small summer squash or zucchini, sliced
2	tablespoons snipped fresh chervil

Servings: 4
Preparation time: 10 minutes
Cooking time: 20 minutes

- Heat butter in a heavy saucepan.
- Add squash and chervil.
- Stir thoroughly, cover and cook over low heat for 20 minutes.

Green Beans with Rosemary

1-1/2	pounds green pole beans, French-sliced
3	tablespoons lemon juice
2	tablespoons snipped fresh rosemary leaves
1	tablespoon snipped fresh sage leaves
1	large clove garlic, pressed
	Salt and freshly ground black pepper to taste

Servings: 4 to 6
Preparation time: 20 minutes
Cooking time: 5 to 8 minutes
Standing time: 2 hours

- Place beans in a steamer over boiling water. Cook, partially covered, for 5 minutes or until just tender. Drain.
- In a serving bowl, combine remaining ingredients. Whisk mixture until it is well combined.
- Transfer beans to herb mixture and toss.
- Let marinate at room temperature for 2 hours.

Risi e Bisi

2	tablespoons butter, preferably herbed
2	slices Canadian bacon, cubed
1	medium onion, chopped
4	cloves garlic, pressed
3	cups chicken stock
3/4	cup raw rice
1	10-ounce package Birdseye Petit Pois Deluxe, thawed
1/3	cup freshly grated Parmesan cheese
2	tablespoons chopped parsley
2	tablespoons snipped fresh basil
2	tablespoons snipped fresh chives
1	tablespoon herbed butter

Servings: 4
Preparation time: 30 minutes
Cooking time: 35 minutes

- In a large heavy saucepan, melt 2 tablespoons butter. Sauté bacon, onion and garlic over medium heat.
- Add stock and bring to a boil.
- Add rice. Cover and simmer until rice is cooked, about 30 minutes.
- Add peas.
- Stir in cheese, parsley, basil, chives and 1 tablespoon butter.
- Transfer to a covered casserole to keep warm in the oven.

Herb Risotto

3	tablespoons butter or margarine	
1	large shallot, finely chopped	
1	cup raw Italian medium-grain rice, washed and drained	
3	cups chicken stock, heated	
2	threads saffron, crumbled	
1	bay leaf, crushed	
12	sage leaves, finely snipped	
12	sprigs thyme, finely snipped	
12	tarragon leaves, finely snipped	
12	marjoram leaves, finely snipped	
	Salt and freshly ground black pepper to taste	

Servings: 6
Preparation time: 30 minutes
Cooking time: 30 minutes

- Heat butter in a heavy saucepan.
- Cook shallot until tender.
- Add rice. Stir until well coated.
- Add 1-3/4 cups stock.
- Cover and simmer gently until almost all the liquid is absorbed.
- Add saffron, bay leaf and herbs to 3/4 cup stock. Stir into rice.
- Cover again and cook gently until stock is absorbed.
- If rice is tender, season with salt and pepper and serve. If not tender, add remaining 1/2 cup stock and continue to simmer until cooked.

Pesto alla Genovese

5 to 6	cloves garlic, pressed
2	cups coarsely cut fresh basil
6	tablespoons freshly grated Parmesan cheese
1	tablespoon unsalted butter
1/2	cup good olive oil

Servings: 4 to 6
Preparation time: 20 minutes

- In a processor, blend garlic, basil, cheese and butter until a paste forms.
- Reduce speed to low and slowly add oil until mixture is smooth.
- Use as a sauce for pasta or vegetables.

Quick Version

1	cup fresh basil leaves
1/3	cup stemmed parsley
1	cup freshly grated Parmesan cheese
6	tablespoons good olive oil

Servings: 3 to 4
Preparation time: 15 minutes

- Put all ingredients in a processor bowl and whirl until smooth.

Herb Quiche

3	tablespoons vegetable or aromatic oil
1	pound fresh spinach, washed, drained and stemmed
1	cup chopped parsley and chervil
1/2	bunch watercress, washed and drained
1/4	cup mixed herbs: finely snipped fresh tarragon, dill, chives, thyme
2	eggs
1	cup light cream
	Freshly ground black pepper to taste
1/2	cup freshly grated Parmesan cheese, reserving 1 tablespoon
1	10-inch pie shell, baked

Servings: 6
Preparation time: 30 minutes
Baking time: 30 minutes

- Preheat oven to 350° F.
- Heat oil until hot in a large heavy saucepan.
- Cook vegetables and herbs for 4 to 5 minutes, stirring continuously.
- Remove from stove, drain thoroughly and chop.
- Beat eggs in a bowl. Add cream, pepper and cheese.
- Mix in spinach mixture and pour into pie shell. Sprinkle with reserved cheese.
- Bake for 30 minutes.

Eggs in Herb Sauce

1	egg yolk
2/3	cup good olive oil or herbed oil
1-1/2	tablespoons white wine vinegar
1/2	tablespoon lemon juice
2/3	cup light cream
1	cup mixed herbs: finely snipped fresh chervil, chives, dill, marjoram, parsley, thyme
1	head lettuce
6	hard-boiled eggs

Servings: 6
Preparation time: 20 minutes

- In a blender, combine egg yolk, olive oil, vinegar and lemon juice.
- Add cream and herbs.
- Whirl blender twice quickly to combine.
- Make a bed of shredded lettuce on each salad plate.
- Cut eggs in half and place, cut side down, on lettuce.
- Pour sauce over all and serve as a first course.

Herbed Chicken

3	tablespoons herbed or vegetable oil
4	broiler quarters
1/2	cup dry white wine
1/4	cup water
	Salt and freshly ground black pepper to taste
1-1/2	tablespoons finely snipped fresh rosemary
2	tablespoons finely snipped fresh orégano
4	tablespoons stemmed and snipped fresh thyme

Servings: 4 to 6
Preparation time: 45 minutes
Baking time: 20 minutes

- Preheat oven to 325° F.
- Preheat a large heavy skillet over medium high heat.
- Add oil, heating until hot.
- Brown chicken lightly in oil, turning once.
- Add wine and water, reduce heat and simmer for 15 minutes.
- Remove all to a baking dish.
- Sprinkle herbs over chicken and pan juices. Cover.
- Bake for 20 minutes. Remove cover for last 5 minutes of baking to brown.

Duck with Honey and Herbs

1	4-pound duck, quartered
1/4	cup clear honey
1	tablespoon each: minced fresh rosemary, marjoram, thyme, summer savory
	Freshly ground black pepper to taste
1/2	cup orange juice, preferably fresh

Servings: 4
Preparation time: 15 minutes
Standing time: 1 to 2 hours
Baking time: 50 minutes

- Prick skin of duck with a sharp skewer to release fat while cooking.
- Warm honey in a saucepan. Add herbs and mix well.
- Add orange juice and simmer gently for 3 to 5 minutes.
- Place duck quarters, skin side up, in a baking dish.
- Pour honey mixture over all. Let stand 1 to 2 hours to absorb flavor.
- Bake in a preheated 325° F. oven for 50 minutes, basting and rearranging pieces to brown evenly.
- Discard pan juices as they are too fatty to serve with duck.

Pork Chops with Basil

3	tablespoons herbed or vegetable oil
4	thick-cut pork chops
3	cloves garlic, pressed
1-1/2	tablespoons snipped fresh basil
1/2	cup dry Marsala wine

Servings: 4
Preparation time: 20 minutes
Baking time: 1 hour

- Preheat oven to 250° F.
- Heat oil in a heavy skillet.
- Brown pork chops. Remove to a shallow baking dish.
- Make a paste of garlic and basil. Spread on top of chops. Cover tightly.
- Bake for 1 hour or until tender.
- Add wine and cook, uncovered, until wine bubbles.

Broiled Herb Fish Fillets

3	tablespoons margarine, melted
3	teaspoons minced fresh dill weed
2	teaspoons minced fresh thyme
1	teaspoon minced fresh tarragon
2	teaspoons lemon juice
1/4	cup dry white wine
2	fish fillets

Servings: 2
Preparation time: 30 minutes
Broiling time: 10 minutes

- Melt margarine in a small saucepan.
- Sauté herbs for 3 to 4 minutes.
- Add lemon juice. Simmer for 3 minutes.
- Pour wine over fish fillets and set aside for 10 minutes.
- Lightly oil a shallow baking dish. Put fish in, skin side down.
- Pour herb mixture over fish.
- Broil 6 inches from heat for 8 to 10 minutes or until fish flakes easily.

Scallops in Herb Sauce

1	pound sea or bay scallops, rinsed and drained
2/3	cup white wine
1/3	cup water
	Freshly ground black pepper to taste
2	tablespoons butter or margarine
1	tablespoon all-purpose flour
1	tablespoon each: finely snipped fresh tarragon, dill, chives, parsley
2/3	cup light cream

Servings: 2
Preparation time: 15 minutes
Cooking time: 10 minutes

- Cut sea scallops in quarters. Bay scallops may be left whole.
- Bring wine, water and pepper to a boil in a small saucepan.
- Add scallops, cover and simmer for 6 minutes, or until tender.
- Remove scallops with a slotted spoon and keep warm.
- Reserve liquid, keeping hot.
- Melt butter in a saucepan. Blend in flour to form a smooth paste.
- Stir reserved liquid in slowly and stir gently to make a smooth sauce.
- Add herbs. Gently simmer 2 to 3 minutes.
- Blend in cream. Return scallops to sauce to heat for a moment.

Parsley and Bread Stuffing

1/4	cup butter or margarine
6	ounces shallots, finely chopped
3	cups fresh white bread crumbs
1	cup chopped parsley
	Salt and freshly ground black pepper to taste

Servings: 3-1/2 cups
Preparation time: 15 minutes

- Melt butter in a skillet.
- Sauté shallots until golden.
- Add bread crumbs and stir until well mixed.
- Remove skillet from heat and stir in parsley.
- Add salt and pepper.
- Let cool completely before using to stuff fish or baking fowl. To stuff a turkey, double recipe.

Entertaining "Jacksonville Style"

A Venetian Masked Ball
to benefit
The Cummer Gallery of Art

Bay Scallops en Coquille*

Grigliata de Mansa

Sauce Béarnaise

Snowpeas with Water Chestnuts*

New Potatoes au Caviar*   Gingered Carrots*

Croissants Ricotta

Strawberries au Chocolat*

Espresso

Pouilly-Fuissé   Château Batailley Pouillae Bordeaux

Domaine Chandon Brut Champagne

Costumed heralds and a trumpet fanfare greet guests at the Gallery entrance. Under banners of Venetian blue and gold depicting the winged lion of Venice, guests are presented with plumed and sequinned masks. Through formal gardens and over a replica of the Rialto Bridge, they make their way to a glittering tented barge, scene of a lively auction to benefit the museum. A seated dinner is held in the permanent collection galleries, where moiré cloths of burgundy, hunter green, Venetian blue, scarlet or gold cover round mirror-topped tables. Mirrored pedestal centerpieces hold plumed masks and clusters of rubrum lilies with ribbon streamers. White candles, white napkins circled with gold ribbon and gold-bordered Tiffany place cards complete the table settings. After dinner, guests return to the floating tent to dance late into the magical evening.

*Starred menu items in this section may be found listed as such in the index.

A Holiday "Spanish Gold" Celebration

to benefit

The Jacksonville Museum of Arts and Sciences

Caviar Egg Ring* with Assorted Crackers

Cold Blanched Vegetables with Arnold's Hollandaise Sauce*

Assorted Hard Rolls and Soft Cheeses

Boiled Shrimp and Crab Claws

Watermelon Basket with Melon Balls and Strawberries

Guava Dainties*

Bourbon Fruitcake Cookies*

Luscious Squares*

White Spanish Rijoa

Celebrating an extraordinary exhibit of Spanish gold salvaged from ancient shipwrecks, the evening reflects the romance of Spanish treasure fleets which sailed the Florida coasts centuries ago. The long cocktail table draped in gold lamé is laden with giant clam shells filled with cold vegetables and sauce. Shell-shaped lucite pieces serve as additional containers. Sand sprinkled with glitter is spread on the table, and at each end a large fish bowl holds shells, jewelry and gold coins. Candles burn in conch shells. Nearby a small dinghy overflows with crab claws and shrimp on cracked ice. The arched windows are decorated for Christmas with gold-swagged wreaths and poinsettias, and a towering tree is hung entirely with gold ornaments and shells sprayed gold. Spanish classical music enhances the feeling of ancient splendor and romance.

A Russian Christmas Evening
to benefit
The Jacksonville Art Museum

Whole Poached Salmon with Horseradish Sauce* and Dill Sauce*

Toast Points with Black Caviar, Sour Cream, Finely Chopped

Onion and sieved Hard-Boiled Egg

Stolichnaya Vodka on Ice

Crab Rangoon* with Hot Mustard Sauce*

Russian Chef's Stroganoff* with Buttered Noodles

Sautéed Cherry Tomatoes*

Salad of Bibb Lettuce and Mandarin Oranges Vinaigrette

Hard Rolls

Miniature Individual Cheesecakes*

Praline Cookies*

Guests arrive through a waterfall of miniature lights covering the tall glass façade of the museum. Tall, heavily flocked, lighted trees create the spirit of a Russian Christmas inside. Heightening the wintry effect, snow-covered branches form arches leading into the exhibit of antique Russian costumes. One gallery is reserved for the traditional hors d'oeuvres served each year at the benefit: Russian vodka, salmon and caviar. Three tables covered in white linen hold the iced Stolichnaya bottles, thin vodka glasses, smoked salmon and toast points and caviar surrounded by crystal bowls of garnish. Another gallery serves the buffet from a silver-covered table bearing massive candelabra with white candles. The centerpiece is a topiary of white chrysanthemums flanked by two Imperial swans on a lake of mirror, circled with green foliage.

Antique Show
to benefit
The Jacksonville Wolfson's Children's Hospital

Marinated Shrimp*

Frosted Artichokes with Caviar* and Melba Toast

Crustless Quiche*

Assorted Fruits and Cheeses

Roast Lamb with Herb Mustard*

Souffléed Corn*

Ratatouille*

Sour Cream Crescent Rolls*

Kahlua Mousse*

Mosel Wehlener Sonnenuhr Kabinett
Rhône Châteauneuf-du-Pape

At the entrance to the exhibit hall, a red carpet and massed red and white poinsettias welcome patrons while lighted ficus trees and palms glow alongside. Folding mirrored panels reflect the light and color around them. Clustering around the intimate vignettes of antique exhibits are huge lighted holly and ficus trees anchored in tubs wrapped in foil. Dinner is served from long tables draped in silver mylar and covered with mirrored panels. Each table holds arrangements of white gladioli and red anthurium lilies in tall glass cylinders. Crystal candlesticks hold white candles.

Symphony Pops French Country Picnic

to benefit

The Jacksonville Symphony Orchestra

"The" Pâté*

Assorted Cheeses

Bread Sticks   French Bread

Lime Chicken with Melon*

Artichoke-Rice Salad*

Buttermilk Orange Cupcakes with Fresh Orange Sauce*

Pecan Tart*

Beaujolais   Loire Valley Anjou Rosé

A French country picnic begins early on a summer evening with cocktails in a terraced garden beside the St. Johns River. Pâté in stoneware pots, cheeses and French bread in baskets are served with refreshing wine spritzers made of white wine and club soda and garnished with slices of lime. The light breeze from the river tugs at the round tablecloths of blue cotton overlaid with blue, coral and white paisley cotton scarves. The tables hold terra-cotta hens filled with white baby's breath and low candles in terra-cotta saucers. Guests gather around each table to serve themselves from picnic baskets packed with entrées for eight. These baskets from the farmer's market are lacquered white and hand painted with blue forget-me-nots. Blue cotton napkins line the baskets and set off simple white picnic ware. As the music begins, the guests settle at the tables to enjoy their "moveable feast" in the cool evening air.

Dinner Dance by the Riverside
to benefit
The American Cancer Society

Shrimp with Mayonnaise Dressing*

Zucchini Frittata*

Party Sandwiches with Vidalia Onion Spread*

Assorted Fruits and Cheeses

Fillet of Beef with Port Butter*

Amelia Island Rice*

Marinated Broccoli Ring*

Hard Rolls with Butter

Meringues Pistachio*

Miniature Cream Cheese Tarts with Cherry Sauce*

Bourbon Balls*

Concannon Sauvignon Blanc   Beringer Cabernet Sauvignon

Pots of coral and pink begonias, maidenhair fern and illuminated ficus trees highlight the entrance of the house and lead the guests to a white tent opening onto the banks of the St. Johns River. Hundreds of balloons in rainbow colors form an archway into the tent and hang in clusters in each corner. Placed around the dance floor, the skirted tables match the balloons in shades of lavender, salmon, yellow and turquoise. Pots of salmon amaryllis fenced by pussy willow stems sit on a base of galax leaves centered on the table tops. Inside the house, dinner is served from a long mahogany Sheraton table. Twin Chinese cachepots rest on circles of mirror; between them, galax leaves and white quince are reflected in a mirrored square. Guests return to the open tent for dinner, music and starlight dancing.

Oyster Roast Celebrating the Florida-Georgia Game

Mosquito Lagoon Duck Breasts* with Béarnaise Sauce

Twelve Bushels of Oysters (to serve fifty)

Cocktail Sauce, Melted Butter, Saltine Crackers

Amelia Island Brunswick Stew*

Georgia Coleslaw*

Swiss Cheese Cornbread*

"The Sisters" Bourbon Pound Cake*

Louis Martini Chardonnay   Imported Beers

Each fall the Florida-Georgia football game is played in Jacksonville. A favorite way to celebrate — or to offer consolation — after the game is with a traditional oyster roast. Outdoors in the cool November air, the celebrated Florida oyster is served both roasted and raw. The oyster tables are set carefully to accommodate the succulent seasonal feast. Long tables wrapped with butcher paper are equipped with galvanized buckets from a hardware store. These are filled with oyster gloves, oyster knives and forks. Stacks of tin pie pans hold the roasted oysters and small buckets are filled with melted butter, cocktail sauce and crackers. The main buffet table wears natural burlap and holds a pair of shiny tin pails filled with bronze chrysanthemums and dried herbs. Candles of varying heights are grouped around the pails. Cinnamon, brown and beige bandannas tied with dried corn husks are heaped alongside tin plates. Brunswick stew and coleslaw are served from shallow galvanized buckets and hot bread is wrapped in bandannas and served from a huge flat basket. A bonfire warms the evening.

Brunch Before the Gator Bowl Game

Bloody Marys with Celery Sticks

Frozen Bourbon Sours*

Crab Swiss Rounds*   *Sausage Filled Mushrooms**

Egg and Artichoke Casserole*

Smithfield Ham and Southern Biscuits*

Asparagus and Cherry Tomatoes with Watercress Mayonnaise*

Fresh Fruit in Grand Marnier Sauce*

Kentucky Butter Cake*

Ruth's Coffee*

Asti Spumante

In late December the Gator Bowl Game brings together top-rated football teams for a spirited contest in Jacksonville's Gator Bowl. A traditional way to prepare for the sporting event is with a sumptuous brunch on the morning of the game. Setting the stage for the party and lending a carnival air, two red balloon topiary trees flank the entrance. To make the trees, balloons are tied together to form rounded shapes, attached to wooden dowels wrapped in florist tape and inserted in earth-filled white ceramic pots. Two clusters in graduated sizes are tied to the same dowel to increase the illusion of topiary trees. The earth around the pots is covered with deer moss. Over the round indoor buffet table, skirted in red patent vinyl, hang multicolored helium-filled balloons. The table is set with clear lucite, glass and white enameled serving pieces. Silverware is wrapped in red and white striped ribbon and the bar is made festive with red plastic ice buckets tied with clusters of balloons.

Luncheon on the Terrace at Ponte Vedra Beach

*Potage Cressonaire**

*Seafood and Pasta Salad Pescara**

*Beans with Dill Sauce**

*Onion Rolls**

*Meringues with Strawberries and Custard**

Rhone Tavel Rosé

Southeast of Jacksonville lies magnificent Ponte Vedra Beach, its white sands stretching across miles of unobstructed view, an ideal setting for an oceanside luncheon. A round table draped in salmon cotton is set with blue and white Canton porcelain on capiz shell mats and salmon and white napkins wrapped in white shell rings. A simple glass bowl filled with coral in delicate shades ornaments the table. The soup course served from a Canton tureen begins a relaxed and unhurried luncheon overlooking a dazzling sweep of beach.

Cookout Supper Before the Tournament Players Championship

Shrimp Butter* with Melba Toast

Chicken Shish Kabobs* with Pineapple

Herbed Rice*

Spinach Salad Mold*

Poppy Seed Pastries*

Fresh Coconut Torte*

California Johannisberg Riesling

The Tournament Players Championship golf tournament is played each spring near Jacksonville at the Tournament Players Club, home of one of the world's most challenging golf courses. The Tournament begins a whirlwind week of casual entertaining. The mild spring weather in northern Florida is perfect for a cookout overlooking the rolling fairways of the TPC course. The table is set with dark green palmetto leaves for placemats. Napkins in shades of orange, yellow and hot pink are tied with palmetto fronds. Plain white china is in pleasing contrast to the centerpiece of multicolored gerbera daisies arranged, as if planted, in a basket filled with deer moss and long shoots of variegated spider plants which trail down the table. Orange candles in hurricane lamps flicker over the tropical setting.

Dinner by the Dunes at Sawgrass

*Cold Zucchini Soup**

*Quenelles Superior**

*Broccoli Soufflé**

*Mandarin Orange Salad**

French Bread

Crêpes Floridian

Puligny Montrachet   Hanns Kornell, Sear Trocken Champagne

Sawgrass, named for the windswept dune grasses which grow along its beaches, is one of Florida's most beautiful resorts. Located 19 miles south of Jacksonville and set in 4,800 acres of unspoiled North Florida terrain, Sawgrass offers excellent golf, tennis, sailing, swimming and fishing. Dinner begins as the sun sets behind the magnificent dunes of South Ponte Vedra Beach. The glass table is set with antique Majolica serving pieces, their rich color accented with green Heisey glass plates and pale yellow mats and napkins. A large straw basket in the center is filled with two full green cabbages and cream hydrangeas. Votive candles, wrapped in hydrangea leaves and tied with yellow ribbon, light the evening on this serene Atlantic beachfront.

Galley Supper en Route to St. Augustine

Blue Crab Soup*

Seasoned Arabic Bread Wedges

Roast Beef Salad with French Mustard Dressing*

Fresh Apple Pound Cake*

Pears Poached in Wine*

California Korbel Brut Champagne

St. Augustine, Florida, our nation's oldest city, lies south of Jacksonville. A favorite way to reach this historical city is by sailing or cruising down the Intracoastal Waterway, enjoying supper on the way. As the simple but delicious fare is served, egrets fly low over the marshes and a breeze ripples the water. Brightly-colored, plastic-coated paper plates and bowls, matching napkins, heavy plastic forks and spoons and lucite serving pieces make the meal both festive and carefree.

Tennis Luncheon at Amelia Island

Chilled Shrimp with Saffron Dressing*

Vegetable Pasta Salad*

Spinach Stuffed Onions*

Unbelievable Garlic Bread*

Famous Mint Iced Tea*

Cold Lemon Soufflé*

White Graves, Château Olivier

Amelia Island, named for the daughter of King George II more than 200 years ago, lies 30 miles northeast of Jacksonville. The southernmost of the large Atlantic Barrier Islands, Amelia is the home of Amelia Island Plantation, a beautiful resort surrounded by towering sand dunes, giant live oaks and tidal marshes. Luncheon on this picturesque island calls for a setting in the brightest of colors. Under a white tent, round tables are covered with cream sailcloth spatter-painted with lavender, coral, pink, green, yellow and turquoise. Single pots of cascading coral impatiens center each table. The buffet table is skirted in cream sailcloth and a short overcloth of lavender. Paired glass globes filled with coral gladioli spash the table with color. Coral impatiens spill out around the bases of tall palms in Italian terra-cotta planters. Tent poles, wrapped in brown crepe paper with enormous palm fronds and crepe paper flowers attached to their tops, create the tropical illusion of dining under palm trees.

Spring Luncheon on the Banks of the St. Johns

Cold Snapper Mold* with Assorted Crackers

Gourmet Beef Salad Vinaigrette*

Feta Phyllo Squares*

Aunt Em's Strawberry Shortcake*

Buena Vista Heritage Chardonnay

Jacksonville blooms in April when the azaleas burst into color and provide a perfect setting for an outdoor luncheon. Each table, spread with a colorful handmade quilt, displays a centerpiece of folk art, wooden watermelons, small painted boxes and decoys. Placed among these treasures are small pots of trailing ivy and spring flowers. From a bleached pine sideboard on the patio, food is served in stoneware crocks, Shaker boxes and primitive bowls. An old wooden tool box holds pewter forks and cotton napkins in a variety of solid colors matching those in the quilts. An antique copper boiler is filled with wine on ice, and mountain-made oriole baskets hold arrangements of wild flowers and baby's breath.

Summer English Country Dinner

Shrimp Pâté* with Melba Toast

Asparagus-Cheese Canapes*

Devonshire Pie*

Tomatoes Stuffed with Summer Squash*

Bibb Lettuce, Spring Onions and Parsley with Golden Dressing*

Fluffy Rolls*

Brandy Alexander Pie*

Chablis Premier Cru   Château Gloria à St. Julien Bordeaux

The timeless charm of the old South is reflected by the Mandarin countryside. The majestic oaks and hanging Spanish moss provide the serene setting for this summer dinner. Creating an English pastoral scene on the polished wood of a Queen Anne table, a pair of small ivy topiary trees flank an antique Chelsea rabbit tureen, porcelain animals, shepherds and shepherdesses. Heavy Sheffield silver plates and antique flatware are arranged on cream lace placemats for a seated dinner. Cream napkins are tied with sprigs of ivy and four silver candelabra with cream candles light the scene.

Fall Game Feast

Boursin Stuffed Mushrooms*

Grilled Quail and Dove* with Cumberland Sauce*

Wild Rice with Fresh Mushrooms*

Orange Avocado Toss*

Dill Muffins*

Chocolate Ricotta Cheesecake*

Côte de Beaune Village

The arrival of the crisp fall air heralds the hunting season in Northeast Florida, and a traditional game dinner celebrates the hunter's bounty. A rustic pine buffet table sports a handsome pair of game birds, fashioned of brass and ostrich eggs and slender brass vases filled with colorful feathers. Beside square teakwood plates, a vine basket is filled with paisley napkins in tortoise-shell rings. Horn and brass candlesticks light the feast.

Gala Holiday Dinner

Yogurt Cucumber Soup*

Shrimp with Creole Mustard*

Chicken Breasts and Artichokes in Champagne Sauce*

Fancy Baked Tomatoes*

Mushroom Salad*

Croissants*

Frozen Grand Marnier Soufflé with Hot Strawberry Sauce*

Alsace Gewurztraminer   Piper Heidsieck Brut Champagne

California Reisling

The long dining table of glass and verd antique marble is set with *point de Venice* lace mats and napkins ringed in silver. *Famille Rose* bough pots placed at each end of the table are filled with sprays of tiny white orchids and rubrum lilies. Candlelight from a pair of 18th century French ormolu girondoles reflects in the mirrored wall behind the buffet. The mirror is framed with swags of green plaid taffeta tied in large festive bows at the ceiling with streamers reaching to the floor. The table, *Famille Rose* plates and burnished silver sparkle with celebration and holiday spirit.

Blast-Off Party

Stellar Cheese Spread Sandwiches

Mixed Fruit Salad

Rocket Ship Cake and Ice Cream

Milky Way Drink

Heralded by invitations written on old fashioned paper airplanes the party promises a "blast-off" into space. Deep blue paper tablecloths are spread on the floor ready for decorating. Little guests armed with white and yellow chalk and foil star stickers gather around in groups to design their own outer space tablecloths. Above them balloons bearing the names of planets and large foil stars hang suspended from the ceiling. When the tablecloths are ready and spread on the tables, lunch is served in "flying saucers" made from two aluminum pie pans filled with lunch and then taped together. "Stellar sandwiches" are created with star, crescent and round cookie cutters. The rocket ship cake is made from a sheet cake. A rectangle using two-thirds of the sheet forms the body of the rocket. Three triangles cut from the remaining one-third form the cone and the two fins. The cake is then iced in dark blue and white. The milky way drink, hot chocolate with marshmallows, completes the menu. Favors are frisbee "flying saucers."

Second-Hand Rose Party

Heart-Shaped Canapes

Tea Cakes, Cookies and Petit Fours

Assorted Nuts

Fruit Punch

The "Second-Hand Roses" arrive ready for a grown-up tea party. Awaiting the little ladies is a room full of trunks overflowing with boa wraps, old furs, sequinned dresses, veiled hats, fans and long gloves gleaned from the attic and local thrift shops. With this collection of finery and long mirrors, the guests create their own costumes. Talented mothers arrange each child's hair with ribbons and bows and silk flowers. Thus attired, they gather at the tea table laid with a white piqué ruffled cloth and a bouquet of pink sweetheart roses. With Mother as maid and Dad as butler, the serving begins with punch ladled into cups of fine china. Tea cakes and cookies are passed on silver trays and instant snapshots are taken of each guest to make the day a truly memorable occasion.

Circus Party

Clown Hat Sandwiches

Carrot and Celery Sticks

Pink Lemonade

Circus Parade Cake

Clown hat invitations made of construction paper announce that the circus will be coming to town to celebrate the honoree's birthday and that many clowns will be needed. The children arrive and enter the "big top" made of crepe paper streamers. The ends of three wide streamers are gathered together and taped to the center of the ceiling; the opposite ends are fanned out over one quarter of the ceiling, draped slightly and fastened. This is repeated three times to tent the room. Helium-filled balloons and felt pennants complete the circus theme. The children's faces are made up as clowns and they choose from a basket of assorted clown hats. With rhythm band instruments and lively marching music, they join in a circus parade. Refreshments are clown hat sandwiches made from triangles of bread decorated with raisins along the bottom and marshmallow "pom poms" at the point of the "hat." The birthday cake is an iced sheet cake bordered with a "parade" of animal crackers overlaid with "bars" of icing and life savers for the wheels of the "cages." The cake is cut so that each child receives a "caged" animal. Each clown receives a favor of a sand bucket filled with peanuts or popcorn.

Index

A

Amelia Island Brunswick Stew.............. 99
Amelia Island Rice...................... 189
Angel Pie............................... 294
Anne Marie's Stuffed Leg of Lamb.......... 127
APPETIZERS
  CANAPES AND SANDWICHES
    Asparagus-Cheese Canapes............. 34
    Chile Rellenos Squares................ 27
    Clams Monterey...................... 18
    Feta Phyllo Squares................... 36
    Mushroom and Sausage Hors d'Oeuvre.... 24
  CHAFING DISH
    Hot Crabmeat Dip.................... 15
    Hot Sausage in Sour Cream............ 24
    Hot Shrimp or Crab Dip............... 16
  COLD FINGER FOOD
    Chilled Shrimp with Saffron Dressing..... 11
    Marinated Shrimp.................... 13
    Shrimp Balls......................... 14
    Shrimp Remoulade.................... 12
    Shrimp with Creole Mustard............ 11
    Shrimp with Mayonnaise Dressing....... 12
  DIPS
    Avocado Appetizer.................... 19
    Dallas Cowboy Dip................... 35
    Gourmet Crab Dip.................... 17
    Herb Dip........................... 322
    Hot Crab Dip........................ 17
    Spinach Flexibility................... 147
  HOT FINGER FOOD
    Bacon and Onion Roll-Ups............. 20
    Bacon Wraps........................ 20
    Baked Brie in Puff Pastry.............. 253
    Blue Cheese Stuffed Mushrooms........ 23
    Boursin Stuffed Mushrooms............ 21
    Chicken Teriyaki..................... 21
    Crab Rangoon....................... 16
    Crab Swiss Rounds................... 18
    Crémaillère......................... 25
    French Fried Mushrooms.............. 22
    Fried Zucchini....................... 33
    Herb Roll-Ups...................... 163
    Kaiser Dippers....................... 26
    Mosquito Lagoon Duck Breasts........ 110
    Oysters Rockefeller................... 19
    Sausage Filled Mushrooms............. 23
    Stuffed Mushroom Caps............... 22
  SPREADS AND MOLDS
    Caviar Egg Ring..................... 27
    Caviar Supreme..................... 28
    Chutney Dip........................ 25
    Cold Snapper Mold................... 39
    Cottage Cheese Mold................. 29
    Frosted Artichokes with Caviar......... 29
    Frosted Pâté........................ 32
    Homemade Boursin Cheese............ 36
    Hot Appetizer Pie.................... 33
    Pâté Burgette....................... 30
    Shrimp Butter....................... 15

Shrimp Pâté............................ 13
Spicy Shrimp Spread.................... 14
Tennis Team Spinach Spread............ 35
"The" Pâté............................. 32
Vidalia Onion Spread................... 26
Yogurt Herb Spread.................... 320
APPLE
  Apple Carrot Muffins................... 168
  Apple Cheddar Bread.................. 164
  Apple Dumplings..................... 256
  Apple Popover Pancake................ 174
  Fresh Apple Pound Cake............... 274
  Sausage and Apple Bake................ 124
  Spiked Apple Crisp.................... 255
Apricots, Baked......................... 155
Arnold's Hollandaise Sauce................ 210
Arroz con Pollo......................... 100
ARTICHOKE
  Artichoke and Seafood Casserole........ 84
  Artichoke and Spinach Casserole........ 135
  Artichoke Puffs....................... 240
  Artichoke-Rice Salad................... 52
  Chicken Breasts and Artichokes in
    Champagne Sauce................... 87
  Crab Stuffed Artichoke Entrée........... 72
  Egg and Artichoke Casserole........... 183
  Frosted Artichokes with Caviar.......... 29
ASPARAGUS
  Asparagus-Cheese Canapés............. 34
  Ham and Asparagus Casserole......... 124
  Rice with Asparagus................... 189
Aunt Em's Strawberry Shortcake.......... 282
Autumn Acorn Squash................... 146
AVOCADO
  Avocado Appetizer.................... 19
  Orange Avocado Toss................. 60

B

Bacon and Onion Roll-Ups................ 20
Bacon Wrapped Dove.................... 109
Bacon Wraps........................... 20
Baked Apricots......................... 155
Baked Brie in Puff Pastry................ 253
Baked Deviled Eggs..................... 184
Baked Oysters.......................... 81
Baked Stuffed Red Snapper.............. 66
Baked Stuffed Shrimp................... 75
Barbecue Sauce........................ 207
Basil and Garlic Butter.................. 320
Bay Scallops en Coquille................. 83
BEANS
  Beans with Dill Sauce.................. 145
  Black Beans and Rice.................. 153
  Dilled Green Beans.................... 144
  Fresh Green Beans with Sour Cream Sauce.... 145
  Green Beans Tarragon................. 144
  Green Beans with Rosemary............ 327
  Red Beans and Rice................... 154
BEEF
  Amelia Island Brunswick Stew.......... 99

Beef Bourguignon........................116
Braised Stuffed Flank Steak..............118
Fillet of Beef with Green Peppercorns......114
Fillet of Beef with Port Butter...........113
Ginger Sauce for Beef....................207
Gourmet Beef Salad Vinaigrette............51
Helwig's Salt Steak......................119
Lazy Day Beef Burgundy...................117
Ram's Steak Sandwich.....................239
Roast Beef Salad with French Mustard
  Dressing..............................50
Russian Chef's Stroganoff................115
Spicy Beef Stew.........................117
Steak "Au Poivre".......................114
Tournedos Madagascar....................115
World Champion Chili....................116
Bermuda Salad............................57
Best Pumpkin Pie........................293
Best Salad Dressing.....................214
Black Beans and Rice....................153
Black Russian Cake......................279
Blazing Spice Wine Punch................243
Bloomingdale's Pound Cake...............275
Blue Cheese Stuffed Mushrooms.............23
Blue Crab Soup..........................224
Blueberry Cake..........................279
Boston Club Punch.......................246
Bourbon Balls...........................314
Bourbon Fruitcake Cookies...............303
Boursin.................................320
Boursin Cheese, Homemade.................36
Boursin Stuffed Mushrooms................21
Braised Stuffed Flank Steak..............118
Brandied Chicken with Currant Jelly Sauce.105
Brandied Peaches........................220
Brandy Alexander Pie....................292
BREADS
 BISCUITS
   Orange Sugar Biscuits.................159
   Southern Biscuits.....................159
 MUFFINS
   Apple Carrot Muffins..................168
   Crisp Miniature Cinnamon Muffins......169
   Dill Muffins..........................169
   Oatmeal Muffins.......................168
   Spice Muffins.........................167
 QUICK BREADS
   Apple Cheddar Bread...................164
   Apple Popover Pancake.................174
   Breakfast Puff........................171
   Butterscotch Breakfast Ring...........172
   Club Waffles and Pancakes.............170
   Cranberry Bread.......................163
   Gram's Pancake and Waffle Batter......171
   Herb Roll Ups.........................163
   Hush Puppies..........................165
   Parsley and Bread Stuffing............332
   Poppy Seed Pastries...................160
   Scottish Scones.......................167
   Sister's Sally Lunn...................166
   Spring Crest Cornbread................161
   Strawberry Preserve Coffee Cake.......170
   Sweet Lemon Bread.....................164

   Swiss Cheese Cornbread................162
   Unbelievable Garlic Bread.............166
 ROLLS
   Fluffy Rolls..........................162
   One Hour Rolls........................161
   Onion Rolls...........................178
   Quick Mayonnaise Rolls................160
   Sour Cream Crescent Rolls.............176
 YEAST BREADS
   Butterflake Treats....................177
   Cinnamon Bread........................173
   Croissants............................174
   Oatmeal Bread.........................165
Breakfast Puff..........................171
Breast of Chicken and Country Ham in
   Grape Sauce...........................92
BROCCOLI
   Broccoli Bisque.......................228
   Broccoli Extraordinaire...............150
   Broccoli Soufflé......................151
   Broccoli Soup.........................228
   Marinated Broccoli Ring...............62
Broiled Herb Fish Fillets...............331
Butter, Basil and Garlic................320
Butter, Mixed Herb......................321
Butterflake Treats......................177
Buttermilk Orange Cupcakes with Fresh
   Orange Sauce..........................287
Butterscotch Breakfast Ring.............172

C

Cabbage, California.....................151
CAKES
   Black Russian Cake....................279
   Bloomingdale's Pound Cake.............275
   Blueberry Cake........................279
   Buttermilk Orange Cupcakes with Fresh
      Orange Sauce.......................287
   Caramel Cake with Caramel Icing.......280
   Coconut Pound Cake....................274
   Fresh Apple Pound Cake................274
   Kentucky Butter Cake..................284
   Lafayette Grill Cake..................276
   Lemon Garden Cake.....................285
   Mrs. Dearing's Mayonnaise Cake........281
   No Mix Chocolate Cake.................277
   Sunshine Cake.........................278
   "The Sisters" Bourbon Pound Cake......273
Calamondin Marmalade....................216
California Cabbage......................151
CANDY
   Bourbon Balls.........................314
   English Toffee........................312
   Foolproof Fudge.......................313
   Mint Balls............................314
   Peanut Butter Balls...................311
   Peanut Butter Fudge...................313
   Pralines..............................312
Cannelloni..............................196
Caramel Cake with Caramel Icing.........280
Caramel Soufflé with English Custard Sauce.251
Caramelized Pears.......................270

CARROTS
  Apple Carrot Muffins 168
  Gingered Carrots 138
Caviar Egg Ring 27
Caviar Supreme 28
Celery, Chinese 152
Celery Seed Dressing 216
Champagne Chocolate Sauce 211
Champagne Mousse 267
Champagne Punch 247
Charlotte Malakoff 260
Cheese Blintzes 268
CHEESE MAIN DISHES
  Cheese Savory 181
  Crustless Quiche 187
  John Wayne Pie 183
  Olive Cheese Strata 181
CHEESECAKE
  Chocolate Cheesecake Muffins 308
  Chocolate Ricotta Cheesecake 286
  Miniature Individual Cheesecakes 305
  Most Requested Cheesecake 286
Chervil Soup 325
CHICKEN
  Amelia Island Brunswick Stew 99
  Arroz con Pollo 100
  Brandied Chicken with Currant Jelly Sauce . . . 105
  Breast of Chicken and Country Ham
    in Grape Sauce 92
  Chicken à la Habakov 104
  Chicken and Spinach Crêpes 96
  Chicken Archduc 88
  Chicken Breasts and Artichokes in
    Champagne Sauce 87
  Chicken Breasts with Almond Sauce 95
  Chicken Connemara 102
  Chicken Dijon 88
  Chicken in Gouda Sauce 98
  Chicken Persian 101
  Chicken Pie with Coachwheel Crust 97
  Chicken Salad Supreme 41
  Chicken Shish Kabobs 91
  Chicken Stack-Up Salad 41
  Chicken Teichgraeber 93
  Chicken Teriyaki 21
  Chutney and Curry Chicken Salad 40
  Coq au Vin Bourguignon 106
  Coronation Chicken 102
  Country Chicken Soup 237
  Durkee Chicken 103
  Fruited Honey Chicken 94
  Gumbo 223
  Herbed Chicken 330
  Hungarian Chicken 91
  Lemon Chicken 94
  Lime Chicken with Melon 95
  Poulet à la Crème Joubine 93
  Spanish Chicken 98
  Tropical Chicken Salad 42
  Vegetable Chicken Soup 238
  Wild Rice and Chicken Tarragon 90
Chile Rellenos Squares 27
Chilled Shrimp with Saffron Dressing 11

Chinese Celery 152
Chocolate-Caramel Layer Squares 307
Chocolate Cheesecake Muffins 308
Chocolate Chip Pie 288
Chocolate Cups 263
Chocolate Mint Ice Cream 267
Chocolate Perfections 309
Chocolate Ricotta Cheesecake 286
Chocolate Toffee Yummies 306
Chocolate Torte 296
Chutney and Curry Chicken Salad 40
Chutney Dip 25
Chutney, Indian Tomato 217
Cinnamon Bread 173
Cinnamon-Sherry Sauce 211
Cioppino 225
CLAMS
  Clams Monterey 18
  Linguine with Red Clam Sauce 196
Club Waffles and Pancakes 170
Cobb Salad 40
Cocoa Clouds 300
Coconut, Fresh Torte 264
Coconut Mousse 266
Coconut Pound Cake 274
Coffee Punch 245
Cointreau Strawberry Sauce 212
Cold Cucumber-Dill Soup 231
Cold Lemon Soufflé 270
Cold Seafood and Pasta Salad 43
Cold Snapper Mold 39
Cold Zucchini Soup 229
Coleslaw, Georgia 53
Company Fish Fillets 67
Conch or Fish Chowder 226
COOKIES
  Bourbon Fruitcake Cookies 303
  Chocolate-Caramel Layer Squares 307
  Chocolate Cheesecake Muffins 308
  Chocolate Perfections 309
  Chocolate Toffee Yummies 306
  Cocoa Clouds 300
  Exquisite Mint Sticks 304
  Guava Dainties 300
  Incredible Edibles 310
  Luscious Squares 306
  Meringues Pistachio 299
  Miniature Individual Cheesecakes 305
  Mint Surprise Cookies 303
  Oatmeal Crisp Cookies 302
  Peanut Buttercups 310
  Pecan Pie Bars 308
  Peppermint Chocolate Meringues 299
  Praline Cookies 301
  Rich Brownies 304
  Russian Rocks 311
  Sugar Cookies 302
  Tea Cakes 301
Coq au Vin Bourguignon 106
CORN
  Corn Relish 220
  Fresh Corn Pudding 140
  Souffléed Corn 140

Coronation Chicken............................102
Cottage Cheese Mold.......................... 29
Country Chicken Soup........................237
Country Vegetable Quiche....................187
CRAB
    Blue Crab Soup...........................224
    Crab Fondue............................. 68
    Crab or Shrimp Mornay................... 69
    Crab Rangoon............................ 16
    Crab Shrimp Quiche......................186
    Crab Stuffed Artichoke Entrée............ 72
    Crab Swiss Rounds....................... 18
    Crabmeat Crêpes......................... 70
    Deviled Crab............................ 68
    Gourmet Crab Dip........................ 17
    Hot Crab Dip............................ 17
    Hot Crabmeat Dip........................ 15
    Hot Shrimp or Crab Dip.................. 16
    Maryland Crab........................... 70
    Shrimp and Crab Soufflé................. 76
    Shrimp and Crabmeat Fondue in
      Bread Cups........................... 74
    Shrimp and Crabmeat Madeira............. 78
    Spinach Shellfish Soup...................226
    Thousand Island Mold with Fresh Seafood.... 46
CRANBERRIES
    Cranberry Bread.........................163
    Cranberry Kumquat Relish................218
    Nantucket Cranberry Pie..................292
Crémaillère................................. 25
Creole, Shrimp.............................. 76
CRÊPES
    Cheese Blintzes..........................268
    Chicken and Spinach Crêpes.............. 96
    Crabmeat Crêpes......................... 70
    Crêpes Floridian.........................254
    Frozen Chocolate Crêpes with Custard
      Sauce................................252
    Manicotti...............................202
Crisp Miniature Cinnamon Muffins............169
Croissants..................................174
Crustless Quiche.............................187
Cucumber, Cold Dill Soup....................231
Cucumber Salmon Mousse..................... 45
Cucumber, Yogurt Soup......................231
Cumberland Sauce............................206

D

Dallas Cowboy Dip........................... 35
DESSERTS
    CAKES, TARTS, TORTES
      Aunt Em's Strawberry Shortcake........282
      Chocolate Cups.......................263
      Chocolate Ricotta Cheesecake..........286
      Chocolate Torte......................296
      Fresh Coconut Torte..................264
      Lighter Than Air Date Torte...........288
      Miniature Cream Cheese Tarts with
        Cherry Sauce......................283
      Most Requested Cheesecake............286
      Pecan Tart...........................293
      Strawberries au Chocolat..............257

CUSTARDS AND PUDDINGS
    Lemon Snow Pudding with Custard
      Sauce................................257
    Meringues with Strawberries and
      Custard..............................258
FROZEN DESSERTS
    Exceptional Chocolate Mousse...........269
    Frozen Chocolate Crêpes with
      Custard Sauce........................252
    Frozen Grand Marnier Soufflé with
      Hot Strawberry Sauce.................259
    Orange Ice.............................269
    Strawberry Sorbet......................262
    The Girdlebuster.......................265
    Watermelon Ice........................265
FRUIT DESSERTS
    Caramelized Pears......................270
    Fresh Fruit in Grand Marnier Sauce......262
    Pears Poached in Wine..................261
HOT DESSERTS
    Apple Dumplings......................256
    Baked Brie in Puff Pastry...............253
    Caramel Soufflé with English
      Custard Sauce........................251
    Cheese Blintzes........................268
    Crêpes Floridian.......................254
    Spiked Apple Crisp.....................255
ICE CREAMS
    Champagne Mousse....................267
    Chocolate Mint Ice Cream..............267
    Honey Ice Cream......................263
    Pineapple Sherbet.....................256
REFRIGERATED DESSERTS
    Charlotte Malakoff.....................260
    Coconut Mousse......................266
    Cold Lemon Soufflé....................270
    Fresh Lemon Charlotte Russe..........261
    Kahlua Mousse........................266
Deviled Crab................................ 68
Devonshire Pie..............................128
Dill Muffins.................................169
Dill Sauce..................................207
Dilled Green Beans..........................144
DIPS—See APPETIZERS—DIPS
DOVE
    Bacon Wrapped Dove...................109
    Dove with Shallots and Wine............108
    Grilled Quail and Dove.................108
DRESSINGS—See SALAD DRESSINGS
DRINKS
    Blazing Spice Wine Punch..............243
    Boston Club Punch....................246
    Champagne Punch....................247
    Coffee Punch..........................245
    Famous Mint Iced Tea..................248
    Frozen Bourbon Sour..................246
    Holiday Eggnog.......................247
    Hot Buttered Rum.....................244
    Hot Mulled Wine......................244
    Jacksonville Sangria....................242
    Ruth's Coffee..........................245
DUCK
    Duck à l'Orange........................110

Duck with Honey and Herbs............330
Mosquito Lagoon Duck Breasts............110
Wild Duck in Red Wine................109
Durkee Chicken.......................103

E

Eggnog, Holiday......................247
EGGPLANT
   Ratatouille.......................153
EGGS
   Baked Deviled Eggs................184
   Caviar Egg Ring.................... 27
   Egg and Artichoke Casserole............183
   Egg Soufflé.......................184
   Eggs in Cheese and Sherry Sauce..........182
   Eggs in Herb Sauce.....................329
   Golden Egg Casserole................185
English Toffee......................312
Ensalada de Fruta................... 54
Escalloped Green Peppers.............154
Exceptional Chocolate Mousse.............269
Exquisite Mint Sticks.....................304

F

Famous Mint Iced Tea....................248
Fancy Baked Tomatoes..................136
Festive Onions......................139
Feta Phyllo Squares.................. 36
Fettuccine Alfredo...................193
Fettuccine Gargonzola................193
Fettuccine with Zucchini, Mushrooms
   and Ham........................194
Filé Seafood Gumbo....................224
Fillet of Beef with Green Peppercorns........114
Fillet of Beef with Port Butter.............113
FISH
   Baked Stuffed Red Snapper............ 66
   Broiled Herb Fish Fillets...............331
   Cold Snapper Mold................. 39
   Company Fish Fillets................ 67
   Cucumber Salmon Mousse............ 45
   Fish or Conch Chowder................226
   Herbed Flounder................... 67
   Quenelles Superior................. 65
Fluffy Rolls........................162
Foolproof Fudge.....................313
French Fried Mushrooms............... 22
French Peas........................156
French Silk Pie.....................291
Fresh Apple Pound Cake...............274
Fresh Coconut Torte..................264
Fresh Corn Pudding..................140
Fresh Fruit in Grand Marnier Sauce........262
Fresh Green Beans with Sour Cream Sauce.....145
Fresh Lemon Charlotte Russe............261
Fried Zucchini..................... 33
Frosted Artichokes with Caviar............ 29
Frosted Pâté....................... 32
Frozen Bourbon Sour.................246

Frozen Chocolate Crêpes with Custard
   Sauce..........................252
Frozen Chocolate Pie with English Custard
   Sauce..........................289
Frozen Grand Marnier Soufflé with Hot
   Strawberry Sauce....................259
Frozen Tomato Salad................ 56
FRUIT
   Fresh Fruit in Grand Marnier Sauce........262
   Fruited Honey Chicken................ 94

G

Georgia Coleslaw.................... 53
Ginger Sauce for Beef..................207
Gingered Carrots....................138
Golden Dressing....................214
Golden Egg Casserole................185
Goodstuff's Bourbon Pie................290
Gourmet Beef Salad Vinaigrette............ 51
Gourmet Braised Turnips...............152
Gourmet Crab Dip................... 17
Gram's Pancake and Waffle Batter...........171
Granola..........................172
Greek Lemon Egg Soup................234
GREEN BEANS—See BEANS
Green Peppers, Escalloped.............154
Green Rice........................191
Grilled Quail and Dove...............108
Grilled Shrimp Marinated in Cognac........ 75
Grits, Sausage Casserole................182
Guava Dainties....................300
Gumbo..........................223
Gumbo, Filé Seafood..................224
Guten Tog.........................240

H

HAM—See also PORK
Ham and Asparagus Casserole............124
Ham Topped Muffins....................242
Hearty Gazpacho....................233
Heavenly Turkey Hash..................107
Helwig's Salt Steak..................119
HERBS
   Basil and Garlic Butter...............320
   Boursin.........................320
   Broiled Herb Fish Fillets...............331
   Chervil Soup.....................325
   Duck with Honey and Herbs............330
   Eggs in Herb Sauce.................329
   Green Beans with Rosemary............327
   Herb Dip........................322
   Herb Quiche.....................329
   Herb Risotto.....................328
   Herb Roll-Ups....................163
   Herbed Chicken...................330
   Herbed Flounder................... 67
   Herbed Rice......................191
   Mixed Herb Butter..................321
   Parsley and Bread Stuffing.............332
   Parsley Sauce.....................322

Pesto Alla Genovese	328
Pork Chops with Basil	331
Quick Herb Sauce	322
Risi e Bisi	327
Scallops in Herb Sauce	332
Sesame Salt	323
Slimmer's Herbed Gazpacho	325
Summer Squash and Chervil	326
Tomato Soup with Basil	324
Tomatoes Stuffed with Herbed Orzo	326
Vinaigrette with Mixed Herbs	323
Yogurt Herb Spread	320
Yogurt Salad Dressing	324
Holiday Eggnog	247
Hollandaise, Arnold's Sauce	210
Homemade Boursin Cheese	36
Honey Dressing	213
Honey Ice Cream	263
Horseradish Sauce	210
Hot Appetizer Pie	33
Hot Brown Sandwich	241
Hot Buttered Rum	244
Hot Crab Dip	17
Hot Crabmeat Dip	15
Hot Fudge Sauce	212
Hot Mulled Wine	244
Hot Mustard Sauce	209
Hot Pepper Jelly	217
Hot Pineapple Casserole	155
Hot Rice Casserole	188
Hot Sausage in Sour Cream	24
Hot Shrimp or Crab Dip	16
Hungarian Chicken	91
Hush Puppies	165

I

Incredible Edibles	310
Indian Tomato Chutney	217
Italian Lemon Rice	188
Italian Rice and Vegetables	192
Italian Scalloped Potatoes	149

J

Jacksonville Sangria	242
Jellied Borscht	233
Jelly, Hot Pepper	217
John Wayne Pie	183

K

Kahlua Mousse	266
Kaiser Dippers	26
Kentucky Butter Cake	284

L

Lafayette Grill Cake	276
LAMB	
Anne Marie's Stuffed Leg of Lamb	127
Devonshire Pie	128
Lamb Moroccan	126
Marinated Leg of Lamb	129
Roast Lamb with Herb Mustard	125
Lasagne	199
Lasagne, Sausage and Spinach	193
Lasagne, Vegetarian	201
Layered Spinach Salad	58
Lazy Day Beef Burgundy	117
Lemon Chicken	92
Lemon Garden Cake	285
Lemon Snow Pudding with Custard Sauce	257
Lentil Soup	236
Lighter Than Air Date Torte	288
Lime Chicken with Melon	95
Linguine with Red Clam Sauce	196
Louis Pappas' Famous Greek Salad	44
Louisville Pie	291
Low Calorie Curry Sauce	205
Luscious Squares	306

M

Mandarin Orange Salad	62
Manicotti	202
Marmalade, Calamondin	216
Marinade, Teriyaki	208
Marinated Broccoli Ring	62
Marinated Leg of Lamb	129
Marinated Shrimp	13
Maryland Crab	70
Mayonnaise, Watercress	205
MEATS — See Individual Listings	
MERINGUES	
Cocoa Clouds	300
Peppermint Chocolate Meringues	299
Meringues Pistachio	299
Meringues with Strawberries and Custard	258
Michael Field's Broiled Shrimp with Tarragon	73
Miniature Cream Cheese Tarts with Cherry Sauce	283
Miniature Individual Cheesecakes	305
Minnesota Sandwich Pickles	219
Mint Balls	314
Mint Surprise Cookies	303
Mixed Herb Butter	321
Mosquito Lagoon Duck Breasts	110
Most Requested Cheesecake	286
MOUSSE	
Champagne Mousse	267
Coconut Mousse	266
Cucumber Salmon Mousse	45
Exceptional Chocolate Mousse	269
Kahlua Mousse	266
Tuna Mousse with Cucumber Sauce	49
Mrs. Dearing's Mayonnaise Cake	281
MUSHROOM	
Blue Cheese Stuffed Mushrooms	23
Boursin Stuffed Mushrooms	21
Fettuccine with Zucchini, Mushrooms and Ham	194
French Fried Mushrooms	22

Mushroom and Sausage Hors d'Oeuvre 24
Mushroom Bisque 230
Mushroom Broth 230
Mushroom Salad 53
Mushrooms Polonaise 147
Sausage Filled Mushrooms 23
Stuffed Mushroom Caps 22
Wild Rice with Fresh Mushrooms 190
Mustard Sauce 206

N

Nantucket Cranberry Pie 292
New Orleans Style Shrimp 77
New Potatoes au Caviar 149
No Mix Chocolate Cake 277

O

Oatmeal Bread 165
Oatmeal Crisp Cookies 302
Oatmeal Muffins 168
Olive Cheese Strata 181
One Hour Rolls 161
ONIONS
   Festive Onions 139
   Onion Pie 139
   Onion Rolls 178
   Spinach Stuffed Onions 138
   Vidalia Onion Spread 26
ORANGE
   Buttermilk Orange Cupcakes with Fresh
      Orange Sauce 287
   Crêpes Floridian 254
   Duck à l'Orange 110
   Mandarin Orange Salad 62
   Orange Avocado Toss 60
   Orange Ice 269
   Orange Pork Chops 120
   Orange Rice 192
   Orange Sugar Biscuits 159
   Watercress and Orange Salad 61
OYSTERS
   Baked Oysters 81
   Oyster and Spinach Soup 225
   Oysters Rockefeller 19
   Oysters Rockefeller Casserole 81
   Oysters with Herb Butter 80

P

Parsley and Bread Stuffing 332
Parsley Sauce 322
Parslied Salad with Homemade Croutons 54
PASTA
   Cannelloni 196
   Cold Seafood and Pasta Salad 43
   Fettuccine Alfredo 193
   Fettuccine Gargonzola 193
   Fettuccine with Zucchini, Mushrooms
      and Ham 194
   Lasagne 199
   Linguine with Red Clam Sauce 196
   Pasta Verde 195
   Sausage and Spinach Lasagne 198
   Seafood and Pasta Salad Pescara 48
   Spaghetti Carbonara 195
   Spaghetti Florentine 194
   Tomatoes Stuffed with Herbed Orzo 324
   Vegetable Pasta Salad 56
   Vegetarian Lasagne 201
   White Party Pasta 200
PÂTÉ
   Frosted Pâté 32
   Pâté Burgette 30
   Shrimp Pâté 13
   "The" Pâté 32
Peach, Spectacular Pie 294
Peaches, Brandied 220
Peanut Butter Balls 311
Peanut Butter Fudge 313
Peanut Buttercups 310
Peanut Soup 238
PEARS
   Caramelized Pears 270
   Pears Poached in Wine 261
Peas, French 156
Pecan Pie Bars 308
Pecan Tart 293
Pennsylvania Dutch Apple Pork Chops 120
Peppermint Chocolate Meringues 299
Pesto Alla Genovese 328
PICKLES
   Minnesota Sandwich Pickles 219
   Sweet Pickles 218
   Watermelon Rind Pickles 219
PIES
   Angel Pie 294
   Best Pumpkin Pie 293
   Brandy Alexander Pie 292
   Chocolate Chip Pie 288
   French Silk Pie 291
   Frozen Chocolate Pie with English
      Custard Sauce 289
   Goodstuff's Bourbon Pie 290
   Louisville Pie 291
   Nantucket Cranberry Pie 292
   Spectacular Peach Pie 294
   "The Sisters" Famous Peanut Butter Pie 295
PINEAPPLE
   Hot Pineapple Casserole 155
   Pineapple Sherbet 256
Poppy Seed Pastries 160
PORK
   Amelia Island Brunswick Stew 99
   Breasts of Chicken and Country Ham
      in Grape Sauce 92
   Fettuccine with Zucchini, Mushrooms
      and Ham 194
   Ham and Asparagus Casserole 124
   Ham Topped Muffins 242
   Orange Pork Chops 120
   Pennsylvania Dutch Apple Pork Chops 120
   Pork Chops Grand Marnier 121

Pork Chops with Basil................331
Pork Tenderloin Casserole............125
Sausage and Apple Bake...............124
Sausage Ring.........................122
Savory Loin of Pork..................122
Shadydale Pork Chops.................121
Stuffed Roast Pork with Onion Cream..123
Potage Cressonaire.......................232
POTATOES
   Italian Scalloped Potatoes...........149
   New Potatoes au Caviar...............149
   Sour Cream Potato Casserole..........148
   Spinach and Potato Casserole.........148
   Vichyssoise..........................232
Poulet à la Crème Joubine............... 93
POULTRY — See Individual Listings
Praline Cookies..........................301
Praline Sauce............................212
Pralines.................................312
Pumpkin Pie, Best........................293
Pumpkin Soup.............................235

Q

Quail and Dove, Grilled..................108
Quenelles Superior....................... 65
QUICHE
   Country Vegetable Quiche.............187
   Crab Shrimp Quiche...................186
   Crustless Quiche.....................187
   Herb Quiche..........................329
   John Wayne Pie.......................183
   Spinach-Feta Cheese Quiche...........186
Quick Herb Sauce.........................322
Quick Mayonnaise Rolls...................160

R

Ram's Steak Sandwich.....................239
Ratatouille..............................153
Red Beans and Rice.......................154
RELISH
   Corn Relish..........................220
   Cranberry Kumquat Relish.............218
RICE
   Amelia Island Rice...................189
   Artichoke Rice Salad................. 52
   Green Rice...........................191
   Herb Risotto.........................328
   Herbed Rice..........................191
   Hot Rice Casserole...................188
   Italian Lemon Rice...................188
   Italian Rice and Vegetables..........192
   Orange Rice..........................192
   Rice and Shrimp Salad................ 42
   Rice with Asparagus..................189
   Risi e Bisi..........................327
   The King's Parsley Rice..............190
   Wild Rice and Chicken Tarragon....... 90
   Wild Rice Salad with Oriental Vegetables..... 55
   Wild Rice with Fresh Mushrooms.......190
Rich Brownies............................304

Roast Beef Salad with French Mustard
   Dressing............................. 50
Roast Lamb with Herb Mustard.............126
Roquefort Dressing.......................213
Roquefort-Mayonnaise Dressing............215
Roquefort-Olive Dressing.................215
Russian Chef's Stroganoff................115
Russian Dressing.........................215
Russian Rocks............................311
Ruth's Coffee............................245

S

SALAD DRESSINGS
   Best Salad Dressing..................214
   Celery Seed Dressing.................215
   Golden Dressing......................214
   Honey Dressing.......................213
   Roquefort Dressing...................213
   Roquefort-Mayonnaise Dressing........215
   Roquefort-Olive Dressing.............215
   Russian Dressing.....................215
   Sour Cream Dressing..................213
   Vinaigrette with Mixed Herbs.........323
   Watercress Mayonnaise................205
   Yogurt Salad Dressing................324
Salade de Maison......................... 60
Salade Niçoise........................... 61
SALADS
   MEAT AND SEAFOOD
      Chicken Salad Supreme............. 41
      Chicken Stack-Up Salad............ 42
      Chutney and Curry Chicken Salad... 40
      Cobb Salad........................ 40
      Cold Seafood and Pasta Salad...... 43
      Cold Snapper Mold................. 39
      Cucumber Salmon Mousse............ 45
      Gourmet Beef Salad Vinaigrette.... 51
      Louis Pappas' Famous Greek Salad.. 44
      Rice and Shrimp Salad............. 42
      Roast Beef Salad with French
         Mustard Dressing............... 50
      Seafood and Pasta Salad Pescara... 48
      Thousand Island Mold with Fresh
         Seafood........................ 46
      Tropical Chicken Salad............ 42
      Tuna Mousse with Cucumber Sauce... 49
      Watercress Salad with Turkey
         and Bacon...................... 47
   RICE AND PASTA
      Artichoke-Rice Salad.............. 52
      Cold Seafood and Pasta Salad...... 43
      Rice and Shrimp Salad............. 42
      Seafood and Pasta Salad Pescara... 48
      Vegetable Pasta Salad............. 56
      Wild Rice Salad with Oriental
         Vegetables..................... 55
   VEGETABLES AND TOSSED GREENS
      Bermuda Salad..................... 59
      Cobb Salad........................ 40
      Ensalada de Fruta................. 54
      Frozen Tomato Salad............... 56
      Georgia Coleslaw.................. 53

Layered Spinach Salad	58
Louis Pappas' Famous Greek Salad	44
Mandarin Orange Salad	62
Marinated Broccoli Ring	62
Mushroom Salad	53
Orange Avocado Toss	60
Parslied Salad with Homemade Croutons	54
Salade Niçoise	61
Salade de Maison	60
Spinach Salad Mold	57
Tabouli	52
Tangy Squash Salad	59
Vegetable Pasta Salad	56
Watercress and Orange Salad	61
Wilted Lettuce Salad	57
Salt, Sesame	323

SANDWICHES
Artichoke Puffs	240
Guten Tog	240
Ham Topped Muffins	242
Hot Brown Sandwich	241
Ram's Steak Sandwich	239

SAUCES
Arnold's Hollandaise Sauce	210
Barbecue Sauce	207
Champagne Chocolate Sauce	211
Cinnamon-Sherry Sauce	211
Cointreau Strawberry Sauce	212
Cumberland Sauce	206
Dill Sauce	207
Ginger Sauce for Beef	207
Honey Dressing	213
Horseradish Sauce	210
Hot Fudge Sauce	212
Hot Mustard Sauce	209
Low Calorie Curry Sauce	205
Mustard Sauce	206
Parsley Sauce	322
Pesto Alla Genovese	328
Praline Sauce	212
Quick Herb Sauce	322
Spinach Flexibility	147
Steak Sauce	208
Sweet and Sour Sauce	209
Teriyaki Marinade	208
Vegetable Wine Sauce	206
Wine Sauce	210

SAUSAGE
Hot Sausage in Sour Cream	24
Mushroom and Sausage Hors d'Oeuvre	24
Sausage and Apple Bake	124
Sausage and Spinach Lasagne	198
Sausage Filled Mushrooms	23
Sausage Grits Casserole	182
Sausage Ring	122
Sautéed Cherry Tomatoes	135
Savory Loin of Pork	122

SCALLOPS
Bay Scallops en Coquille	83
Scallops in Herb Sauce	332
Scallops Provençale	82

Scampi Bread	79
Scampi Jacksonville	80
Scottish Scones	167

SEAFOOD—See Individual Listings
SEAFOOD COMBINATIONS
Artichoke and Seafood Casserole	84
Cioppino	225
Cold Seafood and Pasta Salad	43
Filé Seafood Gumbo	224
Gumbo	223
Quenelles Superior	65
Seafood and Pasta Salad Pescara	48
Shrimp and Crabmeat Fondue in Bread Cups	74
Shrimp and Crabmeat Madeira	78
Thousand Island Mold with Fresh Seafood	46
Sesame Salt	323
Shadydale Pork Chops	121

SHRIMP
Artichoke and Seafood Casserole	84
Baked Stuffed Shrimp	75
Chilled Shrimp with Saffron Dressing	11
Crab or Shrimp Mornay	69
Crab Shrimp Quiche	186
Grilled Shrimp Marinated in Cognac	75
Hot Shrimp or Crab Dip	16
Louis Pappas' Famous Greek Salad	44
Marinated Shrimp	13
Michael Field's Broiled Shrimp with Tarragon	73
New Orleans Style Shrimp	77
Quenelles Superior	65
Rice and Shrimp Salad	42
Scampi Bread	79
Scampi Jacksonville	80
Shrimp and Crabmeat Fondue in Bread Cups	74
Shrimp and Crabmeat Madeira	78
Shrimp and Crab Soufflé	76
Shrimp Balls	14
Shrimp Butter	15
Shrimp Creole	76
Shrimp Pâté	13
Shrimp Remoulade	12
Shrimp Rothbury	77
Shrimp Scampi Puerta Verde	78
Shrimp Vermouth	79
Shrimp with Creole Mustard	11
Shrimp with Mayonnaise Dressing	12
Spicy Shrimp Spread	14
Thousand Island Mold with Fresh Seafood	46
Sister's Sally Lunn	166
Slimmer's Herbed Gazpacho	325
Snow Peas with Water Chestnuts	143
Song of India Soup	234

SOUFFLÉS
Broccoli Soufflé	151
Caramel Soufflé with English Custard Sauce	251
Cold Lemon Soufflé	270

Egg Soufflé..........................184
Frozen Grand Marnier Soufflé with Hot
    Strawberry Sauce.....................259
Shrimp and Crab Soufflé................76
Souffléed Corn.......................140
Zucchini Soufflé......................143
SOUPS
Blue Crab Soup....................224
Broccoli Bisque...................228
Broccoli Soup.....................228
Chervil Soup......................325
Cioppino..........................225
Cold Cucumber-Dill Soup...........231
Cold Zucchini Soup................229
Country Chicken Soup..............237
Filé Seafood Gumbo................224
Fish or Conch Chowder.............226
Greek Lemon Egg Soup..............234
Gumbo.............................223
Hearty Gazpacho...................233
Jellied Borscht...................233
Lentil Soup.......................236
Mushroom Bisque...................230
Mushroom Broth....................230
Oyster and Spinach Soup...........225
Peanut Soup.......................238
Potage Cressonaire................232
Pumpkin Soup......................235
Slimmer's Herbed Gazpacho.........325
Song of India Soup................234
Spinach Shellfish Soup............226
Spinach Soup......................227
"The Sisters" Cheese Soup.........235
Tomato Soup with Basil............324
Vegetable Chicken Soup............238
Vichyssoise.......................232
Winter Green Soup.................236
Yogurt Cucumber Soup..............231
Zesty Spinach Soup................227
Zucchini Bisque...................229
Sour Cream Crescent Rolls.............176
Sour Cream Dressing...................213
Sour Cream Potato Casserole...........148
Southern Biscuits.....................159
Spaghetti Carbonara...................195
Spaghetti Florentine..................194
Spanish Chicken........................98
Spectacular Peach Pie.................294
Spice Muffins.........................167
Spicy Beef Stew.......................117
Spicy Shrimp Spread....................14
Spiked Apple Crisp....................255
SPINACH
Artichoke and Spinach Casserole...135
Chicken and Spinach Crêpes.........96
Layered Spinach Salad..............58
Oyster and Spinach Soup...........225
Sausage and Spinach Lasagne.......198
Spaghetti Florentine..............194
Spinach and Potato Casserole......148
Spinach and Tomatoes..............136

Spinach-Feta Cheese Quiche............186
Spinach Flexibility...................147
Spinach Salad Mold.....................57
Spinach Shellfish Soup................226
Spinach Soup..........................227
Spinach Stuffed Onions................138
Tennis Team Spinach Spread.............35
Zesty Spinach Soup....................227
Spring Crest Cornbread................161
SQUASH
Autumn Acorn Squash...............146
Summer Squash and Chervil.........326
Tangy Squash Salad.................59
Tomatoes Stuffed with Summer Squash.....137
Steak "Au Poivre".....................114
Steak Sauce...........................208
STRAWBERRY
Aunt Em's Strawberry Shortcake....282
Cointreau Strawberry Sauce........212
Frozen Grand Marnier Soufflé with
    Hot Strawberry Sauce...........259
Meringues with Strawberries and
    Custard........................258
Strawberries au Chocolat..........257
Strawberry Preserve Coffee Cake...170
Strawberry Sorbet.................262
Stuffed Mushroom Caps..................22
Stuffed Roast Pork with Onion Cream...123
Sugar Cookies.........................302
Summer Squash and Chervil.............326
Sunshine Cake.........................278
Sweet and Sour Sauce..................209
Sweet Lemon Bread.....................164
Sweet Pickles.........................218
Swiss Cheese Cornbread................162

T

Tabouli................................52
Tangy Squash Salad.....................59
Tea Cakes.............................301
Tennis Team Spinach Spread.............35
Teriyaki Marinade.....................208
The Girdlebuster......................265
The King's Parsley Rice...............190
"The" Pâté.............................32
"The Sisters" Bourbon Pound Cake......273
"The Sisters" Cheese Soup.............235
"The Sisters" Famous Peanut Butter Pie....295
Thousand Island Mold with Fresh Seafood.....46
TOMATOES
Fancy Baked Tomatoes..............136
Frozen Tomato Salad................56
Indian Tomato Chutney.............217
Sautéed Cherry Tomatoes...........135
Spinach and Tomatoes..............136
Tomato Soup with Basil............324
Tomatoes Stuffed with Herbed Orzo....326
Tomatoes Stuffed with Summer Squash....137
Tournedos Madagascar..................115
Tropical Chicken Salad.................42
Tuna Mousse with Cucumber Sauce........49

TURKEY
- Heavenly Turkey Hash 107
- Watercress Salad with Turkey and Bacon 47
- Turnips, Gourmet Braised 152

U
- Unbelievable Garlic Bread 166

V
VEAL
- Veal Lassere 131
- Veal Malagasy 130
- Veal Marsala 129
- Veal Piccata 130
- Veal with Vermouth 132
- VEGETABLES — See Individual Listings
VEGETABLE COMBINATIONS
- Artichoke and Spinach Casserole 135
- Country Chicken Soup 237
- Country Vegetable Quiche 187
- Fettuccine with Zucchini, Mushrooms and Ham 194
- Hearty Gazpacho 233
- Italian Rice and Vegetables 192
- Pasta Verde 195
- Ratatouille 153
- Slimmer's Herbed Gazpacho 325
- Snow Peas with Water Chestnuts 143
- Spinach and Tomatoes 136
- Spinach Stuffed Onions 138
- Tomatoes Stuffed with Summer Squash 137
- Vegetable Chicken Soup 238
- Vegetable Pasta Salad 56
- Vegetarian Lasagne 201
- Wild Rice with Oriental Vegetables 55
- Vegetable Wine Sauce 206
- Vichyssoise 232
- Vidalia Onion Spread 26
- Vinaigrette with Mixed Herbs 323

W
- Watercress and Orange Salad 61
- Watercress Mayonnaise 205
- Watercress Salad with Turkey and Bacon ... 47
- Watermelon Ice 265
- Watermelon Rind Pickles 219
- White Party Pasta 200
- Wild Duck in Red Wine 109
- Wild Rice and Chicken Tarragon 90
- Wild Rice Salad with Oriental Vegetables ... 55
- Wild Rice with Fresh Mushrooms 190
- Wilted Lettuce Salad 57
- Wine Sauce 210
- Winter Green Soup 236
- World Champion Chili 116

Y
- Yogurt Cucumber Soup 231
- Yogurt Herb Spread 320
- Yogurt Salad Dressing 324

Z
- Zesty Spinach Soup 227
- ZUCCHINI
  - Cold Zucchini Soup 229
  - Fettuccine with Zucchini, Mushrooms and Ham 194
  - Fried Zucchini 33
  - Ratatouille 153
  - Zucchini Bisque 229
  - Zucchini Frittata 141
  - Zucchini Pie 141
  - Zucchini Rounds 142
  - Zucchini Soufflé 143
  - Zucchini Tarragon 142

Jacksonville & Company
2165 Park Street
Jacksonville, Florida 32204
(904) 387-9927

Please send me _____ copies of **Jacksonville & Company** @ $12.00 each $_____
Add postage and handling @ $ 1.55 each $_____
Add giftwrap (if desired) @ $ .50 each $_____
Florida residents add 5% sales tax @ $ .60 each $_____
Total enclosed $_____

Name_____
(please print)
Address_____

City_____ State_____ Zip_____

Please make checks payable to **Jacksonville & Company.**

All Proceeds from the sale of cookbooks benefit the community through projects of the Junior League of Jacksonville, Florida, Inc.

Jacksonville & Company
2165 Park Street
Jacksonville, Florida 32204
(904) 387-9927

Please send me _____ copies of **Jacksonville & Company** @ $12.00 each $_____
Add postage and handling @ $ 1.55 each $_____
Add giftwrap (if desired) @ $ .50 each $_____
Florida residents add 5% sales tax @ $ .60 each $_____
Total enclosed $_____

Name_____
(please print)
Address_____

City_____ State_____ Zip_____

Please make checks payable to **Jacksonville & Company.**

All Proceeds from the sale of cookbooks benefit the community through projects of the Junior League of Jacksonville, Florida, Inc.

Jacksonville & Company
2165 Park Street
Jacksonville, Florida 32204
(904) 387-9927

Please send me _____ copies of **Jacksonville & Company** @ $12.00 each $_____
Add postage and handling @ $ 1.55 each $_____
Add giftwrap (if desired) @ $ .50 each $_____
Florida residents add 5% sales tax @ $ .60 each $_____
Total enclosed $_____

Name_____
(please print)
Address_____

City_____ State_____ Zip_____

Please make checks payable to **Jacksonville & Company.**

All Proceeds from the sale of cookbooks benefit the community through projects of the Junior League of Jacksonville, Florida, Inc.